ConStatS:
Software for Conceptualizing Statistics

ConStatS:

Software for Conceptualizing Statistics

A User's Manual by

**George E. Smith, Steve Cohen, Linfield C. Brown,
Richard A. Chechile, David Garman, Robert G. Cook,
James G. Ennis, and Sara Lewis**

Substantial funding for *ConStatS* came from FIPSE
(Fund for the Improvement of Postsecondary Education)
Grant Numbers G008730477 and P116B11580

A Product of

**Tufts University
Curricular Software Studio**

PRENTICE HALL
Upper Saddle River, New Jersey 07458

Library of Congress Cataloging-in-Publication Data

ConStatS : software for conceptualizing statistics : a user's manual /
  by George E. Smith ... [et al.].
      p.   cm.
    "A product of Tufts University's Curricular Software Studio."
    ISBN 0-13-502600-8 (alk. paper)
    1. ConStatS (Computer file)   2. Statistics—Data processing.
I. Smith, George E.   II. Tufts University.   Curricular Software Studio.
QA276.4.C615   1996
519.5'078—dc20   96-26461
                                                           CIP

Acquisition Editor: *Ann Heath*
Editorial Assistant: *Mindy Ince*
Editorial Director: *Tim Bozik*
Editor-in-Chief: *Jerome Grant*
Assistant Vice President of Production and Manufacturing: *David W. Riccardi*
Editorial/Production Supervision: *Jennifer Fischer*
Managing Editor: *Linda Mihatov Behrens*
Executive Managing Editor: *Kathleen Schiaparelli*
Manufacturing Buyer: *Alan Fischer*
Manufacturing Manager: *Trudy Pisciotti*
Marketing Manager: *Evan Girard*
Creative Director: *Paula Maylahn*
Art Director: *Jayne Conte*
Cover Art/Design: *Wendy Alling Judy*

© 1997 by Tufts University
Published by Prentice-Hall, Inc.
Simon & Schuster/A Viacom Company
Upper Saddle River, New Jersey 07458

Printed in the United States of America

10 9 8 7 6 5 4 3 2

ISBN 0-13-502600-8

Prentice-Hall International (UK) Limited, *London*
Prentice-Hall of Australia Pty. Limited, *Sydney*
Prentice-Hall Canada Inc., *Toronto*
Prentice-Hall Hispanoamericana, S.A., *Mexico*
Prentice-Hall of India Private Limited, *New Delhi*
Prentice-Hall of Japan, Inc., *Tokyo*
Simon & Schuster Asia Pte. Ltd., *Singapore*
Editora Prentice-Hall do Brasil, Ltda., *Rio de Janeiro*

To Students and Teachers

Audience and Goals

ConStatS is software for conceptualizing statistics. It was developed by the Curricular Software Studio and teachers of statistics at Tufts University to help students gain a solid grasp of the concepts and principles taught in introductory statistics courses. *ConStatS* is designed to be used as a supplement in one-semester courses in statistics in U.S. colleges and universities, regardless of the departments in which the courses are taught. Its only prerequisite is high school algebra. The range of topics *ConStatS* covers makes it useful for at least the first ten weeks of every introductory course.

The Scope of *ConStatS*

ConStatS consists of 12 separate WINDOWS-based programs: 4 on representing data, 2 on probability, 3 on sampling, 2 on the elements of statistical inference, and 1 for conducting experiments. Each of these programs has elementary pathways that introduce students to the topic, and more advanced pathways that students can use to extend and solidify their understanding. Teachers can thus pick and choose the parts of *ConStatS* they wish to use, so that it can serve the most elementary courses in introductory statistics, as well as the most ambitious ones.

The *ConStatS* Approach

The pathways through the programs in *ConStatS* guide students in devising simulations and experiments that display statistical concepts and principles at work in concrete contexts. *ConStatS* includes data sets from all the disciplines that rely heavily on statistical methods. Teachers can also easily add data sets of their own. For those who wish to use it, the user's manual takes students step by step through setting up and drawing conclusions from at least one example in each program.

ConStatS Workbook

An interactive workbook, written by Steve Cohen and Sara Lewis of Tufts University, is available for purchase with *ConStatS*. The workbook is designed to guide students through each *ConStatS* module and to help them gain maximum benefit from the exploratory style of the software. Each section of the workbook is written to be completed in a 50 minute lab period. The perforated pages and guided questions with space for written answers makes the *ConStatS* Workbook a valuable tool for teachers to use as the basis for assignments using *ConStatS*. ISBN 0-13-522848-4.

System Requirements

ConStatS requires an IBM or compatible personal computer (386 or higher) running Microsoft WINDOWS 3.1 or WINDOWS 95, 4 megabytes of free hard-disk space, and a mouse. *ConStatS* makes extensive use of color, so that a color monitor (preferably VGA or higher) is almost essential.

Technical Support

Call the Prentice Hall Media Group at 1-800-842-2958 to report any damaged or missing components of your *ConStatS* system, or if you believe you have found an error in the software.

TABLE OF CONTENTS

Probability Distributions cont'd.

FOREWORD

The Development of *ConStatS*

ConStatS is a product of nine years of effort by the Curricular Software Studio of Tufts University and members of Tufts' faculty. The goal throughout has been to develop personal-computer based software that will help a much larger fraction of students in introductory statistics courses achieve the level of understanding that only the very best students have been achieving. Skill in manipulating formulas to calculate solutions to problems was *not,* as such, part of this goal. The understanding we aim for includes, first, an ability to recognize what numbers in statistics signify and, second, skill in qualitative reasoning. With these abilities, students will be able to understand the statistical claims they encounter outside courses in statistics.

ConStatS was developed initially under the first of two three-year grants from FIPSE—The Fund for the Improvement of Postsecondary Education—a part of the U.S. Department of Education. This grant extended from 1987 to 1990, with Brian Lekander of FIPSE as Project Officer and George E. Smith of Tufts' Philosophy Department as Project Director (Grant No. G00 8730477). The Abstract from the proposal for this grant shows what we had in mind in 1987:

> Introductory statistics courses, though taught in several different departments in almost all liberal arts colleges and universities, are strikingly unsuccessful. Students come away from them with little understanding of the theoretical framework of statistics, and with continuing conceptual confusions. Even though statistical evidence pervades our lives, liberal arts students shy away from these courses in fulfilling their "core curriculum" requirements in formal or mathematical methods.
>
> In the proposed project Tufts' Curricular Software Studio, together with faculty from all Tufts' departments in which introductory statistics courses are taught, will develop a software package to enable students to conceptualize statistics. The software will allow students to experiment actively on their own time with simulated situations calling for statistical inferences. By using a full range of discipline-specific examples for each topic area covered in the various intro-ductory courses at Tufts, the software will become a centerpiece in the courses taught in every department. The software package will be extensively evaluated in courses both inside and outside Tufts, and then refined and prepared for publication to reach as wide an undergraduate audience as possible.

Looking back nine years later, the only thing wrong with this description was the suggestion that we could achieve what we were setting out to do within three years.

The FIPSE grants were indispensable for developing *ConStatS*. Tufts' Curricular Software Studio, which was founded in 1985 under a grant from the Alfred P. Sloan Foundation, had developed software packages in elementary computer science and population genetics before we applied for our first FIPSE grant. These software packages, however, were modest in scope, and more importantly they could be developed under the direction of a single faculty member specializing in the topic. Software for conceptualizing statistics required a team of faculty members designing separate programs forming a comprehensive package. The first FIPSE grant enabled the Studio to put this team together. It has remained together throughout the effort.

Tufts' Curricular Software Studio is dedicated to a particular view about how personal computers can revolutionize college-level education. Computers can be used to stretch students' imaginations, enabling them to visualize abstract principles and complex processes in concrete form. Everyone carries out thought experiments to some extent while learning. Computer simulations exploiting the interactive, graphics, and computational capabilities of personal computers can extend the range and scope of such experiments in extraordinary ways. Software to this end is best designed in conjunction with specific courses where it can be systematically tested and refined. The ideal way to develop it is for teachers of the courses, who know the material and the places students have trouble, to work hand-in-hand with professional programmers and student programmers working under them. All participants involved in the design and development of the software can then focus on what they do best.

Initial versions of programs on different topics in statistics were developed along the lines of this approach during the beginning phase of our first FIPSE grant. When we tried them in courses, however, they were disappointing. In effect, we had created programs for teachers to use to carry out demonstrations in classrooms, not programs for students to use to devise simulated experiments. The programs permitted a wide range of interesting experiments, but too much was being asked of the students in deciding what experiments to try and how to set them up. Students who had already acquired a good grasp of the basic concepts were able to use the programs effectively. Most students, however, tended to flounder with them. The programs were presupposing too much of the very sort of conceptual understanding that they were intended to help students acquire.

The final design of the programs comprising *ConStatS* is a response to this difficulty. This design strikes a balance between two conflicting considerations. On the one hand, some structure is needed to guide beginning students in devising instructive simulations and experiments. On the other hand, the simulations and experiments need to be ones that the students themselves devise, and not mere demonstrations that they passively watch unfold.

Each of the programs in *ConStatS* contains more than one pathway. The student using the program remains in total control throughout. Nothing happens until the student makes it happen. The pathway most students will initially take through each program is designed to guide them step by step in devising a telling experiment; yet the parameters of the experiment must still be of their choosing. Other pathways are less structured and offer less guidance; they give students who have gained an initial understanding of the topic increasingly free reign to devise a wide variety of simulations and experiments. For those who wish to use it, this user's manual takes students through an example of setting up and drawing conclusions from an experiment on at least one pathway in each program.

Nine programs following this design were developed during the last two years of the initial FIPSE grant: *Displaying Data, Summary Statistics, Transforming Data, Describing Bivariate Data, Probability Measurement, Probability Distributions, Sampling Distributions, Sampling Error,* and *A Sampling Problem.* These were tested in Tufts' classrooms and revised accordingly during the last year of the grant and the year following. Our second three-year grant from FIPSE (No. P116B11580), which extended from 1991 to 1994, then allowed us to conduct a truly ambitious evaluation of these nine programs. FIPSE's project officers for this grant were Eulalia Benejam Cobb and David M. Johnson; the Project Director was Richard Chechile of Tufts' Psychology Department, with George Smith as Co-Principal Investigator; and most of the detailed research effort was carried out by Steve Cohen.

The primary aim of this evaluation was not merely to assess whether *ConStatS* makes a difference. Instead, the aim was to assess the effectiveness of each distinct part of every program in *ConStatS*, determining which parts were and which were not yielding substantial gains in conceptual understanding and then revising those parts of the programs that were not proving as successful as we thought they should be. A huge amount of data was collected—every single step taken and move made by several hundred students in several different universities using the program was traced and recorded. The actions taken by these students were then correlated with the level of understanding of individual concepts they achieved versus the level achieved by students in a control group not using *ConStatS*. This approach is akin to the one engineers take in developing a product: collect a massive amount of data through testing the product and then focus on those parts of the data that can be used to improve the components that are falling short of expectations.

The upshot of this effort is nine programs that have gone through several stages of refinement on the basis of seven years of classroom experience. Three additional programs, Beginning Confidence Intervals, Beginning Hypothesis Testing, and An Experiment in Mental Imagery, have been added, with support from Tufts and Prentice Hall, over the last three years. The design of these three reflects the lessons we learned from the first nine, and they too have been tested in classrooms and refined accordingly. All 12 of the programs are in Microsoft WINDOWS in order to allow users to jump from the middle of one program to any of the others whenever they wish to pursue a line of inquiry. The initial versions of most of the 12 programs in *ConStatS* were developed in Microsoft WINDOWS 1.0. WINDOWS too has gone through several stages of development since we started.

The *ConStatS* Development Team

The team that developed *ConStatS* over the last nine years consisted of 29 people, including 7 faculty and 18 student programmers. The pivotal figure throughout has been Steve Cohen, the Technical Director of the Curricular Software Studio. He worked hand-in-hand with the faculty in designing and testing the individual programs and, in addition to programming substantial portions himself, supervised all the work done by the student programmers. George Smith has been the project director throughout. Five teachers of introductory statistics courses at Tufts have been involved since work began on designing the individual programs: Linfield Brown from the Civil Engineering Department; Richard Chechile and Robert Cook from the Psychology Department; James Ennis from the Sociology Department; and David Garman from the Economics Department. Sara Lewis, who teaches introductory statistics in the Biology Department joined the team in 1991. Durwood Marshall, Tufts Computer Services' statistics specialist, served as a consultant throughout, and Barbara Alarie of Tufts Computer Services provided documentation support. Paul Morris, the Executive Director of Tufts Computer Services, handled many of the business aspects of the project since 1990.

All of the faculty contributed significantly to every one of the programs. As one might expect from a group of faculty, no comments were spared in the meetings devoted to detailed critical reviews of each program. Nevertheless, different individuals carried the primary responsibility for the design and development of each program. The overall pedagogical approach was devised by George Smith, Steve Cohen, and Robert Cook. James Ennis and George Smith were responsible for the basic design of

Displaying Data and *Descriptive Statistics*. Richard Chechile was responsible for *Transforming Data* and *Probability Measurement*. Linfield Brown was responsible for *Probability Distributions*, and he worked jointly with Steve Cohen on *Sampling Distributions* and *Sampling Errors*, and with David Garman and Steve Cohen on *Beginning Hypothesis Testing*. David Garman was responsible for *Describing Bivariate Data*, and he was assisted by Linfield Brown and Steve Cohen on *Beginning Confidence Intervals*. Robert Cook was responsible for *An Experiment in Mental Imagery*, and he assisted George Smith and Steve Cohen on *A Sampling Problem*.

The final draft of the **User's Manual** was written by George Smith, following invaluable suggestions from our editor, Ann Heath, of Prentice Hall. Initial drafts of the chapters were prepared as follows: Chapter 2, Linfield Brown and Kirk Israel; Chapter 3, James Ennis; Chapter 4, Sara Lewis; Chapters 5 and 7, Richard Chechile; Chapters 6 and 12, David Garman; Chapters 8 and 13, Linfield Brown; Chapter 9, Steve Cohen; Chapter 10, Steve Cohen and Sara Lewis; and Chapters 11 and 14, Robert Cook.

Steve Cohen had overall responsibility for the programming of all of *ConStatS*. The 18 student programmers who participated programmed individual parts as follows: Steve Braverman, *Probability Measurement* and *Probability Distributions;* Alex Dymerets, *Sampling Distributions* and *Sampling Errors;* Pierce Park, *Descriptive Statistics* and Tools; Paul Marquis, Tools; John Greebe, *A Sampling Problem* and *Transforming Data;* Marc Greenfield, graphic tools; David Johnson, *Describing Bivariate Data;* Doug Larrick, *Describing Bivariate Data;* Al Lee, *Descriptive Statistics;* Michael J. Saletnik, *Sampling Errors, Sampling Distributions,* and *Descriptive Statistics;* Frank Tsai, *Probability Distributions;* Kirk Israel, *Beginning Hypothesis Testing;* Paul Moreville, *Beginning Confidence Intervals;* Dag Holmboe, *An Experiment in Mental Imagery;* Robert Kogan, *Beginning Confidence Intervals* and *An Experiment in Mental Imagery;* Robert Winter, *Probability Measurement;* Paul Poh, Tools; and David Lindheimer, *Probability Measurement*. Most of these students were either Engineering or Computer Science majors at Tufts. None of them came to the project with the knowledge of statistics that they developed while working on it. Coincidental learning of this sort is no small part of the rationale underlying the Curricular Software Studio.

Acknowledgements

We thank the students and faculty who used prior versions of the software and manual. They offered many suggestions. Several faculty outside the *ConStatS* development team who participated in the evaluation helped improve *ConStatS:* Bill Baum (University of New Hampshire), Jim Ebersole (Colorado College), Cynthia King (Gallaudet University), and Suzanne Lovett (Bowdoin College), as well as Allyssa McCabe (Tufts), Rajaram Krishnan (Tufts), Joann Montepare (Tufts), and Cynthia Thomsen (Tufts). Lucille Palubinskas and Richard Stout supported the evaluation with a thorough review of our test items. Many others offered insightful comments by way of review, including Dan Dennett, Molly Hahn, John McKenzie, Marty Zelin, Jerry Dallal, Candace Schau, Glen Burns, and Kate Beattie. Kate, in particular, became a valuable adjunct to our development team during her year at Tufts.

All the staff who work in and around the Curricular Software Studio made important contributions to the software and the manual. Students working at the front desk in Tufts Academic Computing Services, including Sara Rosenberg, Judi Miller, Carla Schack, Dan Abramovich, Emmanuel O. Roble, Barry Rothberg, Erica Coffin, Erica Bial, and Emily Sossaman helped print, proofread, and prepare parts of this manual, as well as deliver countless sets of *ConStatS* disks. Durwood Marshall offered dozens of ideas in conversations over lunch. Diane Ricciardelli and the Tufts Computer User

Consultants kept the working versions of *ConStatS* up and running in the computer labs. Paula Fisher and Judi Rennie kept our development tools updated. Barbara Alarie solved all our word processing problems. Alan Kasparian, Greg Williamson, and Aaron Lipeles reviewed papers and support materials. Mitch Rosenbaum helped prepare the final version of the manual. And Paul Morris, Executive Director of Tufts Computer Services, along with Erin Rae Hoffer, Associate Director of Academic Computing, provided a supportive work environment.

Many others outside Tufts also helped make *ConStatS* happen. We need to recognize our editor, Ann Heath, and her assistant Mindy Ince, both of whom made useful suggestions and helped us down the home stretch. Jerome Grant, also from Prentice Hall, helped us plan the manual. Jim Hilton (Grossmont College), Timothy Lesnick (Grand Valley State University), and Anthony Orzechowski (Abbot Labs) reviewed ConStatS for Prentice Hall. The FIPSE Program Officers, Brian Lekander, Eulalia Cobb, and David Johnson, provided feedback and flexibility that permitted us to move ahead and feel comfortable experimenting with new ideas.

Finally, a special thank you to Steve Cohen's family, Denise, Jackson, and Charlotte, none of whom were part of the project when it began.

In Conclusion

In its scope and ambition, *ConStatS* is just the sort of project that would not have been feasible to undertake without financial support from FIPSE, an organization whose sole motive is the improvement of postsecondary education. *ConStatS* would also have been impossible without the extraordinary spirit of interdepartmental cooperation that has long marked Tufts. We are all grateful to the Administration of Tufts for promoting this spirit, as well as for the substantial support they gave the project. Both FIPSE and Tufts' Curricular Software Studio hope that *ConStatS* will instill in future generations of statistics students an appreciation and grasp of the subject that they will carry with them long after their student days are behind them.

George E. Smith, Director
Tufts' Curricular Software Studio
April 1996

Chapter 1

*Con*ceptualizing *Stat*istics

An Introduction to *ConStatS*

Why Use *ConStatS*?

A small fraction of gifted students in introductory courses in music theory simply read the textbook, letting their imaginations supply examples to illustrate the concepts presented in the text. For most people, however, the piano is indispensable for learning music theory, not just because teachers can use it to illustrate concepts in class, but much more so because students can experiment on it outside of class, banging out intervals, chords, and themes in one variant after another until they grasp the concepts forming the theoretical framework.

ConStatS is a "concept piano" for statistics. Students in introductory statistics courses can experiment on it to develop a concrete understanding of concepts, principles, and lines of reasoning in statistics in the same way a piano is used to gain a concrete understanding of music theory. It enables more students to come away from these courses with a solid grasp of statistical concepts and an ability to employ them in qualitative reasoning.

The 12 computer programs that comprise *ConStatS* cover the full range of topics in introductory statistics courses—from elementary ways of displaying data and using summary statistics to describe them, to issues in probability, sampling, and bivariate data analysis, and finally to the rudiments of estimation and hypothesis testing. Data sets from a wide range of disciplines are included, and instructors can add their own; students can even generate their own data by conducting a well-known experiment in cognitive psychology on themselves. Each program guides the user in devising examples with the data sets and then in varying these examples in diverse ways. While *ConStatS* carries out all computations and constructs all the graphical displays, it does so only upon request. It is like a piano, but not like a player piano. The student is always in the position of a "researcher," using the software to address questions.

Learning Statistics

Statistics is a science for extracting useful information from data. It is both a theoretical discipline in mathematics and an applied discipline used in many other fields. Those working in the mathematical discipline must have a mastery of the formulas and techniques. But, thanks to computer packages like *SPSS* (*Statistical Package for the Social Sciences*) and the numerous summary reports published by professional statisticians, most of us do not need this level of mastery. What we do need is an ability to assess the results of statistical procedures and to decide what conclusions reliably follow from the information extracted from data by means of these procedures.

This ability has more than one dimension. It includes a reasonable understanding of what numbers used in statistics do and do not tell us about the data and whether these numbers are especially sensitive to certain features in the data. It includes a feel for when numbers in statistics are anomalous or, for other reasons, ought to be provoking questions. In the case of claims put forward on the basis of statistical evidence, it includes our being able to weigh this evidence and to recognize ways in which it may be misleading. And it includes skill in reasoning qualitatively from features of a data set to conclusions. These are the kinds of things the phrase *conceptualizing statistics* covers.

Those who work with statistics acquire this ability from their experiences with specific examples. But this takes time, often years. We need to telescope as much of the benefits of such field experience as we can into introductory courses. This can be done by using *thought experiments* to simulate field experience. *ConStatS* has been designed with the goal of helping students to employ such thought experiments in learning statistics.

Using *ConStatS* to Extend Imagination

Thought experiments involving mathematics place heavy demands on our imaginations. *ConStatS* functions as a *prosthesis to the imagination*, a device that extends our imagination by supplying it with powers that it does not have on its own.

To this end, *ConStatS* takes advantage of the computer in three ways. First, the computer performs all the calculations for us, effortlessly and without error. We can therefore concentrate on the questions of concern. Second, the computer produces striking, informative displays on the monitor screen, exploiting color and animation where appropriate. Visual displays can convey a great deal more information compactly than numbers can. Furthermore, effective visual images are more likely to make a sufficient impression on us for them to be retained in memory and hence available for future comparisons. Third, the computer can juxtapose several different visual displays at once, whether as programmed by *ConStatS* or upon the user's request. *ConStatS* is based in *Microsoft Windows*. When the *Mouse* is used to highlight a specific item in one of the displays, the corresponding item is automatically highlighted in the others in which it appears. This makes it much easier to jump back and forth between displays when comparing them. *Microsoft Windows* also allows the user to pause in the middle of a program, turn to any other program in *ConStatS* in order to clarify something, and then resume at the point where the original program was interrupted. The entire resources of *ConStatS* are always available.

Many other software packages in statistics, such as *SPSS*, exploit the computer in these same ways. Yet they require greater knowledge of statistics to use them effectively for thought experiments. Raising questions, setting up suitable experiments, and figuring out what the outcomes suggest are skills that not everyone has. What separates *ConStatS* from other software packages is that every *ConStatS* program includes pathways that guide the user in posing questions, devising experiments, and evaluating outcomes. These pathways are critically important when students are first learning the topics covered in each program. Just as one can use the piano in learning music theory without being skillful in playing it, *ConStatS* is an effective "concept piano" for statistics because it does not require expertise to use it.

ConStatS is not a prosthetic device that one comes to depend on totally. Students will have increasingly less need for it. The more they grasp the concepts and main patterns of reasoning in statistics—and the more examples they have thought through and visual displays they have in memory—the more they will be able to carry out thought experiments in their head. In this regard, *ConStatS* is intended to be less like a prosthesis and more like a Nautilus machine used to strengthen the imagination.

Can *ConStatS* Make a Difference?

The answer, in a word, is yes. *ConStatS* was evaluated from 1991 through 1994 in a project funded by the Fund for the Improvement of Postsecondary Education of the U.S. Department of Education. The primary goal of this evaluation was not to determine whether *ConStatS* could make a difference—we were already confident of this from using it in courses at Tufts since 1989. Instead, we wanted to know which parts of *ConStatS* were proving most and least successful and what was creating the difference between them so that we could systematically address any shortcomings. We recorded every single keyboard or mouse click of every subject using *ConStatS* in the study, obtaining a massive amount of data on how it was used. With the help of outside experts, we devised 103 short-answer questions testing students' command of specific concepts in statistics and their ability to reason qualitatively.

In this evaluation, *ConStatS* was used by 639 students in 16 separate introductory statistics courses taught in a range of departments in 5 very different colleges and universities. Seventy seven students in 4 different courses participated as control subjects. Some references describing the project and its results are given at the end of this chapter.

Students using *ConStatS* in the evaluation did substantially better than students in the control group on 94 of the 103 questions. The 9 questions on which the *ConStatS* students did not outperform the control group revealed sometimes subtle features of particular parts of *ConStatS* that were not succeeding in the way we had expected them to. For example, in some cases a seemingly insignificant feature of concepts reinforced a misconception students had before they began studying statistics. We subsequently made changes to correct these shortcomings.

The evaluation of *ConStatS* paid no attention to its impact on the ability of students to solve problems or to define terms in statistics. A comparatively elementary question used in the evaluation, designed to test whether students understand what a continuous variable is, is given in Figure 1.1 below. Students were invited to add an explanation of their answer. The question does not ask for a definition.

Circle the variables in the table below which are continuous.

City	Population (Metro area)	Sq. Miles	Number of Buses
Boston	4,055,700	46	502
Dallas	3,655,300	333	806
Denver	1,847,400	111	701
Milwaukee	1,552,000	96	546
St. Louis	2,438,000	61	588

Figure 1.1 A Question to Test Understanding of the Concept of a Continuous Variable

The question offers two appealing foils. Students who think that variables are continuous if they take on large values might choose Population or Number of Buses. Such foils were included to help expose misconceptions. While this question only required students to demonstrate understanding by recognition, many others required students to sketch graphs and resolve dilemmas. Many students expressed surprise over how difficult the test was. (The question in Figure 1.1, by the way, is one on which the students using *ConStatS* had much higher scores than those in the control group.)

A caveat should be added to the conclusion that *ConStatS* does make a difference in conceptual understanding. Very basic mathematical ability is a factor that affects students' success in learning with *ConStatS*. All the students participating in the evaluation were given a 10-question test covering mathematical skills presupposed by *ConStatS*. Students scoring a perfect 10 on this test showed greater gains from using the software, versus the control group, than students scoring 9 or 8. Two basic skills made an especially significant difference. The question shown in Figure 1.2, which tests understanding of fractions and percentages, was missed by 22 percent of the students (in spite of the fact that 375/1000 was scored correct — students were not required to reduce the fraction). Students also had

Convert .375 to a fraction.

Figure 1.2 A Question Testing a Basic Skill Presupposed in *ConStatS*

trouble coming up with a ratio between 5:2 and 20:6. These proved to be the most difficult questions on the basic-skills test. Students who did not score a perfect 10 typically answered one or both of them wrong. We have tried to make some changes in *ConStatS* to help these students. But comfort with the relationship between ratios, fractions, and decimals is so fundamental to understanding probability and statistics that we question whether these changes will have a large effect.

An Overview of *ConStatS*

ConStatS consists of 12 *Microsoft Windows* based programs, grouped into five distinct parts:

Representing Data — different ways in which aggregates of data are represented in statistics, both graphically and numerically.

> *Displaying Data* — univariate data given in tables displayed in histograms, cumulative frequency displays, observed sequence graphs, and bar charts, as an initial step in data analysis.

> *Descriptive Statistics* — univariate summary statistics describing the *center* (e.g., the mean and median), the *spread* (e.g., variance, standard deviation, and interquartile range), and the *shape* of data.

> *Transforming Data* — linear transformations, especially Z scores, and their effects on the center, spread, and shape of distributions of univariate data; also, frequently used non-linear transformations for changing the shapes of distributions.

Describing Bivariate Data — scatter plots and summary statistics for bivariate data, with emphasis on the use of the least squares line, residuals from it, and the correlation coefficient in analyzing data to find relationships between variables.

Probability — basic concepts in probability that are presupposed in advanced topics in statistics, like sampling and inference.

Probability Measurement — numerical probabilities as ratios, and consistency constraints on them, illustrated through having students assign numerical probabilities to alternatives in everyday situations.

Probability Distributions — the key properties of 14 probability distributions used in statistics, including the binomial and the normal, brought out by interactive comparisons between graphical displays of their probability density functions, their cumulative distribution functions, and pie charts.

Sampling — gains and risks in using samples to reach conclusions about populations.

Sampling Distributions — the variability and distribution of the values of different sample statistics for samples of different sizes drawn from populations having different (postulated) underlying probability distributions.

Sampling Errors — the risks of being misled when using sample statistics, obtained for samples of different sizes, as values for the corresponding statistics for the populations from which the samples were drawn.

A Sampling Problem — a game in which a simulated coin can be tossed repeatedly before deciding whether it is fair, or it is 55 percent or 60 percent biased in favor of heads, or 55 percent or 60 percent biased in favor of tails.

Inference — the basic frameworks of reasoning in which statistical evidence is used to reach a conclusion or to assess a claim, illustrated in examples.

Beginning Confidence Intervals — repeated sampling used to show the relationship between the width of an interval, employed as an estimator for the population mean, and the proportion of the times it will cover this mean.

Beginning Hypothesis Testing — a step-by-step tracing of the reasoning involved in the statistical testing of claims about the mean of a single population or about the difference between the means of two populations.

Experiment — experiments in which the user of *ConStatS* is the subject, for purposes of generating original data for use in the *Representing Data* programs.

An Experiment in Mental Imagery — the classic Shepard-Metzler experiment in cognitive psychology involving the rotation of images, yielding as data the time taken for the subject to react versus the number of degrees through which the image is rotated.

Pathways Through *ConStatS*

ConStatS can be used in every introductory statistics course, from the least to the most advanced, regardless of the academic department in which it is taught. Instructors can select data sets from any of several disciplines, or they can add their own. The Tufts faculty who participated in the design of *ConStatS* teach introductory courses in six different departments, catering to students at several different levels of mathematical sophistication, including the math phobic. A high school course could be designed using *Displaying Data*, *Descriptive Statistics*, *Probability Measurement*, and *A Sampling Problem*. Yet, even though nothing in *ConStatS* presupposes more than elementary high school mathematics, advanced math majors will find parts of *Probability Distributions* and *Sampling Distributions* very helpful.

No one-semester introductory course is likely to begin exhausting the resources in *ConStatS*. The range of topics it treats, the number of options with which it can approach these topics, and the diversity of data sets it makes available are too great. The question is how to pick and choose within *ConStatS*.

Each of the 12 programs in *ConStatS* is an independent entity. One can jump in anywhere, using any program by itself or as a starting point before other programs. A modicum of background in sampling is needed to get much out of the programs in *Inference*, some knowledge of probability distributions will enhance the programs in *Sampling*, and familiarity with basic summary statistics and standard graphical displays is needed everywhere except in *Displaying Data* and *Descriptive Statistics*. But this sort of background can be acquired without having to use the relevant programs in *ConStatS*, and students can always turn to the programs in question for more background when they feel the need.

Similarly, most of the individual programs offer more than one pathway through them. Every program has one or more pathways for students who are just beginning to learn the topic. These pathways can be used by themselves, without ever turning to more advanced options. Or, equally, some or all of the beginning pathways can be skipped over, jumping right away to the combined use of all the concepts and techniques covered in the program. There is a huge number of pathways through the *ConStatS* package, and hence a huge number of different ways in which it can be used in courses.

The order in which the 12 programs are listed in the preceding section offers a natural pathway through *ConStatS*. *Displaying Data* and *Descriptive Statistics* lay a foundation. *Transforming Data* can be used only for Z scores and other simple linear examples, and *Describing Bivariate Data*, only for scatter plots and an introduction to correlation and least squares lines. All but the normal and binomial can be ignored the first time through *Probability Distributions*. The mean and one or two other statistics can then be examined in *Sampling Distributions* and *Sampling Error*, in preparation for either or both of *Beginning Confidence Intervals* and *Beginning Hypothesis Testing*. An introductory course following this pathway could then go on to other matters, if time remains, or it could return to any combination of topics covered in the programs that were skipped over the first time through.

There is nothing mandatory about this pathway, however. Any number of others are just as natural. Topics in *Probability* can be treated before those in *Data Representation*. *Transforming Data* can be ignored entirely or restricted to Z scores. *Describing Bivariate Data* can be delayed to the end of a course. *ConStatS* is adaptable to any sequence of topics an instructor of introductory statistics might prefer. The only proviso, based on our experience, is that time spent on *Displaying Data*, on *Descriptive Statistics*, and on the principal distributions in *Probability Distributions* is almost always time rewarded when dealing with more advanced topics later in a course.

WHY's and HELP's

Nothing happens in *ConStatS* unless and until the user initiates an action. Users are never in a passive position, watching a scene unfold before them in the manner of television. This raises the question, what prevents students from getting lost or, worse, from freezing up when faced with alternatives?

Part of the answer lies in the way that the programs in *ConStatS* have been structured. Each program consists of a series of *screens*. Each screen presents the user with a small number of options. Different options on a screen lead to further screens, forming separate pathways through the program. Keeping the number of options small helps students to focus on a specific question or objective when they initiate the action leading to the next screen. Once they have gained some command of the topic, they can turn to screens available on the more advanced pathways. These offer a wider range of options that allow the concepts and techniques covered in the program to be combined in whatever way students might wish—for example, in exploratory data analysis.

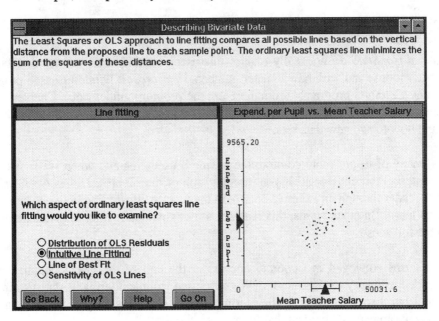

Figure 1.3 A Typical Screen in *ConStatS*

Another way students are helped to move through the programs is the design of the screens. The screen shown in Figure 1.3, from the *Learn about bivariate techniques* pathway in *Describing Bivariate Data*, shows all the standard screen elements. The topic is *Line Fitting*. The student reaches this screen by selecting *fit a line to these variables* from a list of three options on the screen preceding it. Two sentences at the top of the screen provide an overview of the matter at hand. The working data are displayed on the right, and four options are offered on the left, in response to the question, *Which aspect of ordinary least squares line fitting would you like to examine?* This is the first mention of least squares lines in this program.

The *Why?* and *Help* buttons below the four options are present on almost all *ConStatS* screens. They provide a resource to turn to whenever the user is uncertain about which option to choose. One can click on any option—in the case shown, on *Intuitive Line Fitting*—and then on *Why?* to obtain a brief statement of a typical reason why someone might want to select this option. The *Why* message for the case at hand is, *Most people are surprised to find how different their guess can be from the true ordinary least squares line*. These messages are intended to be the sort an instructor might whisper into the ear of a student who seems to be hesitating overly long before proceeding with a choice. If the *Why* message does not give the student a clear idea of why to pursue this option, the *Help* button generally offers more standard didactic information.

Go Back and **Go On** are also present on most *ConStatS* screens. Clicking **Go On** initiates the action corresponding to the option selected, frequently leading to the next screen. Separating the step of clicking on the option and initiating action allows for **Why** and **Help** and also gives students time to think about what is going to happen next and why they have chosen to pursue it. The **Go Back** button can be used to go back to an earlier screen, and hence to an earlier choice, whenever one begins to feel a little lost, or for any other reason. These four buttons leave the user in full control even when proceeding down a comparatively structured pathway.

The User's Manual

The programs in *ConStatS* do not really require this user's manual. All you need is familiarity with using a computer mouse and with how to enter numbers in *Microsoft Windows*-based programs in order to jump into any *ConStatS* program. From there on, the program guides you. Chapter 2 covers these *Windows* techniques and the way they are used in *ConStatS*. It also tells you how to install *ConStatS* on a computer and how to add new data sets.

Nevertheless, many of us are more comfortable having a user's manual when we first use a computer program. Chapters 3 through 14 guide you through each of the 12 programs in *ConStatS* in sequence. They carry the reader through an example or two, in the process illustrating how one can go about using the program to learn. In other words, this really is a user's manual. It shows students how to use the programs in the full sense.

A glossary of terms employed in *ConStatS* appears at the end of the User's Manual, along with an appendix intended primarily for instructors. We have used technical terms in statistics in as standard a way as we can, but textbooks differ in their terminology. The glossary should bridge any differences between the terminology used here and that found in textbooks.

References for Chapter 1

Cohen, S., Chechile, R. A., Smith, G. E., Tsai, F., and Burns, G. (1994) "A Method for Evaluating the Effectiveness of Educational Software," Behavior Research Methods, Instruments, and Computers, 26, pp. 236-41.

Cohen, S., Smith, G.E., Chechile, R.A., Burns, G., Tsai, F., (in press) "Identifying Impediments to Learning Probability and Statistics from an Assessment of Instructional Software," Journal of Educational and Behavioral Statistics.

Chapter 2

Running *ConStatS* on the Computer

System Requirements

ConStatS requires the following minimum system configuration:

- an IBM or compatible computer (386 or higher)

- Microsoft Windows 3.1 (or higher)

- 4.5 megabytes of free hard disc space

- a mouse.

A color VGA or SVGA monitor is strongly recommended, as *ConStatS* makes extensive use of color.

Installing *ConStatS*

ConStatS comes with an installation program. This program must be run from within Windows. To install *ConStatS* from Windows:

1. Open the *Windows Program Manager*.
2. Place *ConStatS Disk 1* in the computer's floppy drive, typically the *A*: drive.
3. Select **Run** from the Program Manager's *File* menu and a *Run Dialog* Box will appear.
4. Type **a:setup**, in the *Command Line* and select **OK**. (If you are not installing from the *A:*drive, substitute the appropriate drive letter for **a:** in the command.)
5. The *ConStatS Installer* will appear on the screen, as shown in Figure 2.1. By default, *ConStatS* will be installed into the directory *CONSTATS* on the *C:* drive. If you prefer *ConStatS* to be installed in a different directory or disk drive, type the desired disk drive and directory name in the box labelled *Destination Directory*.

Figure 2.1 The ConStatS Installer Showing C:\CONSTATS as the Destination Directory

6. Click on the **Install** button when you are ready to proceed with the installation. (If at any time during the installation you wish to stop or quit, simply click on **Cancel**. A *Confirm Cancel* message will appear on the screen. Select **Yes** to quit the *ConStatS* installation, or **No** to continue with the installation.)

7. As files are loaded into the *Destination Directory*, the arrow on the *ConStatS Installer* screen will move from left to right toward the *bulls-eye target*.

8. At some point during the installation, you will be prompted to insert the second *ConStatS* disk. Remove *ConStatS Disk 1* from the floppy drive. Insert *ConStatS Disk 2*, and select **OK** to continue with the program installation.

9. When all files have been copied to the *Destination Drive*, the *Install* program will offer to create a *Program Group* and a *Program Icon* in *Program Manager*. Select **Yes** to add these to *Program Manager*; otherwise select **No**. (Creating a *Program Icon* simplifies running the *ConStatS* program.)

10. After successful installation, an *Install Complete* message will appear on the screen. Select **OK** to acknowledge completion.

11. To run *ConStatS* after installation, click on the *ConStatS* icon in the *Program Manager* window.

The *ConStatS* Environment

The *ConStatS* program runs under Microsoft Windows and takes advantage of many Windows conventions. The Windows operations most frequently employed in *ConStatS* are:

1. *Using a mouse* to start a program or to select an option. Use the mouse to move the pointer to the desired selection, and then click the left mouse button to activate your choice. ("Clicking" is shorthand for depressing and releasing the left mouse button.)

2. *Moving windows*. Windows appear as rectangular boxes on the screen. They can be moved to another position on the screen, or from front to back on the screen. To reposition a window, move the mouse pointer to the *Caption Bar* at the top of the window. Depress and hold the left mouse button as you move the mouse, and the window will move on the screen. Release the mouse button when the window is in the desired position. To see a window that has been partially obscured by other windows on the screen, click the mouse button once anywhere on the window. It will jump in front of the other windows. To see a window that is completely obscured behind other windows move the other windows out of the way.

3. *Re-sizing windows*. To re-size a window, move the pointer to an edge or corner of a window until the pointer changes to a double-headed arrow. Depress and hold the left mouse button, and as you move the mouse, the window will change size. Release the mouse button when the window has the desired size.

4. *Icon Arrows*. The small up- and down-arrow buttons in the upper-right hand corner of some windows are called *Icon arrows*. Clicking on the down-arrow collapses the window into a small icon at the bottom of the screen. To restore a window, click once on the icon; a short menu list will appear; clicking on the *Restore* option will then restore the window to the screen. The up-arrow makes the window in which you are working fill the entire screen.

The programs in *ConStatS* are designed for experimentation and exploration without the normal restrictions of a rigid step-by-step demonstration. They also provide more assistance and coaching than is available in typical statistics software packages. Each program consists of a sequence of screens that guide the user toward a given objective, such as exploring different graphical displays of a data set or constructing an experiment to investigate the sampling distribution of the mean.

All of the program screens in *ConStatS* share a common structure, illustrated by the screen from the *Displaying Data* program shown in Figure 2.2. Each screen consists of a *main window* (generally at the top of the screen), with one or more *supporting windows*. The main window contains a *text box* (called scaffolding), an *options list*, and four *command buttons* along the bottom of the window. The text box states the purpose of the current screen. The options list represents the selections available to the user in order to proceed to the next screen. The command buttons allow the user to move through the program and provide assistance when difficulty arises. The *supporting windows* may contain text, graphs, or data sets, as seen at the bottom of the screen in Figure 2.2. They may also ask the user to supply information, such as the numerical value of a sample size or probability.

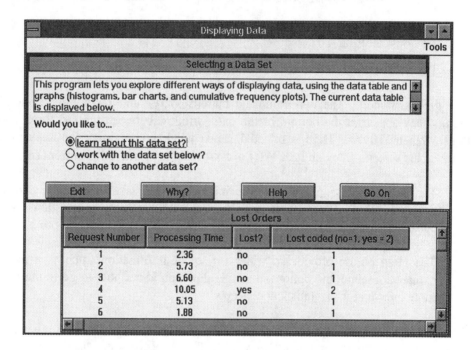

Figure 2.2 Sample Screen from the Data Display Program

Use the mouse and keyboard to move through the *ConStatS* programs as follows:

1. *Choose an option.* Screen options are presented as a list with *radio buttons*, small circles to the left of an option name. To select a particular option, use the mouse to move the pointer to the desired option, and click on it. The option becomes highlighted and the radio button becomes filled in. To de-select the option, click on it again. In Figure 2.2, the option **learn about this data set?** has been selected.

2. *Enter a numerical value.* (Not shown in Figure 2.2.) In various places throughout *ConStatS*, you will need to provide data. A typical prompt might be:

Enter the number of intervals you want: [   ]

To enter a number, move the pointer to the *edit box,* illustrated at the right, and click the mouse button. When the flashing vertical line (cursor) appears in the edit box, enter the desired number using the keyboard.

3. *Move through the program.* Use the two command buttons, **Go On** and **Go Back** (or **Exit**) to move forward and backward from screen to screen. They appear at the bottom of the main window of each *ConStatS* screen.

> The **Go On** button implements a selected option and moves you forward to the next screen. (You can usually double-click an option and automatically move forward.)

> The **Go Back** button returns to the previous screen, allowing you to review or change a previous selection.

> The **Exit** button (not shown in Figure 2.2) is used to exit the *ConStatS* program.

4. *Ask for Assistance.* The two command buttons **Why?** and **Help** provide helpful information. They appear at the bottom of the main window between the **Go Back** and **Go On** buttons. When **Why?** or **Help** is selected, a text window containing the relevant assistance appears on the screen. Click on **Exit Why** or **Exit Help** to return to the current screen.

> The **Why** button explains why you might want to make a particular choice that the program offers. Typically, it consists of a brief statement or question asking you to consider what insights you might gain by choosing the highlighted option.

> The **Help** button provides a wider variety of information, such as a more detailed explanation about the options, a simple direction about how to go to the next step, or more information on statistical concepts.

5. *Tools.* There are two *Tools* sections. Some of the *ConStatS* programs have a separate *Tools* option at the top of the screen (as in Figure 2.2). This *Tools* option is used to control the speed of a process. For example, histograms can be drawn at four different speeds: *Step, Slow, Fast,* and *Results.* Sampling experiments can also take place at different speeds. The *Tools* menu on the main *ConStatS* menu bar has several options. Use this menu to *Copy* a section of the screen to the Windows clipboard, to switch between Windows Colors and *ConStatS* colors, and to exit the program.

Changing the Default Data Sets in the *Data Representation* Programs

The four *Data Representation* (DataRep) programs in *ConStatS* (*Displaying Data, Descriptive Statistics, Transforming Data,* and *Describing Bivariate Data*) make extensive use of data sets. Each of these programs begins with a default data set, but gives the user the option of selecting a different one. The four *Data Representation* programs each have a default data set identified as follows:

ConStatS Program	Name of Default Data Set
Displaying Data	DEFAULT1
Descriptive Statistics	DEFAULT2
Transforming Data	DEFAULT3
Describing Bivariate Data	DEFAULT4

You can specify the set of 4 default files to be used by clicking on the **Data/Examples** menu on the main *ConStatS* menu. Selections include the *ConStatS* defaults, selections of data sets drawn from specific statistics texts, and a *Custom* option that reflects user preferences for default data sets.

The file CUSTOM1 contains the user selected names of the data sets that are used as the four defaults. CUSTOM1 is a text file that may be modified with any standard text editor, such as Windows Notepad or MS-DOS EDIT. The structure of the CUSTOM1 file is as follows:

First Line: **Number of data sets** to be identified as default data sets. In the current version of *ConStatS*, this number should be 4.

Lines 2 to 5: **Names of the files** containing the data sets to be used as default (one name per line). The data file named on line 2 becomes DEFAULT1, the default data set for the *Displaying Data* program. The data file named on line 3, becomes DEFAULT2, the default data set for the *Descriptive Statistics* program, etc.

After this file is edited, it must be saved in ASCII format in the *ConStatS* directory. Figure 2.3 shows an example CUSTOM1 file. In this example, INCOME.DET is DEFAULT1 (the default for *Displaying Data*), US_EDUC.DST is DEFAULT2 (the default for *Descriptive Statistics*), etc.

4
income.det
us_educ.dst
macro.det
fortune.det

Figure 2.3   Example CUSTOM1 File

Creating New Data Sets

You can add new data sets to *ConStatS* by creating a data file containing the desired information. The data file can be prepared using any text editor, such as Windows Notepad or MS-DOS EDIT. It must conform to the following line-by-line structure. See Figure 2.4 for an example of a data file.

First Line: **Data Set Description**. Text describing the data set. The text may be as long as 512 characters, and must occupy only the first line of the file. In Figure 2.4, the description is:

Long distance phone bill for a single individual.

13

<u>Second Line</u>: **Data Set Characteristics**. Four components separated by spaces or tabs:

1. **Caption**: Alphanumeric text, having a maximum of 40 characters and appearing in double quotes, that will serve as the caption for the data table. ("Long distance phone bill" in Figure 2.4)

2. **Data code**: A number that *ConStatS* uses to interpret the contents of the file. Always enter 100 when constructing a data set.

3. **Number of variables**: An integer value. (4 in Figure 2.4)

4. **Number of data values** for each variable: An integer value. (14 in Figure 2.4)

<u>Third Line</u>: **Variable names**. Variable names can be a maximum of 40 characters, but brief names (less than 10 characters) work best. They must appear in double quotes and be separated by spaces or tabs. The number of names on this line must agree with the number of variables specified in the third component on line 2. (In Figure 2.4 the variable names are "Call", "City called", "Length (in minutes)", and "Cost (in $$)".)

<u>Fourth Line</u>: **Variable precision**. An integer code describing the precision to which values of each variable will be displayed. A 0 indicates an integer; a 1, 2, or 3 indicate the number of decimal places for real variables. The number of items on this line must agree with the number of variables specified in line 2. The codes apply to the variables in the order they are listed on line 3, and must be separated by spaces or tabs. (In Figure 2.4 they are 0, 0, 0, and 2.)

<u>Fifth Line</u>: **Type of variable**. An integer code that describes the type of variable. A 0 indicates an alphanumeric variable, a 1 indicates a numeric value. The number of items on this line must agree with the number of variables specified in line 2. The codes apply to the variables in the order they are listed on line 3, and must be separated by spaces or tabs. (In Figure 2.4 they are 1, 0, 1, and 1.)

<u>Remaining Lines</u>: **Values for each of the variables**. Values are entered one line at a time. Each line contains one value for each variable. Each value on a line must be separated by tabs or spaces. Alphanumeric values must be in double quotes. The number of items on this line must agree with the number of variables specified in line 2 and be entered in the order the variables are listed on line 3. The number of lines must agree with the number of data values specified in line 2. (The remaining lines in Figure 2.4 provide the values in this example.)

Once created, the data file must be saved as an ASCII file in the *ConStatS* directory. For compatibility with the *ConStatS* protocol for naming files according to academic discipline, the data file extension must be one of the following:

.dbt = data for Biology	.dpt = data for Psychology
.det = data for Economics	.dst = data for Sociology
.dgt = data for Engineering	.dzt = Generic

14

Long distance phone bill for a single individual.
"Long Distance Phone Bill" 100 4 14

"Call"	"City called"	"Length (in min.)"	"Cost (in $$)"
0	0	0	2
1	0	1	1
1	"Albany"	3	2.00
2	"Seattle"	6	1.60
3	"Charlotte"	10	2.60
4	"Milwaukee"	12	2.80
5	"Baltimore"	17	1.90
6	"Seattle"	16	8.40
7	"Albany"	15	2.40
8	"Phoenix"	12	2.50
9	"San Francisco"	16	4.60
10	"Seattle"	32	3.30
11	"Charlotte"	28	3.30
12	"Seattle"	41	9.50
13	"Baltimore"	37	.90
14	"Charlotte"	44	5.80

Figure 2.4 Example of a *ConStatS* Data file

Adding or Modifying Examples in *Sampling* and *Inference*

Two *Sampling* programs, *Sampling Distributions* and *Sampling Errors*, allow users to define random variables and population distributions. Both the *Inference* programs permit users to add problem contexts. Instructions for adding random variables and problem contexts are in the Appendix.

PART ONE

REPRESENTING DATA

Statistics is a science for extracting useful, instructive information from data. The trouble with data is that there are usually ever so many of them. Picture trying to extract information about differences in incomes between last year and this by looking through a list of 80 million incomes for the last two years. Ways of *representing data* are needed in which the data are aggregated into more compact, distilled forms, preferably forms that accentuate features of particular interest. This need explains why so much of statistics is devoted to descriptive tasks, including ways of displaying data graphically and ways of summarizing them numerically, like the mean and the median. This is what *Representing Data* is all about.

ConStatS includes four programs under *Representing Data*. *Displaying Data* covers the principal ways of presenting data graphically for one variable at a time, with emphasis on histograms. *Descriptive Statistics* covers "statistics" used in summarizing data in a single variable—e.g., the mean, the median, the standard deviation, the interquartile range, etc. These two programs are basic. A central concern in both is, what information is retained and what information is lost with different ways in which univariate data are commonly represented? *Descriptive Statistics* is also concerned with how sensitive the different summary statistics are to individual data or groups of data, this with the goal of developing a feel for the numbers themselves.

Transforming Data covers ways of mathematically transforming data into different forms that are often easier to work with for certain purposes. It treats basic ways of transforming data, like changing units or switching to standardized Z scores used in many disciplines. It also offers the more advanced option of exploring nonlinear transformations. Finally, *Describing Bivariate Data* covers scatter plots for graphically displaying data in two variables, correlation coefficients, and least squares (i.e., linear regression) lines. In addition to introducing these techniques, it includes the more advanced topic of their use in searching for relationships between variables. It includes an option of transforming the data in either or both variables under investigation (but this option can be passed over throughout).

Chapter 3

Displaying Data

What May Be Investigated with the *Displaying Data* Program:

- How to *interrogate* data, in pursuit of useful information
- How to construct a histogram displaying data for a variable from a table
- How to display data in the form of CDF (cumulative distribution function) plots
- What information is lost in different types of univariate displays of data

Why Use This Program?

We have all heard, "A picture is worth a thousand words." This cliché helps explain why pictorial displays of data are important in statistics. Nevertheless, one should never lose sight of the fact that pictorial displays of data can be deceiving. Consider an example. A teacher gives an hour test to 20 students. The grades, in the order in which the tests were turned in, are 92, 89, 79, 90, 82, 80, 97, 76, 61, 75, 89, 81, 80, 90, 74, 78, 75, 79, 91, 62. In order to convert the grades to A's, B's, etc., the teacher groups them into those above 90, those above 80, etc., and prepares the graph shown on the right displaying the results of the test. This graph gives the impression that the

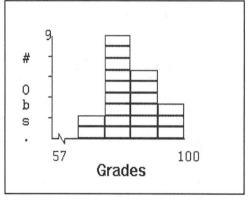

results were just the sort teachers hope for: most of the students are in the middle, and just a handful, more or less in balance, at the two extremes. But there is nothing magical about grouping grades into 90s and 80s. Suppose instead the teacher had used intervals of 6 points each: 95-100, 89-94, 83-88, etc. The corresponding graph, at the right, gives a totally different impression, that the test was the kind a teacher most dreads: the class splits into two halves, with no one in the middle. This second graph displays exactly the same data as the first; yet it conveys a completely different picture of what happened on the test. How can this be? More to the point, which graph is more correct? Which one would give the students more helpful information about how they did on the test? (Could this be what the critics mean when they talk about "lying with statistics"?)

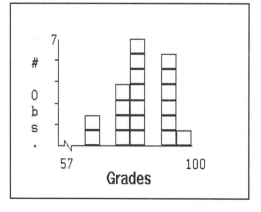

The discipline of statistics is about extracting useful information from data. Data can be presented in many different ways. The most direct way is to list them in a table. As you will see, this is the primary form in which you will find almost all of the data in *ConStatS*. One trouble with tables—to use still another cliché—is that, as the number of entries in the table grows, one has increasing trouble "seeing the forest for the trees." We want to be able to see main trends and important features immediately. Graphical displays are better for this purpose. The *Displaying Data* program lets you experiment with the most common ways of graphically displaying data involving a single variable. Technically, these are called *univariate displays*.

The two graphs on the preceding page are examples of *histograms*. The histogram is the most widely used type of univariate display and is employed most often throughout *ConStatS*. It is therefore important for you to understand histograms and their limitations before you proceed to the rest of the program. Every type of pictorial display of data sacrifices some information in order to highlight other information. You want to see what sorts of information histograms are especially good at highlighting; but you also want to become very aware of what sorts of information tend to be lost when a *data table* is turned into a histogram. Skill in reading a histogram includes an ability to recognize when you ought to go back and look at the data more closely because the histogram could well be giving you a misleading impression. The best way to learn to read histograms is by learning to construct them from tables of data. The *Displaying Data* program makes it easy to do this, letting you experiment with multiple histograms for the same data.

There are other ways besides histograms for displaying data involving a single variable. For example, you can simply plot the data in the order in which they were obtained—in effect, versus time. Or you can show the pattern with which they progress from the lowest value to the highest in a *CDF*, or *cumulative distribution function*, display. Each method has its own way of highlighting information that tends to be lost in histograms while sacrificing some of their advantages. The *Displaying Data* program allows you to experiment with these methods, comparing them side-by-side with histograms in order to see what each does well. Because every *data set* can be a story unto itself, the best way to use *Displaying Data* is to examine lots of different data.

How to Explore Data with the *Displaying Data* Program

Before starting the *Displaying Data* program, select **Data/Examples** from the *ConStatS* menu, highlight **ConStatS Default**, and release the mouse button. To run the *Displaying Data* program, select **DataRep** from the *ConStatS* menu. Choose **Displaying Data** and then click on the **Go On** button. The screen shown in Figure 3.1 will appear, presenting you with three options: *learn about this data set*, *work with the data set below*, and *change to another data set*. As you can see by clicking on **change to another data set** and **Go On**, a large number of other data sets are available. The example below uses the *US Education* data set shown in the figure. As the description of this data set says, the obvious questions it raises are about why each variable has a handful of states falling clearly outside the cluster formed by the rest—i.e., what are called "outliers." To access the description of this data set, click on **learn about this data set** and **Go On**.

Look over the data before proceeding. Only a small portion of the table is visible initially. Clicking on the arrows in the corners lets you scroll through it, horizontally or vertically. You can also expand the window for the moment (by using the mouse to drag the left corner) in order to see more at one time. The important things to note are the variables for which data are given, listed at the top of each column, and the type of data given for each.

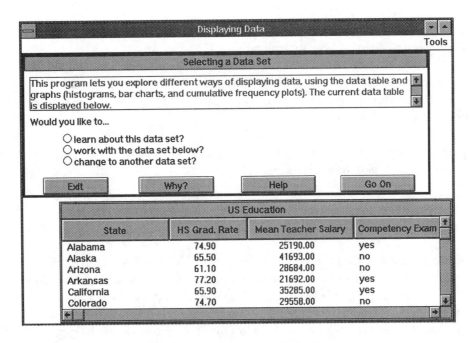

Figure 3.1 Selecting a Data Set

When you are ready to continue, choose **work with the data set below** and click on the **Go On** button. The screen shown in Figure 3.2 offers the three main pathways that you can proceed along in the *Displaying Data* program:

1. You can explore the data-table by clicking on **examine the data in the table**.

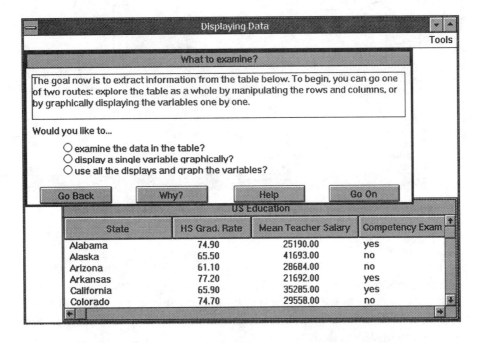

Figure 3.2 The Three Main Pathways in *Displaying Data*

2. You can construct graphical displays of any variable in the data-set by clicking on **display a single variable graphically**.

3. You can use the table and the different ways of graphing variables simultaneously to engage in what is known as "data analysis" by clicking on **use all the displays and graph the variables**.

The third option, although ultimately most interesting, presupposes the other two; we will come back to it after discussing the table and the different displays.

Examining the Data in the Table

Choose **examine the data in the table** and click on **Go On**. You will have three options: *review data tables*, *check the extreme [high and low] values*, and *sort the table*. Select the first and click on **Go On** for a quick review of terminology used to discuss data tables, in particular *rows*, *columns*, and *variables*. Then click on **Go Back.** The other two options let you focus on some aspect of the data. Click first on **check the extreme [high and low] values** and **Go On**. The screen shown in Figure 3.3 will appear. Click on a variable (heading of a column) and the highest and lowest value will be shown. The

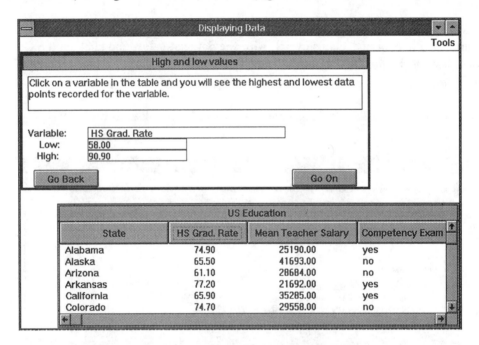

Figure 3.3 High and Low Values

interesting question is how different these two are. For example, the figure indicates that the lowest high school graduation rate for any state is 58.0% and the highest, 90.9%—a striking difference. Proceed through each variable to see whether the difference between the high and low of any of the others is so extreme. In particular, check the high and low for *Expenditures per Pupil*, the other variable we will use extensively in the example below.

22

After looking at the high and low values for each variable, click on **Go Back** to return to the primary options. Then click on **sort the table** and **Go On**. You will again be asked to select a variable, which you do by clicking on a heading. The point of *sorting* the table is to rearrange the rows so that the entries in a column have been put in order. You can sort for only one variable at a time. Click on **HS Grad. Rate** and **Go On**, and the screen shown in Figure 3.4 will appear.

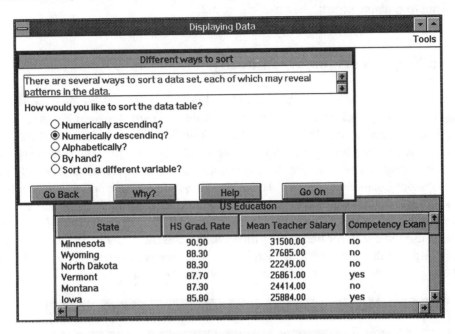

Figure 3.4 Sorting the Table

This *Different ways to sort* screen gives you five options. In the example shown in the figure, we chose to sort the table from the highest to the lowest values of *High School Graduation Rate* (by clicking on **Numerically descending** and **Go On**). The six states with the highest graduation rates can be seen right away. You can scroll through the table to see the whole progression from top to bottom. If you want to know which states have the lowest graduation rates, click on **Numerically Ascending** and **Go On** (or simply double click on **Numerically Ascending**) and the order will be reversed.

Use the *Alphabetically* option to restore the table to its original form after first double clicking on **Sort on a different variable** and then clicking on **State**. The *By Hand* option lets you re-order the rows in the table, one by one, in any way you wish. For example, you might want to group the states separately by region. Doing that takes more time, although still much less time here on the computer than it would to write out the whole table by hand in a different order.

Once you feel comfortable with the five sorting options, choose *Sort on a different variable* to proceed through every variable in the table. Each time you sort on a variable, scroll through the table in order to take a quick glance at where various states lie. For example, you might check your home state in every case. Or you might look to see whether the three states with the highest graduation rates—Minnesota, Wyoming, and North Dakota—and the three with the lowest—Florida, District of Columbia, and Georgia—show up near the top or bottom of any of the other variables.

23

Scroll to the left to see all the other variables. In the case of each variable ask yourself why the top and bottom six states appear where they do. You will find lots of other questions surfacing along the way. Raising questions is the main goal at this point.

Take your time examining the data in the table. When you are ready to go on, click **Go Back** twice to return to the *What to examine* screen, shown in Figure 3.2.

Displaying a Single Variable Graphically

The next step is to consider different ways of graphically displaying the *US Education* data. Click on **display a single variable graphically** in the *What to examine* screen shown in Figure 3.2 and **Go On**. You will be asked to select the variable you want to work with, which you do by clicking on a heading. To continue with the example here, click **Expend. per Pupil** and **Go On**. The screen shown in Figure 3.5 then offers four display options. The *bar chart* option is for non-numerical data only (such as the *Yes*-and-*No* data under *Competency Exam*). The *in the observed sequence* option is for plotting the data in the sequence in which they were observed, and hence in effect versus time. When the data involve some significant temporal sequence, such as US Gross National Product or the Dow-Jones Average, this option should be used to check for trends over time. In the present example, the data are sequenced in the alphabetical order of the states; plotting them in this sequence is pointless. You should explore both the bar-chart and observed-sequence options on your own at a later time.

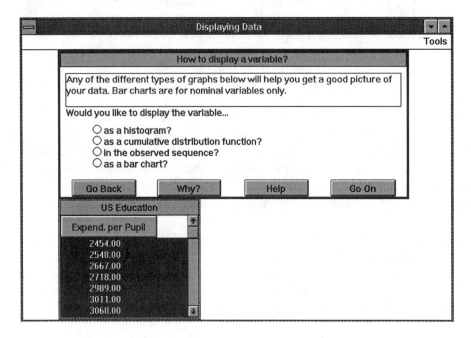

Figure 3.5 Selecting a Type of Display

The best way through the program the first time is to postpone the *cumulative distribution function* option until you have experience with histograms. Click on **as a histogram** and **Go On**. The program leads you step-by-step through the construction of a histogram displaying the *Expenditure per Pupil* data. The first time through the process, pause at the end of each step to make sure you see just what has been done. As the data are plotted, scroll down to see where the next set of points on the graph are coming from. The data in the listing are in ascending order, but they are being grouped to form stacks of data points on the histogram. As a result, the differences among the values within any one such group disappear in the histogram. This loss of information is the price that has to be paid to obtain a better picture of the *distribution* of the data—i.e., of how the data are *distributed* from low to high.

Continue through all of the steps until the histogram for *Expenditures per Pupil* is completed, as in Figure 3.6. The distribution is distinctive. All but seven of the states have expenditures per pupil in the lowest five intervals. The remaining seven extend across five intervals at the high end, producing a *skewed* distribution. This pattern was not immediately evident just from scanning the table.

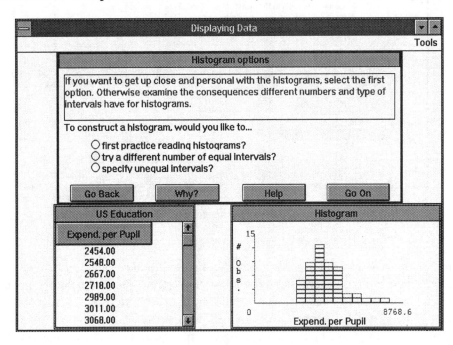

Figure 3.6 Histogram for Expenditures Per Pupil

The *Tools* option in the upper right gives you a choice of four speeds when constructing a histogram: *Step*, *Slow*, *Fast*, and *Results*. Stick with *Step* the first time through. Once you feel confident about how a histogram is constructed, select one of the alternatives to automate the process. The *Tools* option also lets you open (and close) a window showing the full data table if you should wish to see it. Keep this in mind.

The screen shown in Figure 3.6 offers three options for looking more carefully at the histogram you have just constructed. *First practice reading histograms* lets you review the elements that entered into the construction of the histogram. Selecting it will produce a window presenting five alternatives for review, as shown in Figure 3.7. Each is instructive, the third and fourth especially so. They allow you to highlight individual data points or groups on the graph (by clicking on them); by scrolling up or down along the data column, you can find the corresponding entry or group of entries in the table, enabling you to see exactly where each data point on the graph came from. In the example shown in the figure, we clicked on a point in the middle of the graph, and then found that it represents the specific entry of $3,919 per pupil.

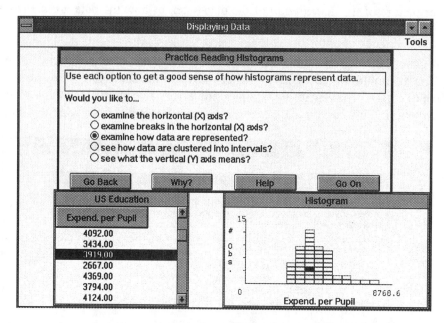

Figure 3.7 Practice Reading Histograms

The other two options offered in the screen shown in Figure 3.6 allow you to examine what effect the specific intervals have on the pattern displayed in the histogram. The example of the hour test at the beginning of the chapter shows that different choices of intervals can result in different pictures. Has that happened here? *ConStatS* normally employs 10 equal spaced intervals when constructing histograms. This is a "default" value built into the program in order to avoid burdening you with having to choose every time. There is nothing about the default value of 10 that makes it more correct than various other numbers, say 12 intervals. Too few or too many intervals obscure the pattern in which the data are distributed. The preferred intermediate number between too few and too many depends on the data, as well as on what information you are trying to extract by displaying them in a histogram.

You can explore unequal intervals on your own after finishing this example. Click on **try a different number of equal intervals** and **Go On**. The screen shown in Figure 3.8 will let you try different numbers of equal intervals. Try the two automated choices first, *1* and *6*. Needless to say, a single interval is too few to display any pattern at all. But what about 6? What information is disappearing when the number of intervals drops from 10 to 6? Can you think of any conclusions that you would reach from the histogram with 6 intervals that differ from ones that you would reach from the one with 10 intervals? Next select the option of entering your own number of intervals. Try numbers progressively from 4 to 20. As Figure 3.8 shows, the straightforward pattern obtained with the default value of 10 intervals breaks down to some extent with 20 intervals. If you wanted to publish a histogram of these data on expenditures, what number of intervals would you now choose—and why?

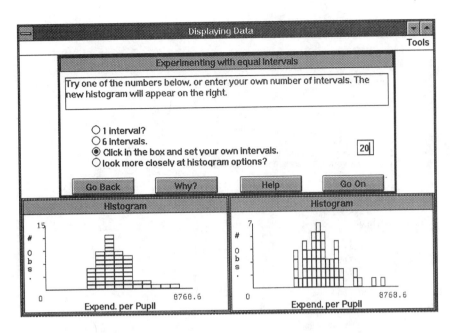

Figure 3.8 Experimenting with Equal Intervals

The last option offered in the screen shown in Figure 3.8, *look more closely at histogram options*, leads to a screen giving you some additional options. The first two of these, *display a subset of the data* and *create a relative frequency distribution*, allow you to construct variants of the histogram you have. For example, you can use the *subset* option to construct a new histogram of *Expenditures per Pupil* in which the 7 states at the high end are excluded from consideration. The *relative frequency distribution* option, by contrast, replaces the histogram with a plot indicating the fraction of the total states lying in each interval, with the total of the fractions summing to 1; this kind of plot makes it easier to compare the distribution of the data in the histogram with different theoretical probability distributions. In addition to these two options, the screen lets you *use a different type of graph for this variable* or *work with a different variable or data set*. If you have this screen in front of you, click on the button for the former of these and **Go On** in order to return to the screen shown in Figure 3.5. Alternatively, if the screen in front of you is the one in Figure 3.8, click twice on **Go Back** to return to this screen.

The one remaining univariate display available from the screen shown in Figure 3.5 is the *cumulative distribution function*. If you are just learning about this type of display here, click on **Tools** and make sure the speed is set to *Step* before continuing. Then click on **as a cumulative distribution function** and **Go On** in order to proceed step by step through the process of constructing a *CDF* display of *Expenditures per Pupil*. The individual data entries are plotted starting from the lowest expenditure per pupil and proceeding to the highest. The vertical location of each successive point on the plot corresponds to the count of the number of points plotted so far. The resulting graph therefore displays, for each level of expenditure per pupil, the number of states with that level *or less*. Since the data cover the 50 states and the District of Columbia, the last point on the plot must be at 51 on the Y-axis. The completed CDF is shown in a window labeled *Sample CDF* in the lower right hand corner (see Figure 3.9). It is called "Sample CDF" because it displays a CDF for data, in contrast to a CDF display of a theoretical probability distribution. One virtue of CDFs is that they make it easy to compare distributions of data with different probability distributions.

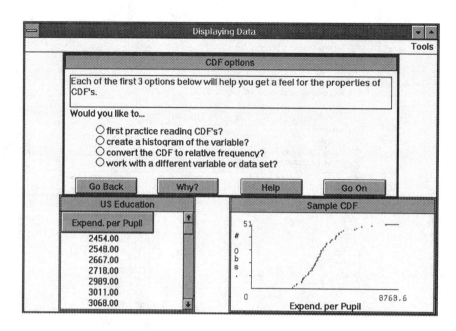

Figure 3.9 CDF for Expenditures Per Pupil

As Figure 3.9 shows, the screen offers three options for experimenting further with the CDF you have just constructed. The *first practice reading CDF's* option lets you review just how the data get represented in the CDF. In particular, two of the options available to give practice in reading CDF's, *see what the ordinate represents* and *examine how data are represented*, allow you to click on individual points on the plot in order to see exactly what they represent.

A second important virtue of CDF data displays is the added insights they can provide into histograms of the same data. Picture a single histogram interval somewhere near the middle of the X-axis in the CDF plot in Figure 3.9. You can tell how many states will be stacked in this interval in any histogram simply by counting the number of points that lie in this interval on the CDF. Even easier, you can see immediately whether a large number or a small number of states will be stacked in this interval in the histogram by the slope of the CDF plot. Wherever the expenditures per pupil in several states cluster closely together, the slope of the CDF plot becomes steep. Wherever the expenditures from state to state are more spread out, so that fewer states fall in any one interval, the slope of the CDF plot levels out toward the horizontal. The nearly horizontal segment of the CDF plot extending across the right hand side at the top corresponds to the skewed tail at the high end of the histogram you obtained earlier for *Expenditures per Pupil*. The fact that the distribution is skewed toward the high end is already evident in the CDF plot, because there is no comparable horizontal segment balancing it on the left hand side at the bottom.

We can exploit this systematic relationship between CDFs and histograms to anticipate what the histogram will look like with different numbers of intervals. Earlier we did this by trial and error, trying different numbers of intervals. Now click on **create a histogram of the variable** and **Go On**. The CDF plot shifts to the lower left corner on the screen. The instruction that appears at the top tells you to click along the X-axis of the CDF plot to define intervals for a histogram. As you do so, look at the CDF plot to see whether you may be accidentally grouping states together whose expenditures per pupil are significantly different. (You can erase any interval boundary you have marked by clicking on it again.)

28

Once you have marked off a complete set of intervals, click on **Plot the data using the current intervals** and **Go On**, and a screen similar to Figure 3.10 appears. Experiment with different intervals on the CDF or click on the horizontal X-axis of the histogram to mark intervals directly on it. After experimenting a bit with the intervals, you will be in a good position to decide how many equal intervals you want to use in any histogram of these data that you will be presenting to others.

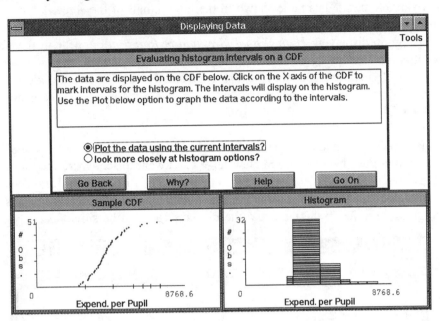

Figure 3.10 Using a CDF to Construct a Histogram

Recall the example at the beginning of the chapter of the teacher who plotted the grades from an hour test on a histogram, grouping 90s, 80s, etc. A CDF would have made it glaringly evident from the outset that there were no grades in the middle 80s and that the teacher's histogram would give a quite misleading picture of how the grades were distributed. A histogram cannot show the differences in the individual data within any one interval. Hence, you cannot tell from a histogram alone whether the data within an interval form a group or whether data that are plotted in two different adjacent intervals have more in common with one another than those within the individual intervals. With a CDF, by contrast, you can see immediately how near to one another consecutive data points lie and any gaps among them.

Using the Displays in Data Analysis

The two main pathways in *Displaying Data* that we have been examining are intended to help you become familiar with data tables and different types of univariate displays. The third pathway allows you to explore different ways of using these resources when dealing with data. Early in the chapter we used the cliché, "having trouble seeing the forest for the trees," to describe the principal shortcoming of data tables. Graphical displays of data tend to have just the opposite shortcoming. They bring out patterns of different kinds in the data, making the forest clear, but in the process they downplay the individual data, diverting attention away from the trees. Obviously, the best approach when looking through data in search of issues and insights is to use tables and displays in combination with one another, flipping back and forth among them. The third pathway in *Displaying Data* offers several ways of doing this. We shall illustrate two of them here.

Click on **Go Back** to return to the *What to examine* screen shown in Figure 3.2. Click on **use all the displays and graph the variables** and **Go On** to open the pathway. Options become available when you click on a variable in the data table shown in the bottom half of the screen. Click on **HS Grad. Rate**, next on **Display** in the small window that opens, and then on **Histogram** in the next small window. A histogram displaying *High School Graduation Rates* will appear in the upper left hand corner. Now click on **Display** again, and then on **CDF**. A CDF of these data will appear. Use the mouse to drag the CDF to the right, so that the histogram and the CDF lie side by side, as in Figure 3.11. Notice that the CDF brings out right away why there is a gap in the middle of the histogram: the same gap occurs in the CDF.

You can use the two displays and the table together to "interrogate" the data. For example, suppose you have a particular interest in New York and New Jersey and want to see where they lie in the displays. Scroll the table down until these two states are visible, then click first on **New Jersey** and then on **New York**. As shown in Figure 3.11, the rows in the table and the corresponding data points in the display become highlighted. Entries in the table and the displays can also be simultaneously highlighted by

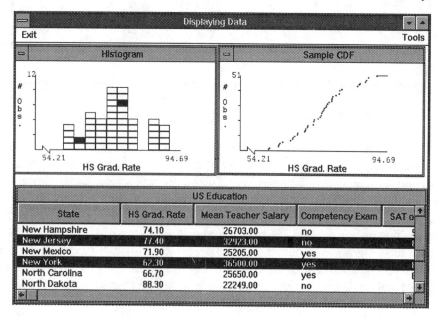

Figure 3.11 Interrogating a Variable

clicking on data points in the histogram. Clicking on any highlighted entry, either in the table or the display, will remove the highlighting from it. This facility lets you get answers to lots of different types of questions. For example, click on **New Jersey** to eliminate the highlighting on it, then click on the remaining five data points that form the last two intervals at the low end of the histogram. Now you can scroll along the table to see which six states are at the bottom of *High School Graduation Rate*.

Displays and the table can be used together in another way. Close the *HS Grad. Rate* CDF, drag the histogram of these data over to the right, and scroll across the table and click on **Expend. per Pupil**. Now click on **Display**, followed by **Histogram**. Histograms for the two variables will appear side by side, as in Figure 3.12. Click on individual data points in either histogram to see where the corresponding entry appears in the other one. In Figure 3.12 we have clicked on the five highest expenditures

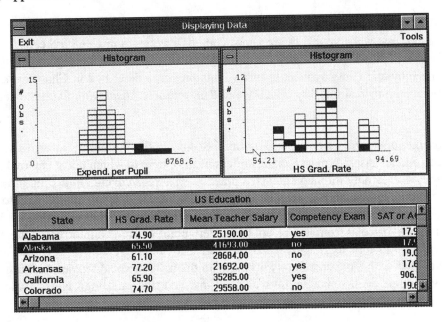

Figure 3.12 Interrogating Two Variables At Once

per pupil. Perhaps somewhat surprisingly, only one of these five fall at the high end of *High School Graduation Rate*, and three of them fall decidedly near the low end. By turning off this highlighting and then clicking on the nine entries at the high end of *HS Grad. Rate*, you can see whether states with high graduation rates spend more or less per pupil. In short, the two simultaneous histogram displays allow you to begin looking to see whether there is any systematic relationship—any *correlation*—between the data in the two variables.

These are just two examples of the many combinations you can use to interrogate data. For a striking third example, click on **Competency Exam**, and then display the data in it in a bar chart adjacent to one of the histograms. By clicking on all the *Yes* entries, in the bar chart, you can see if there is any relationship between requiring such an exam and the other variable. Other examples abound.

Using Displays of Data: Some Further Experiments to Consider

The preceding example covers many of the options in *Displaying Data*. But it has been limited to two variables from a single data set, and one of these variables has been considered only briefly. The challenge of finding informative ways of displaying data can take on entirely different forms with other data. The important thing to do from here, therefore, is to go back through the program with other data.

For starters look at some of the other variables in *US Education*. Many insights about secondary education in the United States are buried in this data table. Then try at least one other data set, *Macroeconomic data*. The data here are historically sequenced, in contrast to the data in *US Education*. Hence, they can be used to explore the advantages of some of the options ignored above, especially the option of displaying the data *in the observed sequence*. Alternatively, choose a data set on a topic of special interest to you, one that you already have some provocative questions that you would like to find answers to.

Working with your own data is often more fun than working with data put together by someone else. This is even more true when your data are about you. The program in *ConStatS* called *An Experiment in Mental Imagery* allows you to carry out a well known experiment in cognitive psychology with yourself as the subject. You may want to turn to this program, described in Chapter 14, to generate a data set on your own mental imagery capacity and then return to *Displaying Data* to examine this data set in detail.

Extracting useful information from data is an art. So too is finding highly informative ways of displaying data to others. As with most arts, regardless of the extent to which talent can make a difference, real proficiency comes only through extensive practice. The *Displaying Data* program is available at every point as you continue on into other programs in *ConStatS*. You can always turn to it even while in the middle of another program simply by clicking on **DataRep** and then selecting it. When you are finished with it, you can exit from it to return to the very point where you interrupted the other program. We encourage you to turn to *Displaying Data* each time you start with a new data set, if only to familiarize yourself with the data before working with them. You should invariably turn to *Displaying Data* when you come upon something in a data set that you find puzzling. Never underestimate how much you can learn just from examining data closely.

Chapter 4

Descriptive Statistics

What May Be Investigated with the *Descriptive Statistics* Program:

- What the measures of central tendency (mean, median, mode) capture
- What the measures of spread (variance, standard deviation, interquartile range) capture
- How most of these summary measures involve a balance of some sort
- What is gained and lost in using combinations of these measures to summarize data
- How sensitive the different summary statistics are to extreme observations

Why Use This Program?

When summarizing their admissions practices to prospective applicants, colleges normally list the median and interquartile range of the SAT or ACT scores of their students. When asked what starting salaries their graduates received last year, however, they are more inclined to give the mean and the standard deviation. Why the difference?

In both cases colleges are using a couple of numbers to summarize a large body of data—which is why such numbers are called *summary* or *descriptive statistics*. These statistics are much easier to work with than a several-page listing of data, or even a histogram. In particular, it is much easier to answer questions about how different colleges compare with one another by comparing summary statistics than by comparing histograms. The mean and median represent the *center* of a body of data—they are answers to the question, around what value do the data tend to be centered? The standard deviation and the interquartile range represent the *spread* of a body of data—they are answers to the question, how spread out are the data? The mode is another measure of center, and the variance and the range are other measures of spread. There are also measures of the *shape* of a body of data, such as the skew, which is an answer to the question, how non-symmetrically are the data distributed?

Why do colleges use the median and interquartile range for test scores, but use the mean and standard deviation for starting salaries? Keep this question in mind while using the *Descriptive Statistics* program to examine how different summary statistics represent data. Why is there more than one measure of center and spread? Numerical measures of the center and spread do not always give an accurate picture of the total data. In cases where the distribution of the data has gaps or multiple peaks, descriptive statistics can be quite misleading, with few data lying in the vicinity of either the mean or the median. While the mean and median have similar values in the case of symmetrically distributed data, they can be very different when the data are skewed. How well any particular measures of center and spread represent the overall body of data therefore depends on the specific data in question. In some cases certain combinations of descriptive statistics give a more informative picture of the overall data, and in other cases other combinations do so.

There is also the matter of what one wants to emphasize about a body of data. Different summary statistics emphasize different aspects of data. Some summary statistics are sensitive to a small handful of the data; their numerical values can change by a large amount when a few data are altered or omitted from a data set. For example, because the mean takes into account how much the data deviate from one another, while the median is based only on the rank ordering of the data, the mean is much more sensitive to data lying extremely far from the center. Consequently, the median provides a more resistant measure of the center because its value is relatively unaffected when a few data are altered or omitted. The mean invariably lies closer than the median to the long tail of a skewed distribution. In effect, therefore, the mean places greater emphasis on this tail.

Maybe colleges think that the median and interquartile range offer the most accurate representation of test scores, while the mean and standard deviation do so in the case of starting salaries, or maybe they are trying to emphasize different aspects of the test scores and the starting salaries. To see what might be going on in this case—and countless others in which descriptive statistics are being used to replace a data set—you need to understand what it is about data that makes certain descriptive statistics more appropriate to use than others. What is gained in using the mean, or the median, as a substitute for the data, and what is lost? Similarly, what is gained and lost in using different measures of spread to indicate how widely the data are spread? Under what circumstances do different combinations of summary statistics give a seriously misleading picture of data? The *Descriptive Statistics* program allows you to carry out experiments that will help answer such questions. With it you can develop more feel for the values of summary statistics, as well as a sense of when to be cautious in relying on these values in answering questions.

How to Use the *Descriptive Statistics* Program—An Overview

Before starting the *Descriptive Statistics* program, select **Data/Examples** from the *ConStatS* menu, highlight **ConStatS Default**, and release the mouse button. To run the *Descriptive Statistics* program, select **DataRep** from the *ConStatS* menu, click once on **Descriptive Statistics** and then **Go On**. You will be offered a default data set, *US Education*. You can select a different data set if you wish, but we will use this one here. Click on **Use the current data set**, followed by **Go On**, and the screen shown in Figure 4.1 appears. This screen presents you with four options:

1. *Examine measures of Center and Spread.* This option allows you to explore how the different summary statistics typically strike a balance of some sort involving either deviations or ranks; you can first examine deviations and ranks, if you wish, and then try your hand at estimating or "eyeballing" the values for different statistics.

2. *Describe distributions using Summary Statistics.* This option allows you to experiment with how well different combinations of summary statistics capture bodies of data by trying to picture the overall data set, given only summary statistics.

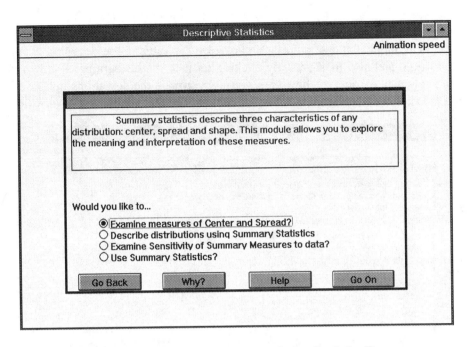

Figure 4.1 Basic Options in the *Descriptive Statistics* Program

3. *Examine Sensitivity of Summary Measures to data.* This option allows you to assess how sensitive different summary statistics are to individual data through experiments in which you can temporarily remove data from the data set.

4. *Use Summary Statistics.* This option allows you to examine data, histograms displaying them, and descriptive statistics summarizing them in various combinations for any variable in any of the available data sets.

Since this is the natural sequence in which to begin using each of the options, they will be covered in this order below.

Examining Measures of Center and Spread

To select this option, click on **Examine measures of Center and Spread,** as shown in Figure 4.1, and then **Go On.** Select the variable *High School Graduation Rate* by clicking on **HS Grad. Rate** in the data table and **Go On.** You will then have the option of working with measures of center or measures of spread. Use the **Why?** and **Help** buttons if you are uncertain about why you might want to proceed with one of these options instead of the other. Here we will first work with statistics for the center and then turn to the spread.

Click on **Work with center statistics** and **Go On.** You can now examine the mean, the median, or the mode. Click on **Examine deviation and rank** and **Go On** to see what each of these are. A histogram of the high school graduation rates of the different states appears giving you the option of looking at deviations or ranks. Choose the former by clicking on **Examine Observation Deviations** and **Go On** (an observation is an individual data point). You can see the value of the deviation of any single data point from the mean, and also its square, by clicking on it in the histogram, as shown in Figure 4.2. After you try a few data entries, see how well you can estimate the deviations before clicking on the data entry in the histogram. Now turn to *Ranks* by clicking **Go On**, **Examine Observation Ranks**, and

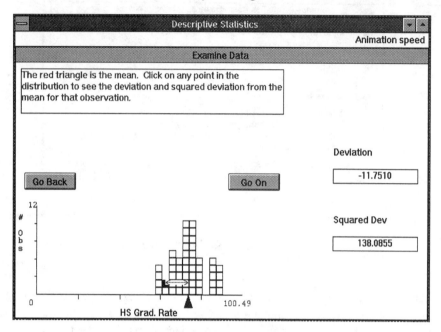

Figure 4.2 Examining Deviations from the Mean

Go On. You can see the rank and the percentile of any data entry in the histogram by clicking on it. Again try your hand at estimating the rank and percentile before clicking on the entry. When you are ready, click **Go On**, and then **Continue** and **Go On** to return to the screen that presents you the option of working with the mean, median, or mode.

Click on **Work with the mean** and **Go On** to try your hand at estimating the mean. The screen in Figure 4.3 appears. Estimate the mean either by clicking on *Estimate* and entering your estimate of the value directly, or by clicking on the pointer below the histogram and dragging it along the X-axis of the histogram to where you think the mean is located. For example, enter *75* in the *Estimate* box. Click **Go On** to see how close your estimate is. The data entries above and below your mean will then be shown in different colors, and the sum of the deviations below and above your estimate will be displayed on the right hand side of the screen, as shown in Figure 4.4. Your estimate will be precisely correct when the two columns on the right are exactly in balance with one another. You can examine how each data entry affects this balance by double clicking **Analyze Current Estimate**, or you can proceed directly to another estimate by double clicking **Try another estimate**. Continue until you get the true value.

You can carry out similar experiments with the median or mode by clicking on **Go Back**, **Work with the median** or **Work with the mode**, and **Go On**.

36

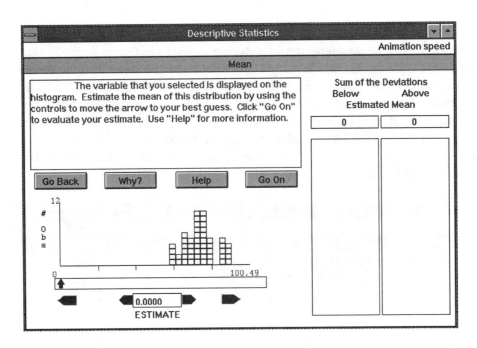

Figure 4.3 Making Your Estimate of the Mean

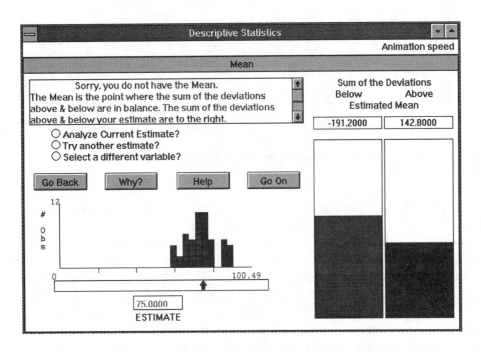

Figure 4.4 Evaluating Your Estimate of the Mean

To examine measures of spread at this point, click **Go Back** until you come to the screen where you can choose to work with either center or spread statistics. Click on **Work with spread statistics** and **Go On**. Now you can work with the standard deviation in conjunction with the mean, the interquartile range in conjunction with the median, or the range in conjunction with the mode. Before turning to the standard deviation, click on **Examine squared deviations** and **Go On**, in order to examine the relationship between the deviations, which are put into balance by the mean, and the squared deviations, which are put into balance by the standard deviation (as well as by its square, the variance). Double click on **Examine Observation Squared Deviations** and you can watch a histogram of the squared deviations be developed entry by entry. (You can control the speed of this process by using the **Speed** and **Pause** buttons or by clicking on **Animation Speed** in the upper right.) When the histogram is completed, you can examine the contribution made by each observation by clicking on it in either of the two histogram displays, as indicated in Figure 4.5.

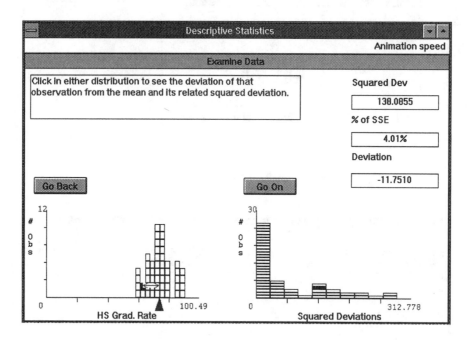

Figure 4.5 Examining the Squared Deviations

Finally, to try your hand at estimating measures of variance, click on either **Go On** or **Go Back**, then on **Continue** and **Go On** to return to the screen offering the different measures of spread. Click on **Standard Deviation with Mean** and **Go On** to obtain the screen shown in Figure 4.6. To make an estimate of the standard deviation, either click on one of the parts of the vertical arrow below the histogram and drag it to indicate what you think is the one-standard-deviation interval on either side of the mean, or enter a numerical value of your estimate of the standard deviation in the *Estimate* box. Now click **Go On** and the screen shown in Figure 4.7 will appear. Here you can see how your estimate has succeeded in balancing squared deviations below and above the square of your estimate—that is, below and above the estimate you have implicitly made of the *variance*. Here again you can analyze the result, try a new estimate, or see how well you can do with an entirely different variable. "Eyeballing" standard deviations is more difficult than "eyeballing" means, so you may well want to try your luck with a second variable.

You can also try your hand with the *Interquartile Range* by clicking on **Go Back** until the screen presenting the different options for spread appears, and choosing it—or, if you prefer, the *Range*.

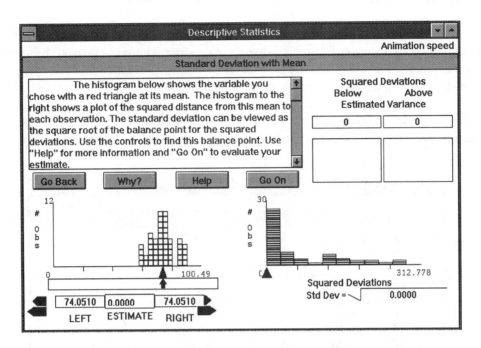

Figure 4.6 Making Your Estimate of the Standard Deviation

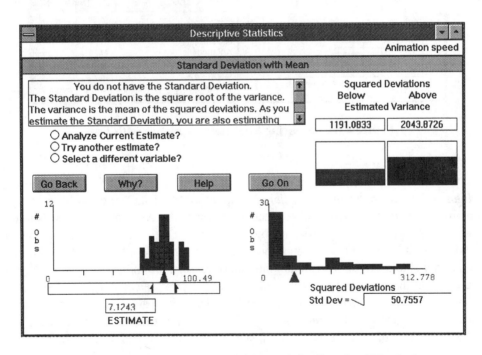

Figure 4.7 Evaluating Your Estimate of the Standard Deviation

Exploring How Well Summary Statistics Represent Data

Click on **Go Back** until the principal options screen shown in Figure 4.1 appears. Then click on **Describe distributions using summary statistics**. As before, choose a variable by clicking on its name in the data table. The *US Education* data set includes variables with a relatively symmetrical distribution (high school graduation rate) as well as ones with a skewed distribution (for example, expenditure per pupil). For purposes of seeing how this part of the *Descriptive Statistics* program works, select *Expenditure per pupil* (by scrolling across the data table until this variable appears and then clicking on **Expend. per Pupil** and **Go On**.) The screen shown in Figure 4.8 appears.

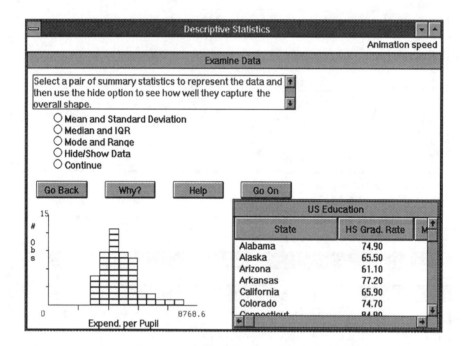

Figure 4.8 Comparing Summary Statistics with Data

You can now select any one of three combinations of summary statistics for representing the overall data set, *Mean and standard deviation, Median and Interquartile Range*, and *Mode and Range*. Double clicking on any one of these options will produce a display of the two statistics in question superposed on the histogram of the data. Specifically, the mean is indicated by a triangle below the X-axis, accompanied by a blue horizontal line on either side indicating the interval defined by one standard deviation on either side of it; the median and interquartile range are indicated by vertical lines; and the mode, by a dot, and the range, by vertical lines. Once you have selected a pair of statistics and seen their relation to the data, double click on **Hide/Show Data** to make the data disappear. Then ask yourself how well anyone could picture the data if the only information they had were the summary statistics. Restore the display of the data by double clicking again on **Hide/Show Data**.

Try each pair of summary statistics with this variable, and then try some other variables in the data set. The *Cities* data set is useful for this exercise since it includes a number of variables that are highly skewed to the right (serious crimes, population, and money spent).

Assessing the Sensitivity of Summary Statistics to Individual Data

Click on **Go Back** until the principal options screen shown in Figure 4.1 appears. Then click on **Examine Sensitivity of Summary Measures to data,** and as before choose a variable by clicking on its name in the data table. *Expenditure per pupil* is again a good choice to start with. Having selected it, click **Go On.** The screen shown in Figure 4.9 will appear.

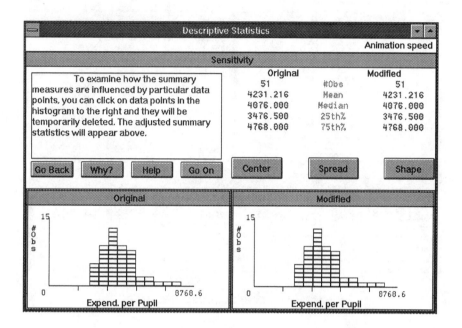

Figure 4.9 Assessing Sensitivity to Individual Data

You can now see the effect any one data point has on any summary statistic by clicking on it in the histogram on the right, dropping it from the data set. The values of the statistics after the change are compared with the original values in the upper right portion of the screen. Eliminate and restore data entries by clicking on them. You can examine different sets of summary statistics by clicking on **Center, Spread**, or **Shape**. In the present case see how much the various numbers change when you eliminate the three extreme data entries forming the tail on the right.

Using Summary Statistics: Some Further Experiments to Consider

You can follow up each of the exercises laid out above simply by selecting a different variable and repeating the steps. Once you feel comfortable with the different summary statistics, however, you may prefer to turn to the last of the principal options shown in Figure 4.1, *Use Summary Statistics.* This option will allow you access in a single place to many of the resources available separately in the three options already described. Use **Go Back** to return to the screen shown in Figure 4.1. By clicking on **Go Back** then, you can choose a different data set. For purposes of illustration, let's stay with the *US Education* data set for the moment. Click **Use Summary Statistics** and **Go On.** Before selecting any variable, click on **StatsOnHist** from the top menu, and click on **Mean & StdDev** and **Median & IQR.** Next click on **Mean Teacher Salary** in the data table, followed by **Display**, followed by **Histogram**.

Notice that for this slightly skewed distribution, the mean is located on the tail side of the median, and the interval defined by the standard deviation includes the interquartile range. To simultaneously display summary statistics for this distribution, click **Mean Teacher Salary** again, then **Statistics**. Move the summary statistics window to the right by dragging the window title bar, yielding the screen shown in Figure 4.10.

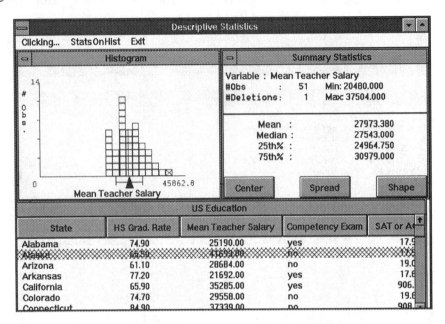

Figure 4.10 Using Summary Statistics

You can now examine the effects of eliminating any data entry in the histogram or in the table by clicking on it. For example, click on the data entry for *Alaska* in the table—or click on the extreme right entry in the histogram, which happens to be Alaska—and new values of the summary statistics appear in the *Summary Statistics* window and on the histogram. Figure 4.10 shows the cross-hatching of both the extreme data entry and the entry for Alaska. Removing this entry changes the mean and the standard deviation more than the median and interquartile range.

This effect would be even more apparent with a more highly skewed distribution. You can make it more apparent here by removing all four of the data entries on the far right of the histogram. Click on **Spread** to see the numbers for measures of spread. Click on **Shape** to see the value for *skew*; then click on the removed data entries one by one, restoring them one at a time, to see the effect on this value. Clicking on another variable, followed by **Display** and then **Histogram** will yield a histogram display of that variable side-by-side with this one. You can then click on individual data entries to compare the effects each has on the two related variables.

The best way of developing a deep feel for the virtues and limitations of each of the summary statistics is to explore several different data sets with the resources available in the *Use Summary Statistics* option—after getting a basic grasp of the statistics in the earlier options.

Chapter 5

Transforming Data

What May Be Investigated with the *Transforming Data* Program:

- What the effects are of adding a number to all the data in a set or multiplying
  them all by a number — i.e., of *linear transformations*
- Why transforming data into *standardized Z scores* yields an appropriate universal
  basis for comparing shapes of distributions
- How some common *nonlinear transformations* of data alter the shapes of distributions

Why Use This Program?

European economists frequently criticize the United States economy, complaining that the distribution of incomes in the United States is far too skewed to foster proper growth and efficiency. When they are trying to be especially nasty, they suggest that the distribution of incomes in the United States looks less like the distributions found in other highly industrialized nations, and more like those in developing nations.

How might we go about assessing the truth of this complaint? We could find histograms of family income in the United States and Mexico in newspapers from 1993 and 1994, when the North American Free Trade Agreement was being debated. But could we just compare these histograms? Incomes in the United States will be given in dollars, those in Mexico in pesos. Perhaps we should first put them on a common basis. This is easy to do: simply multiply the incomes in the United States by the exchange rate—pesos per dollar—to change them into pesos, or divide the incomes in Mexico by this same exchange rate to change them into dollars. Either way, we will have *transformed* the currency in one of the histograms into that of the other.

This is an everyday example of *transforming data*, specifically an example of a *linear transformation*. How does such a transformation affect the distribution displayed in the histogram in which the currency is changed? And how does it affect such summary statistics as the mean and standard deviation used to describe that distribution? The *Transforming Data* program allows experiments to be carried out that will help answer questions like these.

Once the data displayed in one of the histograms have been transformed so that both histograms employ the same currency, can they be used to compare the extent to which the incomes in the two countries are skewed? The mean family income in Mexico is sure to be much lower than that in the United

States, and the respective standard deviations are likely to be very different. Perhaps the visible differences in the two histograms reflect only these differences in center and spread, and not any difference in the extent to which family income in the United States is more, or less, skewed than family income in Mexico. If we could somehow remove the differences in the means and standard deviations of the incomes displayed in the two histograms, any differences that remain would definitely reflect shape. The established way of doing this in statistics is to *transform* both sets of data into so-called *Z scores*. The *Transforming Data* program will help you to see what is involved in transforming data into *Z scores* and why it is quite often useful to do so.

Transforming data into *Z scores* is another instance of a *linear transformation*. In statistics the critical feature of linear transformations of data is that they leave the shape of the distribution intact. Other mathematical moves that can be made with data, such as replacing them by their square roots or by logarithms of them, do not leave the shapes of the distributions intact. These fall under the rubric of *nonlinear transformations*. The *Transforming Data* program will also let you experiment with nonlinear transformations to see how they alter the shapes of distributions and why altering them in this way can sometimes be helpful.

The terminology—*Z scores* and *linear* and *nonlinear transformations*—makes the topic of transforming data sound exceedingly mathematical. The important thing to learn here, however, is not the mathematics involved in changing data from one form to another. The important things to learn are first, the general qualitative effect transformations of different kinds have on data; and second, the circumstances in which the effect in question is worth the trouble. The *Transforming Data* program allows you to learn both of these without any deep or detailed study of mathematical operations.

How to Carry Out Experiments with the *Transforming Data* Program

Before starting the *Transforming Data* program, select **Data/Examples** from the *ConStatS* menu, highlight **ConStatS Default**, and release the mouse button. To run the *Transforming Data* program, select **DataRep** from the *ConStatS* menu. Click once on **Transforming Data** and **Go On**. The *US Education* data set is again offered as the default choice. You are given the options of learning about it, working with it, or changing to another. To proceed with the example here, click on **Work with this data set** and **Go On**. Then, in response to the request for a specific variable, scroll the table over and click on **Expend. per Pupil**. The data are displayed in a histogram in the upper right hand corner, giving you a chance to decide whether you want to proceed with this as the *Working variable*. We have elected to use it here in part to take advantage of the familiarity already gained with it, but also to be working with skewed data.

After you click **Go On**, the screen shown in Figure 5.1 at the top of the next page appears, without the window on the right presenting *Summary statistics*. The "scaffolding" message in red at the upper left hand corner correctly reminds us of the sole reason for interest in ways of transforming this variable: *Transforming a variable mathematically often yields insights hidden in the original.* To this end, we should pause briefly to review the *Expenditures per Pupil* data. The histogram reminds us that the top five intervals at the right contain only 7 states, while the remaining 43 states and the District of Columbia fill the bottom five intervals at the left. Click on **See summary statistics** and **Go On**. Now you can review the summary statistics for the variable by clicking on the **Center, Spread**, and **Shape** buttons. Notice that the mean expenditure per pupil is 4231.22 and, indicative of the skew to the high end, the median of 4076 is below it. The standard deviation is 1152.41 and the interquartile range is 1291.50. (All of these numbers are in dollars.) The value of *Skew*, as shown in the figure, is 1.04857.

Unlike the others, this number is dimensionless—i.e., it has no units. A value of 0 indicates no skew; the more positive the value, the greater the skew toward the high end; and negative values signify skew toward the low end.

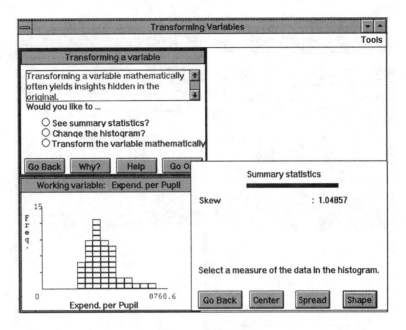

Figure 5.1 Reviewing the Data Before Transforming Them

Once you have reviewed the data, noting the summary statistics, click on **Go Back** in the *Summary Statistics* window. As we found earlier, this histogram is not misleading, and hence there is no reason to change it. So, click on **Transform the variable mathematically** and **Go On** to obtain the screen shown in Figure 5.2, the basic decision screen for transforming variables.

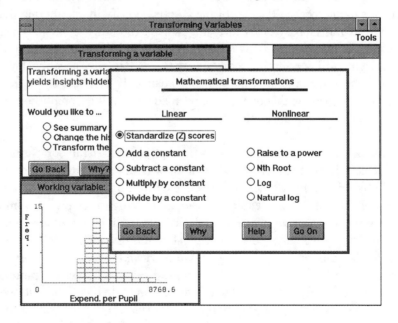

Figure 5.2 Options for Transforming the Variable

For starters, just to see what happens, let's change the units used in *Expenditures per Pupil* from dollars to thousands of dollars by dividing all the data by 1000. Click on **Divide by a constant** and **Go On**. Enter *1000* in the box in the window that opens up and click **Go On**. This will produce the screen shown in Figure 5.3.

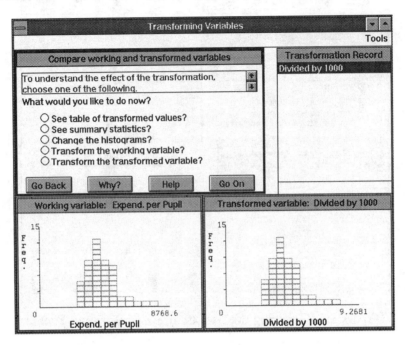

Figure 5.3 Comparing the Working Variable and the Transformed Variables

The computer has made a coincidental small adjustment to the X-axis on the right, changing the highest value at the end of the axis from 8.7686 (i.e., 8768.6/1000) to 9.2681. The two histograms are otherwise identical save for the number at the end of the X-axis. Verify this by noting that corresponding intervals in the two histograms have exactly the same number of entries in them. Or even better, click on any data point in either histogram. This will highlight it and the corresponding data point in the other histogram, and you will see that the correspondence is exact. The only thing that this transformation has in fact done to the original histogram is to change the numbers on the X-axis from dollars to thousands of dollars—something that could have been equally well accomplished simply by shifting the decimal point over in the histogram on the left.

The window on the upper left of Figure 5.3 presents five options to assist in comparing the working and the transformed variables. Double click first on **See table of transformed values** (or click on it and **Go On**) to compare side-by-side listings of the original and the transformed data. Next, double click on **See summary statistics**, and then click on **Center, Spread**, and **Shape** to review the summary statistics in each category. The *Mean*, the *Median*, the *Standard deviation*, and the *Interquartile range* values after the transformation are simply the corresponding original values divided by 1000. The value for *Skew*, by contrast, is exactly the same as before. Click on **Go Back** in the *Summary statistics* window to return to the screen in Figure 5.3. The *Change the histograms* option allows the number of intervals in either or both histograms to be altered. Here, there is no reason to do this. The last two options, *Transform the working variable* and *Transform the transformed variable*, open the way to further transformations; choosing the latter will make the transformed variable the new working variable.

Finally, a record of the sequence of transformations that have been examined since starting with the original working variable is maintained in the window on the upper right. Double clicking on entries in this list shifts back to an earlier point in the sequence in order to initiate a different sequence of transformations from that point. Accordingly, since nothing you have done so far will be lost if you continue on, you need not be reluctant to try still another transformation in order to see what will happen.

Experimenting with Linear Transformations

In *linear transformations* a constant is added to (or subtracted from) the data, the data are multiplied (or divided) by a constant, or combinations of these two are performed. (The screen in Figure 5.2 also offers *Standardize [Z] scores* as an option under *Linear*; we will see why after we try the elementary operations.)

Someone from the Netherlands might ask what the expenditures per pupil in the United States amount to in Dutch guilders. Suppose the exchange rate is 1.65 guilders per dollar. Click on **Transform the working variable** and **Go On** to gain access to the window of transformation options shown in Figure 5.2. Then click on **Multiply by constant** and **Go On**, enter this exchange rate in the box in the small window and click **Go On**. The result will be a histogram in the *Transformed variable* window in which the expenditures per pupil in dollars are displayed in Dutch guilders (as shown at the bottom of Figure 5.4). The two histograms have exactly the same shape, just as they did after dividing by 1000.

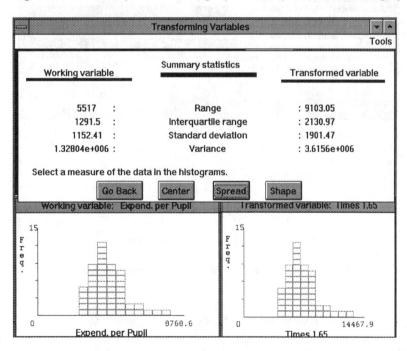

Figure 5.4 The Effect of Multiplying by a Constant

The only effect multiplying by 1.65 has had on the histogram is a change in the numbers along the X-axis. Double click on **See summary statistics** and then on the **Spread** button to obtain the upper half of Figure 5.4. You can verify with a calculator that the values for the *Range*, *Interquartile range*, and *Standard deviation* of the transformed variable are 1.65 times the corresponding original values, and the value for the *Variance* has increased by the square of 1.65. Click on **Center** to verify similarly that all

47

the *Center* statistics of the transformed variable are 1.65 times the original values, just as they were 1/1000 of the original values when we divided by 1000 before. Clicking on **Shape**, by contrast, reveals that the value for *Skew* has once again not changed. In short, it looks like the main effect of multiplying or dividing by a constant is to scale the numbers on the X-axis and, save for the special case of the *Variance*, the statistics for *Center* and *Spread*. The shape of the histogram remains exactly the same before and after the data are multiplied or divided, as does the primary descriptive statistic for *Shape*. Test this conclusion by examining a range of further examples in which data are multiplied or divided by a constant.

What happens when a constant is added or subtracted? Suppose that the federal government contributes $2400 per pupil in all the states. To find the contributions made by each state, then, we should subtract $2400 from each state's expenditures per pupil. Close the *Summary statistics* window on the screen shown in Figure 5.4 by clicking **Go Back**. Then double click first on **Transform the working variable** and then on **Subtract a constant**; enter 2400 in the box and click **Go On** to produce the histogram displaying the contributions made by the individual states, shown in the lower right of Figure 5.5.

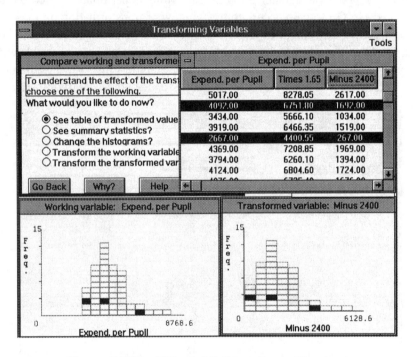

Figure 5.5 The Effect of Subtracting a Constant

The apparent change in shape between the two histograms is again because the computer has adjusted the X-axis of the *Transformed variable* slightly. The number at the end of this X-axis is 6128.6, instead of 6368.6 (i.e. 8768.6 minus 2400). In effect, the X-axis on the right and the intervals along it have been stretched a little. To see that the shapes are the same, note that the number of intervals and the number of entries in each of them are the same in both. Even better, double click on **See table of transformed values** and highlight select entries in the table by clicking on them to verify that they appear in exactly the same places in the two histograms (as the figure illustrates). The only real effect of subtracting 2400 from the data has been to slide the body of the histogram over to the left along the X-axis—or, what amounts to the same thing, to slide the Y-axis over to the right.

Now, double click on **See summary statistics** to examine the effect on them. Each of the measures of the *Center* of the *Transformed variable* is exactly 2400 lower than the corresponding value for the *Working variable*. By contrast, subtracting $2400 from the data has had no effect on any of the measures of *Spread*, and the one measure of *Shape* has once again remained the same. In other words, this transformation has simply shifted the *Center* of the distribution over to the left on the X-axis. Generalizing from a single example is dangerous. Nevertheless, it looks like the only effect of adding or subtracting a constant will always be to slide the body of the histogram over to the right or left along the X-axis without changing its shape or spread in any way. The values of the mean and median will change by having this same constant added to or subtracted from them, but all the values of the standard deviation, the interquartile range, the variance, and the skew will remain the same. As before, you should test this by examining several other cases of addition and subtraction.

The linear transformations we have tried so far have all been motivated by some sort of practical considerations, such as wanting to separate total expenditures per pupil from the contributions made by the states. The results we have obtained, however, show that linear transformations can also be used for a different sort of purpose. The effect of multiplying or dividing by a constant is to multiply or divide both the mean and the standard deviation by this number. The effect of adding or subtracting a constant is to add or subtract this number to the mean without changing the standard deviation. In both cases the shape of the distribution remains the same. What this means is that we can use these operations in combination to produce any values for the mean and the standard deviation that we might wish without changing the shape of the distribution! For example, suppose someone asks you to transform the contributions per pupil made by the states, shown in the lower right of Figure 5.5, so that the mean is 0 (i.e., the Y-axis lies at the mean) and the standard deviation is 1.0. First, double click on **See summary statistics** to determine the values of the *Mean* and *Standard deviation* for the *Transformed variable*, namely 1831.22 and 1152.41. Next, click on **Go Back** and double click on **Transform the transformed variable** and **Subtract a constant** in order to subtract 1831.22. This will produce a histogram in which the Y-axis is in the center of the data. Finally, with *Transform the transformed variable* still highlighted, click **Go On** and double click on **Divide by a constant** in order to divide by 1152.41. The result, which you can confirm by double clicking on **See summary statistics,** is a transformed variable which has (to within computer accuracy) a mean of 0.0 and a standard deviation of 1.0. The shape of the histogram has not changed at all.

Experimenting with Standardized Z Scores

The steps taken at the end of the last paragraph transformed the data giving the contributions the states make to their expenditures per pupil into a special form used widely in statistics called *Z scores*. Numerical[1] data can always be transformed into *Z scores*. Once put into this standardized form, the resulting data will always have a *mean* of 0.0 and a *standard deviation* of 1.0. Consequently, any differences between two data sets in this form will have nothing to do with either the mean or the standard deviation. Nor will they have anything to do with any differences in the specific units employed in the original data sets, e.g., dollars versus guilders, or for that matter, dollars versus high school graduation rates. The differences that remain between two data sets after they have been transformed into *Z scores* reflect differences in the shapes of their respective distributions. In other words, transforming data into *Z scores* provides a universal way to compare the shapes of distributions of diverse data sets.

---

[1]   Technically speaking, data specified on *interval* and *ratio* scales.

As we saw before, transforming data into *Z scores* is just a special case of a linear transformation. Nevertheless, because *Z scores* are so important in statistics, they deserve separate attention. Before examining them more closely, however, let us change to a different variable. Click on **Go Back** to return to the first *Transforming Variables* screen. Click on **Work with this data set** and **Go On.** Then click on *Mean Teacher Salary* in the table and **Go On**. Not surprisingly, the distribution of these data is also skewed toward the high end; but the pattern at the low end looks complicated, with more states in the lowest interval than in the second lowest. To make this more evident, double click on **Change the histogram** and then on **Make cut in x-axis** and **Go On** to introduce a cut in the X-axis, as shown in the lower left of Figure 5.6. (Clicking on **Go Back** in the *Change histogram options* window will close this window.) As a final step before transforming these data, double click on **See summary statistics** and review these statistics. Note in particular that the mean value of *Mean Teacher Salary* is 28242.40, the standard deviation is 4743.92, and the skew is 0.598.

To transform these data into *Z scores*, double click on **Transform the variable mathematically**. Because Z scores come up so often, *Standardize [Z] scores* is automatically highlighted in the *Mathematical Transformations* window. Click the **Go On** button in this window. The screen that then appears, shown in Figure 5.6, will let you proceed step by step through the calculation for transforming

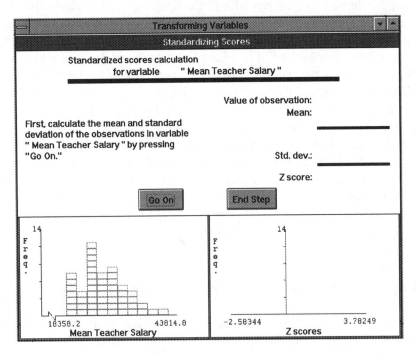

Figure 5.6 Transforming into Z Scores

the data into *Z scores*. Click **Go On** repeatedly to trace through this process for at least the first few data points, noting where the result is placed on the histogram on the lower right. Once the process becomes clear, click on **End Step** to obtain the finished result shown in Figure 5.7.

As a first step toward reviewing the results of this transformation, double click on **See summary statistics** in order to confirm that the value of the *Mean* for the *Transformed variable* is indeed 0.0, the value for the *Standard deviation* is 1.0, and the value for the *Skew* has not changed. As the figure shows, the value for the *Range* has been transformed from 21213 to 4.47161, and the value for the *Interquartile* *range* has been transformed from 6124 to 1.29091. The numbers at the two ends of the X-axis have been similarly transformed into -2.58344 and 3.78249. What do these transformed numbers mean? The way to get at this question is to ask what the number 1.0 means on the transformed X-axis. The answer is, *one standard deviation away from the mean.* But then all the transformed numbers must be giving the number of standard deviations the data point lies above or below the mean. A quick scroll through the table shows that the lowest and highest mean teacher salaries, $20480 and $41693, have been replaced by the numbers −1.64 and 2.84. In other words, the lowest mean teacher salary lies 1.64 standard deviations below (to the left of) the mean for all the states, and the highest lies 2.84 standard deviations above (to the right of) it. *Z scores* provide a meaningful universal basis for comparing distributions because it always makes sense to ask how many standard deviations above or below the mean any data point in the data set is?

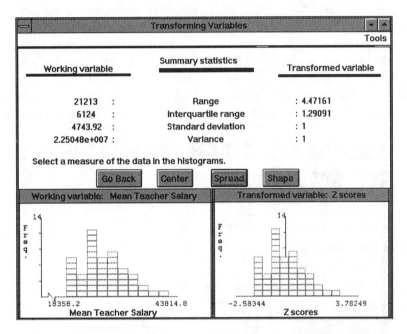

Figure 5.7 Comparing the Z Scores with the Original Data

In sum, *Z scores* are a way of *representing data* that emphasizes the *distribution* of the data points. Given only the Z scores, and no information about the original mean and standard deviation, one cannot say what the numbers in the original data set were. Given the original values of the mean and standard deviation as well, however, the original numbers are easy to recover: simply multiply each Z-score by the standard deviation, then add the original mean.

Experimenting with Nonlinear Transformations

Linear transformations preserve shape. Naturally, then, the whole point of nonlinear transformations is to alter the shapes of distributions. The two most common reasons for wanting to do this are (1) to transform a skewed distribution into a more symmetrical one in order to make it eligible for some other step in statistics that requires at least an approximation to symmetry; and (2) to expose special systematic relationships between two variables that remain hidden from view when the variables are in their original forms. The example below involves an attempt to remove skew. An example in which a hidden linear relationship between two variables is exposed can be found in the next chapter, *Dis-*

playing Bivariate Data. Nonlinear transformations is an advanced topic. The example below provides only an introduction to it.

Use **Go Back** to return to the opening screen in *Transforming Data*. Select *Change to another data set*, scroll through the list of data sets until you find *lynx.dbt*, and click on it to highlight it. As the description of it indicates, this data set gives the number of lynx trapped per year in the MacKenzie River District of the Northwest Territory of Canada from 1821 to 1934. Click **Go On** to return to the initial screen.

Examine the data table before continuing. It has only two variables, *Year* and *# Trapped*. Scrolling down the table reveals that the smallest number trapped any year was 39 (in 1889) and the largest number was 6991 (in 1904). More important, notice the pattern in the data: every few years the number trapped climbs to a peak and then declines.

Click on **Work with this data set** and **Go On.** Select **# Trapped** as the variable and click **Go On**. As the histogram in Figure 5.8 shows, these data are extremely skewed toward the high end, with more than a third of the data points falling in the first interval. To complete the screen in the figure, double click on **See summary statistics** and click on **Shape**. The 1.33 value for *Skew* is considerably greater than

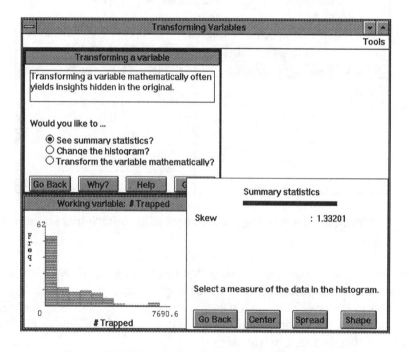

Figure 5.8 # Trapped—A Highly Skewed Data Set

the 1.05 value we had before with *Expenditures per Pupil*. The question is whether we can find a nonlinear transformation that will largely eliminate this skewing—i.e., that will reduce this 1.33 value for *Skew* to near 0. Click on **Transform the variable mathematically** and **Go On** to gain access to the nonlinear transformation options, as shown earlier in Figure 5.2.

ConStatS offers four common ways to transform data nonlinearly. Transformations involving logarithms will be postponed until the next chapter. The other two, *Raise to a power* and *Nth Root*, are related to one another. For example, taking the square root of a number is the same as raising it to the power of 0.5. (Roots and fractional powers cannot be taken of negative numbers. So, when the data set contains negative numbers, which ours does not, a linear transformation will have to be applied to the data first to remove them.)

To get some idea of what can happen, let us start by squaring the numbers. Double click on **Raise to a power**, enter *2* in the box, and click **Go On** to obtain the result shown in Figure 5.9. Squaring has made

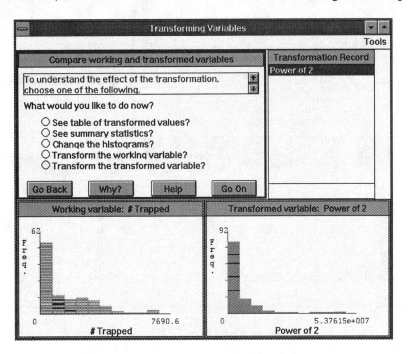

Figure 5.9 The Effect of Raising to the Power 2

the data even more skewed. Click on *See Summary Statistics* to see that the value of *Skew* has jumped from 1.33 to 2.98. Moreover, the fraction of the total data entries in the lowest interval has increased significantly. By clicking on data points along this lowest interval of the *transformed variable*, you will find that several of them came from the 2nd and 3rd intervals of the *working variable*, as indicated in the figure. This suggests that raising to a power greater than 1 increases positive skew by clustering data points more to the left in the transformed histogram. You should test this by trying some other powers greater than 1.

The natural thing to try in order to reduce the skew, therefore, is powers less than 1—i.e., roots. Double click on **Transform the working variable** and **Nth Root**, and enter 2 in the box. The result is a clear reduction in skew. A check of *Summary Statistics*, however, will show that the value for *Skew*, roughly 0.5, is still well above 0. Now continue the process, trying the 3rd root (which drops *Skew* to around 0.27), the 4th (which drops it to less than 0.13), the 5th (which drops it below 0.05), and the 6th (which finally produces a small negative value for *Skew*).

The results of this experiment are shown in Figure 5.10. The outcome, you should notice, is distinctly bi-modal. In other words, the data are tending to cluster around two separate centers. By clicking to highlight the entries in the lower of the two peak intervals on the right—i.e. the fourth interval—you will find that all of them come from the lowest interval on the left (as displayed in the figure). Why this second center is showing up we leave for you to think about, with the suggestion that you turn to the table to see where the highlighted points come from in the up-and-down cycles in the data.

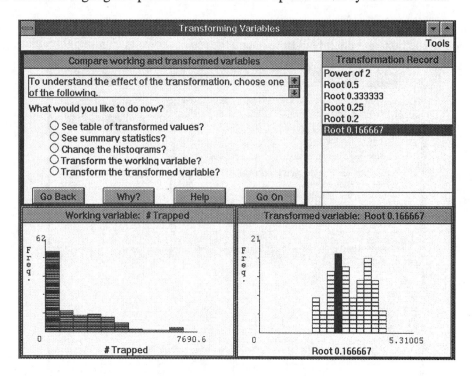

Figure 5.10 The Effect of the 6th Root

Some Suggestions for Further Experiments

The mathematics that comes into play with nonlinear transformations is sufficiently advanced that we suggest you postpone trying further experiments in this domain until a need arises in a concrete context. As indicated above, one such occasion can be found in the next chapter, *Displaying Bivariate Data*. Although the mathematics is more elementary, much is to be said in favor of delaying further experiments with general linear transformations too. With the exception of *Z scores*, the need for a linear transformation usually stems from some specific practical consideration, like switching from dollars to yen. When the occasion arises, you can always turn to the *Transforming Data* program and conduct experiments with definite questions in mind.

Z scores, however, come up very often in statistics. We therefore suggest that you concentrate your immediate further experiments with the *Transforming Data* program to Z scores for some further variables. A good goal is to get comfortable with thinking of distributions in terms of the number of standard deviations each point lies above or below the mean.

Chapter 6

Describing Bivariate Data

What May Be Investigated with the *Describing Bivariate Data* Program:

- How to display data in two variables—i.e., *bivariate* data—on a scatter plot

- What information different bivariate summary statistics convey about the data

- What a regression line fitted to bivariate data does and does not capture

- How sensitive regression lines and other bivariate statistics are to individual data

- How to use regression lines and transformations to look for relationships between variables

Why Use This Program?

At the end of Chapter 3, we placed histograms of *High School Graduation Rate* and *Expenditures per Pupil* side by side and highlighted the five states with the highest expenditures per pupil in an effort to see whether a positive relationship holds between these two variables.[1] To our surprise, we found that only one of these five states had a graduation rate near the top end, and three of them had graduation rates near the bottom end. Some people might be tempted to jump from this provocative finding to the conclusion that spending more per pupil does not help the graduation rate. Doing so, however, would be more than a little premature. There might still be enough of a positive relationship between these two variables in the other 45 states and the District of Columbia to outweigh the absence of any relationship in these five. Since these five states are outliers on the expenditure scale, there might well be something peculiar about them that makes them exceptions. (Indeed, Alaska is one of them.) To have a solid basis for concluding that expenditure per pupil has no positive effect on graduation rate, we need some way to take all the states into consideration. We could continue to highlight states one by one to see where each is located in the two histograms; but, in the absence of a tight relationship between the two variables, this is not likely to produce an unequivocal answer. How then should we go about describing any relationship that may exist between these two variables and measuring its strength? The *Describing Bivariate Data* program is intended to show you how to answer questions of this sort.

The *ConStatS* programs covered in the three preceding chapters focus on methods for representing data that apply to one variable at a time. Yet many of the most interesting empirical questions that require the application of statistics are about relationships between variables. For these questions we need methods for dealing with *bivariate* data. With bivariate data, each data entry consists of values for two

---

[1]   See Figure 3.12, p. 31.

55

variables at once, in the way that the entry for Alaska consists of a graduation rate of 65.5% and an expenditure per pupil of $7971. (Technically speaking, the entry for Alaska in the *US Education* data table is *multivariate* insofar as it includes several other variables, and there are correspondingly multivariate methods in statistics; but multivariate statistics is an advanced topic, and fortunately the key methods you will be examining in *Describing Bivariate Data* can readily be extended to multivariate cases.)

In Chapters 3 and 4 we used histograms and CDF plots to display the distributions of univariate data graphically, and summary statistics for center, spread, and shape to describe the main features of the data numerically. In this chapter we use *scatter plots* for displaying the distributions of bivariate data graphically and some *bivariate summary statistics* to describe them numerically. In particular, the analogue of the mean for bivariate data will be a straight line in the midst of the data called the *regression line*, and the sum of the squares of the deviations of the data points from this line will provide an analogue for the variance. The *regression line* is also called a *least squares line* because it minimizes the sum of the squared deviations (in precisely the way that the mean minimizes this sum in the case of univariate data). *Regression lines* are often shown on scatter plots in order to emphasize the prevailing trend in the data visually. The experiments that can be carried out with the *Describing Bivariate Data* program will help to clarify just what information is contained in scatter plots, regression lines, the sums of squared deviations, and the correlation coefficient, as well as how sensitive these ways of representing bivariate data are to individual data points.

When we turn to bivariate data we usually want to discover the nature of the relationship, if any, between two variables. In the example above, we most want to know the extent to which the variation in the high school graduation rate from state to state is purely a reflection or consequence of the variation in their expenditures per pupil. It turns out that the regression line and the deviations from it provide an especially instructive way of assessing the nature and the strength of the relationship between two variables. This is true in spite of the fact that regression lines are always straight lines, while the relationships between variables are often not linear. Transformations can be used to re-express nonlinear relationships as linear ones—e.g., by squaring the values for x to form the transformed variable $X_T = x^2$, a nonlinear relationship between y and x can be re-expressed as a linear one between y and X_T. *Transformations* play a more prominent role in the *Describing Bivariate Data* program. The experiments that can be carried out in the program with the help of them will illustrate how *regression* can be used to discover whether much of the variation in one variable is simply a reflection of variation in another.

How to Explore Data with the *Describing Bivariate Data* Program

Before starting the *Describing Bivariate Data* program, select **Data/Examples** from the *ConStatS* menu, highlight **ConStatS Default**, and release the mouse button. To run the *Describing Bivariate Data* program, select **DataRep** from the *ConStatS* menu, and click on **Describing Bivariate Data** and **Go On**. The initial screen, besides displaying *US Education* as the default data set, offers four options: *Learn about this data set*, *Change to another data set*, *Learn about bivariate techniques using this data set*, and *Examine the data using bivariate techniques*. The last two options are the two main pathways through the program, the former for becoming familiar with the different bivariate techniques and the latter for using these techniques in combination with one another to analyze data.

Click on **Learn about bivariate techniques using this data set** and **Go On**. You must select a pair of variables from the data set, one to be represented on the vertical Y-axis and the other, on the horizontal X-axis. Having raised a question about the relationship between graduation rates and expenditure levels, let us start with this pair. Click on **Y Variable** and **HS Grad. Rate**, then **X Variable** and (after scrolling) **Expend. per Pupil**. A *scatter plot* displaying this pairing of bivariate data appears in the upper right corner, as shown in Figure 6.1 below, with the Y-axis labeled *HS Grad Rate* and the X-axis,

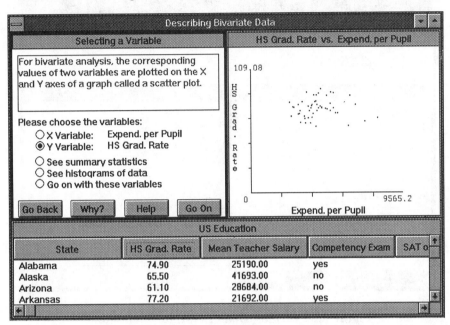

Figure 6.1 Selecting a Pair of Variables

Expend. per Pupil. Use the options in the *Selecting a Variable* window to review your choices before proceeding. For instance, double click on **See summary statistics** to open separate windows for reviewing the univariate statistics for each of the variables. Double click then on the **See histograms of data** to open separate windows displaying the histograms. (To close these "review windows," click on the — button in the upper left corner and then on **Close**.) Once you feel comfortable with these variables, double click on **Go on with these variables**.

The next screen gives you the option of transforming either or both of the variables before going on. The reason for raising this issue at the outset is the emphasis placed on looking for linear relationships between variables in bivariate data analysis. The pattern of the data in the scatter plot may be giving reason to transform one or both of the variables—e.g., to replace the Y variable by its square root—to obtain more of a tendency toward a linear relationship between the variables right from the beginning. As is evident in Figure 6.1, in the case of the two variables we are now working with, so little pattern is visible in the scatter plot that this option does not seem worth pursuing at this point.

Click on **use the current X and Y** and **Go On**. A window reminds you that transforming data into a preferred form will often facilitate bivariate data analysis. (This window will invariably appear every time you turn down the option of transforming data in the *Describing Bivariate Data* program. While you should take the message to heart, do not let it block you from continuing with the variables in their present form.) Click on the **Exit** button in the message window to go on to the main decision screen on this pathway, shown in Figure 6.2. As the text at the top of the screen indicates, the most important of the three options for purposes of looking for relationships between variables is *fit a line to these variables*. We shall examine the other two options first in preparation for it.

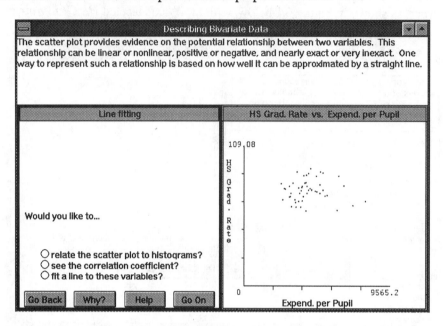

Figure 6.2 Learning about Bivariate Techniques

Reviewing the Scatter Plot and the Correlation Coefficient

Click on **relate the scatter plot to histograms** and **Go On**. The screen that appears, as shown in Figure 6.3, lets you tie each bivariate data point on the scatter plot to the univariate data point representing this same data entry on each of the histograms. For example, click on each of the five points that look to be outliers on the right side of the scatter plot; as you do so, this point will be highlighted, as will the corresponding points on the two histograms, producing the combination of highlights shown in Figure 6.3. These are the same five points on the high end of the histogram for *Expenditures per Pupil* that were highlighted back in Figure 3.12. On the scatter plot we can see immediately, without needing to compare two separate plots, that the five states with the highest expenditures per pupil have graduation rates ranging on the vertical scale from fairly high to among the lowest of any state. Click again on these points to cancel the highlighting on them. Then click on a number of points forming the main cluster of the bivariate data on the scatter plot to see where they lie on the histograms. (You can also click on data points in either histogram to highlight or to cancel highlighting of them on all three displays.)

The strong point of the two histograms is the clarity with which they display the distribution of the data in the two individual variables. The two univariate distributions are not so easy to see from the scatter plot alone. The scatter plot, by contrast, brings out a distribution of another sort, namely the extent to which the bivariate data points tend to fall in a narrow band suggesting a single distinct line, either straight or curved. The more the points band together to form a single line across the plot, the stronger the relationship is between the two variables. If the line is straight, then the relationship between the two variables is linear; if it is curved, the relationship is nonlinear. No line, curved or straight, seems to be suggested by the data shown in the scatter plot below. This gives us much better grounds for concluding that no strong relationship holds between the two variables than we had before when we were looking only at the two histograms and considering only the five states with the highest expenditures per pupil.

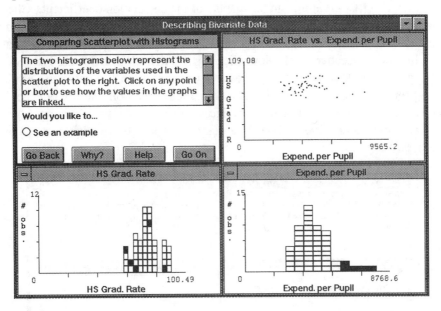

Figure 6.3 Comparing the Scatter Plot with Histograms

Visual impressions can be misleading. Although there is no conspicuous relationship between the two variables in the scatter plot above, some relationship might still be present, masked by scatter in the data arising from the effects of other variables. The *correlation coefficient* gives a numerical measure of how strong a *linear* relationship exists between data in two variables. Values of the correlation coefficient range between −1 and +1. A value of +1 indicates that the data points form a perfect straight line with a positive slope; a value of −1 indicates a perfect straight line with a negative slope; and a value of 0 indicates that there is no *linear* relationship whatever between the data in the two variables. Another way to think of this is that an exact 0 correlation coefficient means that no line drawn through the data will give any help at all in predicting the value of the second variable from the value of the first; a positive correlation coefficient indicates a tendency for high values in one variable to go hand in hand with high values in the other, and likewise for low values; and a negative correlation coefficient indicates a tendency for high values in one variable to be accompanied by low values in the other, and vice versa. To determine the *correlation coefficient* for the data shown in the scatter plot above, click **Go Back** to return to the screen shown in Figure 6.2, then click on **see the correlation coefficient** and **Go On**. Remarkably, the value shown for these data is 0.000.

(We should pause to make clear just what this 0.000 does and does not mean. First, the value is almost certainly not perfectly 0. The computer rounds off numbers, so that all we can be sure of is that the value is less than 0.0005. Second, it does not mean that expenditures per pupil never have any effect on graduation rates. It only means that there is no linear relationship to be found between the two in the data for 1988-89. Third, we should keep in mind that all sorts of diverse categories of expenditures may be lumped together in *Expenditures per Pupil*. If this broad category were broken down into narrower variables, ways might well emerge in which increased expenditures on pupils improve graduation rates. Caution is needed in jumping to conclusions.)

Because of the absence of any detectable linear relationship in the data for *High School Graduation Rate* and *Expenditures per Pupil*, we would be better off switching to different variables before turning to line fitting. Click on **OK** to return from the display of the correlation coefficient. Click on **Go Back** twice to restore the screen shown in Figure 6.1. Next click on **Y Variable** and on **Expend. per Pupil**. At this juncture, with *Expenditures per Pupil* as both the *X* and the *Y variable*, the bivariate data form a perfect straight line on the scatter plot! Now click on **X Variable** and **Mean Teacher Salary**. The resulting scatter plot suggests a fairly strong, positive linear relationship between these two variables. To confirm this, double click on **Go on with these variables**, then on **use the current X and Y**, and finally on **see the correlation coefficient** to produce the screen shown in Figure 6.4. The value of 0.831 for the *correlation coefficient* is indeed substantial. These two variables are more suitable for learning about line fitting.

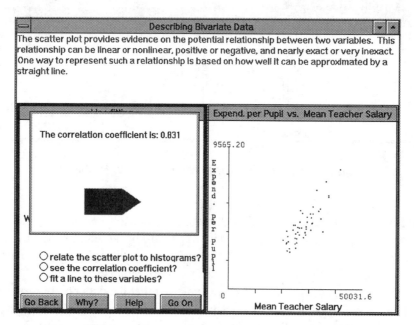

Figure 6.4 Two Variables with a High Correlation Coefficient

Before going on, review this new bivariate data set briefly. Click on **OK**, then on **relate the scatter plot to histograms** in order to repeat the exercise you did earlier, connecting the points in the scatter plot to points in the two histograms. The patterns formed by highlighting in the two histograms should be much more similar to one another than they were earlier.

Fitting Least Squares Regression Lines to Bivariate Data

Click on **fit a line to these variables** and **Go On** in the main decision screen for learning about bivariate techniques (Figure 6.2). Indicators of the mean and standard deviation have now been added on the vertical and the horizontal axes of the scatter plot. These can serve as guides in the line fitting process.

The window on the left presents four options. *Distribution of OLS Residuals* and *Sensitivity of OLS Lines* open pathways for exploring properties of the *Ordinary Least Squares* straight line running through the data. We will return to these two below after learning more about this line. *Intuitive Line Fitting* and *Line of Best Fit* offer two ways of fitting lines by trial and error, the former relying entirely on intuition and "eyeball," and the latter adding a comparison between two numbers to guide the process.

The first time you go through the program, the best place to start is intuitive line fitting. Click on **Intuitive Line Fitting** and **Go On**. A screen like the one in Figure 6.5 will appear, but with no lines drawn yet on the scatter plot and with the *Set Center* button highlighted. The numbers initially shown

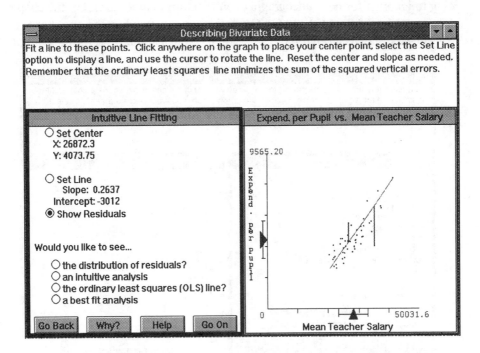

Figure 6.5 An Example of an Intuitive Line Fit

below *Set Center* are the mean values for the two variables. One way to get a line on the plot that you can then move around is to click on **Set Center;** a horizontal line will pass through the point of the two means. Another way, with *Set Center* highlighted, is to move the cursor to the point on the plot that you think is the center and click; a horizontal line will pass through the point. Move this line to where you think it gives the best approximation to the data. To change its slope, click on **Set Line**, and then drag its edge with the cursor (or click on a spot) to make it pivot about its center. To move the center, click on **Set Center** and then on a location on the scatter plot. You will undoubtedly not end up with the very same line as in the figure. Regardless, click on **Show Residuals** and then on the points above and below the line that appear furthest from it; the vertical gap between these points and the line will become highlighted, as in the figure.

These vertical gaps between the points and the line amount to *errors* when the line is used to predict the *Y value* of the point, given only its *X value*. In order for the likely error to be smallest when using a line through the data for making predictions in this way, the line has to be the one for which the *sum of the squares of the errors* is smallest. This is the sense in which the *ordinary least squares* line is optimal: it offers a better approximation than any other straight line to the vertical locations of the data points. The issue, therefore, is how well the line you chose as best succeeded in minimizing the sum of the squares of the vertical gaps between the points and the line. Look over these residuals to decide how well you did. Even better, double click on **the distribution of the residuals** to see a histogram of them in which any residuals you highlight on the scatter plot will be highlighted. How well do you think you did, using intuition alone? We would not be at all surprised if you did better than we did with the line shown in Figure 6.5. To see the true *ordinary least squares* line through these data, double click on **the ordinary least squares [OLS] line**.

Although the option *an intuitive analysis* offers a more systematic way of carrying out an intuitive line fit, we are going to ignore it for now, encouraging you to return to it at the end of the chapter. Click on **Go Back** and then on **Line of Best Fit** and **Go On** in the screen preceding the one shown in Figure 6.5. The screen that appears, shown in Figure 6.6, lets you try your hand at line fitting again, but this time

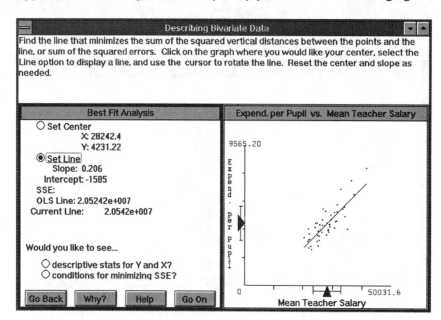

Figure 6.6 Using the Sum of the Squared Errors to Fit a Line

using a comparison between the sum of the squared errors for your line and for the *ordinary least squares* line to guide you. This time start with the line passing through the point of the two means. Click on **Set Center** to obtain your initial horizontal line. Notice, on the left, that the sum of the squared errors (*SSE*) is 7.4838e+017 with this *Current Line* and 2.05242e+007 for the *OLS Line*. Now click on **Set Line**, as before, to pivot the line about this center. As you do so, watch the sum of the squared errors for the *Current Line*. As you increase the slope, this number will go down until it reaches the number for the *OLS Line*; if you increase the slope still further, the number will start going up again. If you are having trouble reducing the number to the *OLS Line* value, check to make sure that your *Center* is at the point of the two means. You should be able to get the value for the sum of the squared errors as near that for the *OLS Line* as we did in the figure.

Notice the difference between the line in Figure 6.6 and the purely intuitive one shown in Figure 6.5. We let the salient point at the far upper right of the plotted data influence us too much when we were relying on intuition alone.

Using the combination of a *Slope* and a *Center* on which the line pivots is an unusual way of specifying the location of a straight line on a plot. One normally does not think of straight lines as being anchored in this way at a "center." This approach nevertheless has more behind it than its merely being convenient on the computer. It reflects two properties of the *ordinary least squares* line that legitimate its claim to being *best fit*. To see this, click on **conditions for minimizing SSE** and **Go On** on the screen in Figure 6.6. The window this opens at the top of the screen (displayed in Figure 6.7) indicates that the *sum of the squares of the errors* is minimum when (1) the sum of *the errors* is 0 and (2) the *correlation coefficient* between the errors and the *X variable* is 0. (If the sum of the errors is not 0, then the errors above and below the line are not in balance, and shifting the line can put them in better balance. Similarly, if the correlation coefficient between the errors and the X variable is not 0, then there is a systematic relationship between the X variable and the errors, a relationship that can be taken advantage of to improve the fit of the line.)

Click on your line to see what values you presently have for the *Sum of the errors* and the *Correlation of errors and X*. If the *Center* of your line is still at the point of means of the two variables, then the *Sum of the errors* is exactly 0; and if its slope approximates the one for which the *sum of the squared errors* is minimum as well as the one shown in Figure 6.6 does, then the *Correlation of errors and X* will be a small number. Now, with *Set Line* highlighted, change the slope. Increasing the slope makes this *correlation* increasingly negative, while decreasing it makes it positive. But, so long as the center remains at the point of the means, changing the slope has no effect on the *sum of the errors*. Now, click on **Set Center** and move the center a little. This produces a result like the one in Figure 6.7.

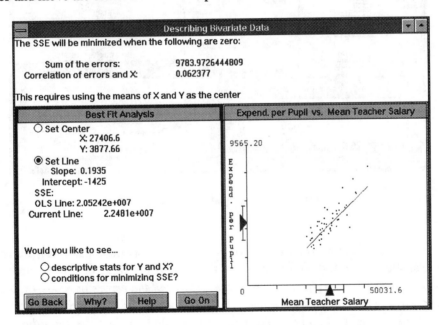

Figure 6.7 Conditions for Minimizing the Sum of the Squared Errors

A moment's reflection will persuade you that the sum of the vertical errors is not going to be 0 unless the *Center* is on the mean of the Y variable. Locating the *Center* on the mean of the X variable too has the further effect of decoupling the two conditions for minimizing *SSE*, so that only the slope has to be varied to remove any *correlation* between the vertical errors and the X variable. Move your line around a little to see how this *sum*, this *correlation*, and the difference in the *SSE* values between your line and the *OLS* line change.

Regardless of how strong a relationship exists between the X and Y variables, there will always be a *least squares line* through any set of bivariate data. This line is often shown on scatter plots, if only to exhibit the prevailing trend in any linear relationship between the variables. Its presence on a scatter plot, however, says nothing about the strength of this relationship. To examine the strength of the relationship, we need to look more closely at the residuals.

Click on **Go Back**, then on **Distribution of OLS Residuals** and **Go On** to see a screen for investigating the *residuals* associated with the *least squares line* for the two variables at hand or, thanks to the *change the variables* option, for any other pairing of variables in the data set that you may wish to examine. To obtain the full array of resources for examining residuals shown in Figure 6.8, double click on **see bivariate statistics** and then on **see histograms of the residuals**. (Drag the *Residuals* window and right edge of the *Squared Residuals* window to the left to obtain the cleaned up arrangement shown in the figure.)

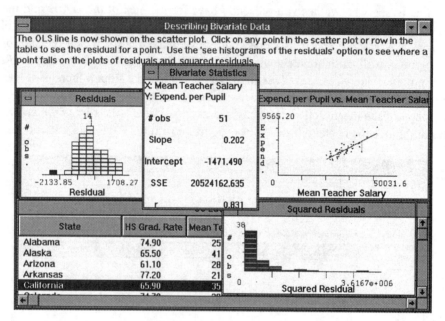

Figure 6.8 Investigating the Residuals

The *OLS* line is the analogue for bivariate data of the *mean* for univariate data. It is numerically given by the pair of statistics, *Slope* and *Intercept* (where the latter is the value of the Y variable at the point where the line intersects the Y axis). The *sum of the squares of the errors* or *SSE*—or, even better, the average squared error obtained by dividing the *SSE* by the number of observations—is the analogue for bivariate data of the univariate *variance*. The smaller this value, the less the *spread* of the data points relative to the least squares line. Finally, *r* stands for the correlation coefficient.

The collection of resources shown in the figure allows you to investigate the residuals in a variety of ways. For example, you can click on any data point in the scatter plot, in the *Residuals* histogram, in the *Squared Residuals* histogram, or the table, and it and the corresponding points will be highlighted. (You can gain access to any individual state by name or to the other data entries for that state by scrolling the table.) The fact that so many of the data points cluster toward the extreme left of the *Squared Residuals* histogram reflects the high correlation coefficient for *Mean Teacher Salary* and

Expenditures per Pupil. This clustering prompted us to click on the outlier at the extreme right of this histogram, which turned out to be California.

The fact that the square of the residual for California is such an outlier raises a question about how this one state affects the *OLS* line. To explore this sort of question, close the *Residuals* window. Click on **Go Back** to return to the four *Line fitting* options. Now click on **Sensitivity of OLS Lines** and **Go On** to obtain the screen shown in Figure 6.9.

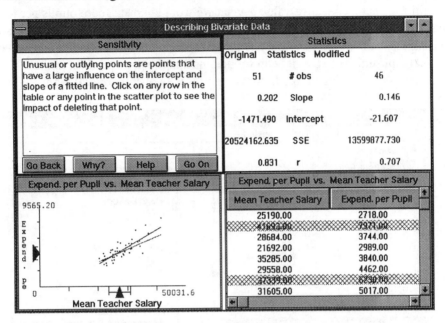

Figure 6.9 Exploring the Sensitivity of the OLS Line

Clicking on any data entry either on the scatter plot or in the table will temporarily remove it, resulting in a new *OLS* line and before-and-after bivariate statistics. The point for California is highlighted in the scatter plot of Figure 6.8. Click on this point and the correlation coefficient jumps from 0.831 to 0.862 once California is eliminated; but the *OLS* line changes only slightly.

Restore California (by clicking on it again) and click on the five states with the highest expenditures per pupil to obtain the more noticeably displaced *OLS* line seen in the figure. (Notice, in the process, that removing these five states significantly reduces the correlation coefficient; these five contribute heavily to the strength of the relationship.) Why deleting California, with its large squared residual, has so little effect on the *OLS* line we leave for you to ponder. Try clicking on different states in an effort to determine what the distinguishing characteristics are of the points that have the greatest effects on the *OLS* line and on *r*.

Using Bivariate Techniques in Data Analysis

So far we have explored the *Describing Bivariate Data* pathway for learning about bivariate techniques. The other main pathway through this program allows the techniques to be used in various combinations with one another in data analysis. Click on **Go Back** repeatedly until the initial screen in the program appears; then click on **Examine the data using bivariate techniques** and **Go On**. A screen will appear allowing you to choose any two variables from the current data set for *X* and *Y* and offering you five options: *Display*, *Statistics*, *Clicking*, *Transform*, and *Exit*. (*Exit* takes you back to the initial screen of this program.)

For a first example, choose *HS Grad. Rate* for *Y* and *Pupils per Teacher* for *X* to see if this variable has much of an effect on graduation rates. Click on **Display** and then **ScatterPlot** for a scatter plot, with an *OLS* line displayed, and on **Statistics** and **Bivariate** to obtain the bivariate statistics. The correlation coefficient is still low, but its negative value is what we would expect: more pupils per teacher tends to reduce graduation rates, to the extent it does anything at all. Next click on **Clicking** and **Deletes** to explore the sensitivity of both the *OLS* line and the correlation coefficient to the individual states. Finally, click on the point furthest to the right above the line and the point furthest to the left below the line to obtain the screen shown in Figure 6.10. Removing these two shifts the *OLS* line and nearly doubles

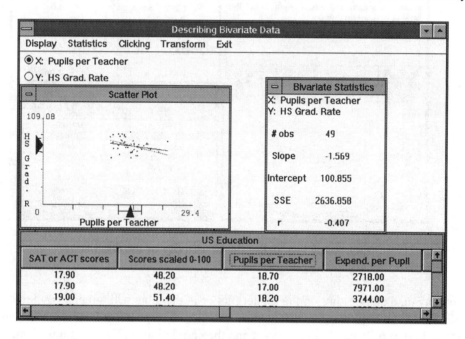

Figure 6.10 Using Bivariate Techniques to Interrogate Data

the strength of the correlation between these variables. Scrolling through the table will reveal that the two exceptional points represent Utah and the District of Columbia. Whether they should be regarded as exceptions to a rule we leave to you.

For an example employing transformations, click on **Exit** and **Yes** to return to the initial screen. Double click on **Change to another data set**, scroll to *macro.det*, highlight it, and click **Go On**. Finally, double click on **Examine the data using bivariate techniques**. Select **Year no.** as *X* and **Nominal GNP** as *Y*. Then click on **Display** and **ScatterPlot** to obtain Figure 6.11.

Drag this *Scatter Plot* window over to the right. With *Y* still highlighted, click on **Transform**, then on **Natural Log** and **Go On**. As the message indicates, the transformed variable has been added to the

66

data table at the far right. Scroll over to reach it (*Nominal GNP T*), click on it to make it the *Y variable*, and then click on **Display** and **ScatterPlot** to obtain the before-and-after transformation plots side by ‑

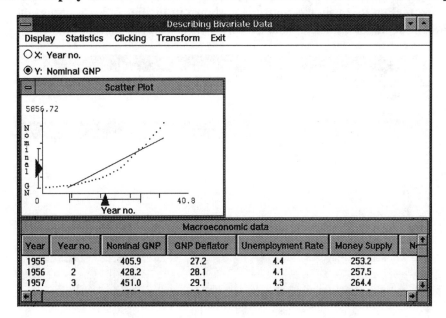

Figure 6.11 Nominal GNP Before Transformation

side, as in Figure 6.12. The result speaks for itself. The logarithmic transformation has exposed an exceptionally strong linear relationship (r = 0.995).

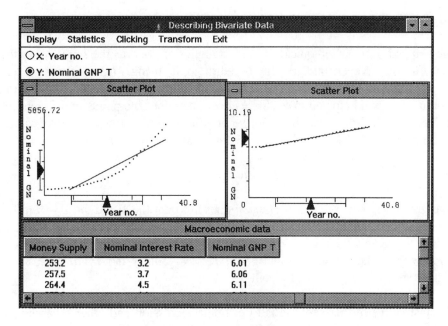

Figure 6.12 The Effect of a Logarithmic Transformation

Does this mean that every variable in this data set should be so transformed? Not necessarily. As a final step, change the *X variable* to *Money Supply*, the *Y variable* back to *Nominal GNP*. Click on **Display** and **ScatterPlot** to obtain the comparison shown in Figure 6.13. A strong linear relationship can exist between two variables that do not themselves vary linearly with time.

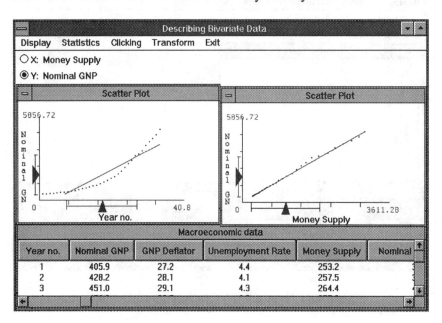

Figure 6.13 A Final Comparison

Some Suggestions for Further Experiments

One thing we skipped over far too quickly in the examples above was the *Intuitive Analysis* option in *Intuitive Line Fitting*. We encourage you to return to it, using *Mean Teacher Salary* as *X* and *Expenditures per Pupil* as *Y*, as before. The option will lead you step by step through a procedure for "eyeballing" a line that will help you to see more clearly how the data points in different intervals along the X-axis affect the *OLS* line. Then try intuitive line fitting with different pairs of variables with the goal of developing more feel for where the *OLS* line must lie from looking at the scatter plot alone. Using the *Sensitivity* option on different pairs of variables is another way for developing more feel for where the *OLS* line has to lie, given only the scatter plot.

As we emphasize above, *least squares regression* does not treat the *X* and the *Y variables* on the same footing with one another. One good way of examining the consequences of this asymmetry is to reverse the two variables to see how the *regression line* and the *bivariate statistics* change. For example, make *Expenditures per Pupil* the *X Variable* and *Mean Teacher Salary* the *Y Variable*, and compare the results with those shown in Figures 6.4 through 6.9.

An extremely instructive further exercise is to examine regression and other bivariate statistics for *Z scores*. For example, transform both *Expenditures per Pupil* and *Mean Teacher Salary* into *Z scores*, then use the Z score form of the former as *Y* and that of the latter as *X* and compare the results obtained via the *Distribution of OLS Residuals* option with those shown in Figure 6.8. Then make the same move with other pairs of variables to confirm the distinctive features of regressing on Z scores.

68

PART TWO

PROBABILITY

Probability enters into statistics in two ways. First, the variables to which one applies statistical methods are *random* variables. That is, they not only take on different values, but the probabilities with which they take on different values form a distinct pattern, called a *probability distribution*. The weights of newborn babies range from around 2 pounds to perhaps as high as 14 pounds. But the probability that a newborn baby selected at random will weigh less than 4 pounds or more than 12 pounds is very small compared with the probability that he or she will weigh between 7 and 9 pounds. The overall pattern of these probabilities constitutes the *probability distribution* for baby weights. Second, statistical data usually come from some sort of *random* sample drawn from a larger population. There is always a chance of any such sample's failing to be representative—i.e., of its giving misleading information about the population. A central concern of statistics is to provide methods for determining the probabilities of samples being misleading. These methods allow one not only to assess risk, but also to limit it when relying on samples. An understanding of statistical methods—or, for that matter, of statistical claims—thus requires some background in probability.

ConStatS includes two programs on probability. *Probability Measurement* covers requirements that have to be met in order for probability *numbers* to be meaningful—requirements that ought to come into play every time one is considering claims in statistics involving such numbers. It leads students through step-by-step procedures for arriving at meaningful estimates of numerical probabilities in various situations. It emphasizes (1) the fact that probability numbers take on meaning only against a background of mutually exclusive outcomes comprising a situation, and (2) the fact that the probabilities of these outcomes represent nothing more than ratios among their relative likelihoods. These points are elementary, and the program is correspondingly basic. Nevertheless, many confusions on more advanced topics in statistics may stem from insufficient appreciation of them.

The second probability program, *Probability Distributions*, covers 14 theoretical probability distributions that come up in statistics. It introduces students to the topic by presenting graphical displays of examples of four common distributions, two discrete and two continuous. From there students can explore any one of these distributions, or any of the others. Students can vary the values of the defining parameters for the distribution, obtaining before-and-after graphical displays of the probability density functions. They can also link sectors on the graphical displays of the probability density function and the cumulative distribution function to one another, with the corresponding probabilities appearing on a pie chart. Both ways of exploring probability distributions help students to think about these mathematical abstractions in concrete, pictorial forms. Finally, the program includes an option for fitting probability distributions to bodies of data. This option also allows different probability distributions to be compared with one another.

Chapter 7

Probability Measurement

What May Be Investigated with the *Probability Measurement* Program:

- What is required for *numerical* probabilities to be meaningful

- How to go about assigning numerical probabilities in a systematic manner

- How demands of consistency impose constraints on numerical probabilities

- Why ratios of likelihoods are sufficient to determine numerical probabilities

Why Use This Program?

Picture the manager of a presidential election campaign who has contracted for a poll in order to see where her candidate stands one month before the election. The polling organization asks 1,500 voters selected at random around the United States how they would vote if the election were held today. After the results are collected and reviewed, the pollster telephones the campaign manager, announcing, "I have great news for you. If the election were held today, your candidate would receive 54 percent of the vote, with a margin of error of 3 percentage points." She asks, "You're saying that he would definitely get somewhere between 51 and 57 percent of the vote?" He responds, "No, not exactly. Polling is not an exact science. I'm saying that the probability is two-thirds that he would get between 51 and 57 percent of the vote. There is still a one-third chance that the result would fall outside this range." Does she have reason to be annoyed? She has just spent thousands of dollars to obtain some information, only to be told that there is a one-third chance that it is in error.

This example raises a host of questions, many of which reach to the heart of the discipline of statistics. For example, where does this one-third probability number come from? What would have to be done to reduce the probability of error from one-third to something much lower, say one-tenth? Must we always face some non-negligible risk of error when basing conclusions on statistics? Questions of this sort are central to the programs in *ConStatS* on *Sampling* and *Inference*. Before turning to them, we best make sure we understand what the number 1/3 represents in the example. Does it mean that, if the election were held today, the probability of the candidate's losing is 1/3? If not, then what is the probability of his losing, and what is the outcome for which the probability is supposedly 1/3? The *Probability Measurement* program will help you to answer questions like these.

We all interject talk of probability in our everyday conversations. "The chances of my getting into that medical school are slim, but I still have a better than even chance of getting into one of the schools I have applied to." "Why do you buy lottery tickets? Do you think you have some real chance of winning?" "The chances are good that my scores will be much higher if I take the SAT tests again."

None of these remarks is at all mysterious. To ask someone who makes one of them what the qualitative claim about probability that they are making amounts to is to ask a pedantic question. The situation is different, however, when the claim involves some specific probability number. You and a friend are in a casino watching a blackjack game. The friend whispers, "The probability of the next card the dealer deals being an Ace is now 1/8." It is not at all pedantic to ask, "Why 1/8 instead of 1/10, or 1/13?" If no proper answer is forthcoming, you have every right to complain to your friend that he is just tossing numbers around that have no real meaning.

How does a probability number have a real meaning? The claim that the probability of an Ace is 1/8 does not have to be true in order to be meaningful. But, then, what conditions have to be satisfied for the claim to be meaningful? Can any numbers, or any numbers between 0 and 1, be assigned as probabilities? Must these numbers satisfy some requirements before they have legitimate claim to representing probabilities? The *Probability Measurement* program sheds light on these questions by leading you step by step through the process of assigning (or estimating) numerical probabilities for various hypothetical situations. No attention will be given to whether the probability numbers you put forward are true. The issue is whether they are meaningful—that is, do they have a legitimate claim to be representing *probabilities*?

Because we are all so accustomed to informal talk about probability, we rarely feel much need to pause over the meaning of claims involving specific probability numbers. As the presidential election poll example illustrates, statistics is filled with such claims. To be under the illusion that we understand them when we do not is to risk serious mistakes. The *Probability Measurement* program addresses the concept of probability at a quite elementary level. Do not be deceived by this. The payoffs from the program will prove to be anything but elementary.

How to Carry Out Experiments with the *Probability Measurement* Program

To run the *Probability Measurement* program, select **Probability** from the *ConStatS* menu, then click on **Probability Measurement** and **Go On**. The screen in Figure 7.1 will appear.

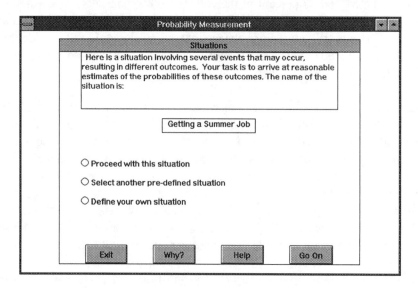

Figure 7.1 Selecting a Situation to Consider

72

First, some jargon. Probability numbers are assigned to possible *outcomes* in specific *situations*. Five hypothetical situations are built into the program, and you can also design your own. You will estimate the probabilities of the outcomes in the situation you choose. Having a feel for the situation—that is, being able to think of it concretely, with yourself in it—will put you in a position to make more informed judgments than you can if the situation seems alien to you. Because of this, specifying your own situation may well be best in the long run.

Our example, however, uses the program's "default" situation, *Getting a Summer Job*. (You can click on **Select another pre-defined situation** and **Go On** to obtain a list of the four other situations built into the program if you instead want to pursue one of them. Instructions for specifying your own situation can be found at the end of the chapter.) Click on **Proceed with this situation** and **Go On**, yielding the screen shown in Figure 7.2.

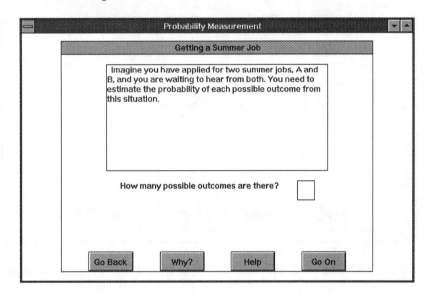

Figure 7.2 Identifying the Number of Possible Outcomes

Identifying the possible basic outcomes is always the first step in assigning numerical probabilities. We add the word "basic" to emphasize that the outcomes of interest at this stage must satisfy two conditions: (1) they must *exhaust* the situation, in the sense that at least one of them will end up occurring; and (2) they must be *mutually exclusive*, so that at most one of them will end up occurring. In the presented situation, you have interviewed for two summer jobs, and you are now waiting to hear from each. Being offered Job A and being offered Job B are not two "basic" outcomes, because they are not mutually exclusive; you might be offered both jobs.

The screen is asking you to identify only the number of possible outcomes. The program expects 4 outcomes: (1) *You are offered both jobs*; (2) *You are offered Job A, but not Job B*; (3) *You are offered Job B, but not Job A*; and (4) *You are not offered either job*. (If you enter a number greater than 4, you will be given this list and asked to add to it. If you enter a number less than 4, you will be given this list and asked which one of the four is impossible. To say that an outcome is impossible is to assign it a probability of 0. In other words, 4 need not be the correct number here, for the situation as you visualize it may call for a number other than 4.) In this example, enter 4 and click **Go On**. The computer program lists the outcomes. Once comfortable with the list, click **Go On**.

The next screen offers information about the two jobs. Click first on **Job A** and **Go On**, read all the information available about it, then click on **Exit.** Do the same for **Job B**. The available information is admittedly limited, but no more so than in most real-life situations.

Once you have reviewed the available information, click on **Estimate Probabilities** and **Go On**. The next screen, shown in Figure 7.3 below, asks you to rank the possible outcomes, listed at the top, in order from the least to the most probable. This step is not indispensable in estimating probabilities. Nevertheless, research has shown that including this step helps people avoid inconsistent estimates. In

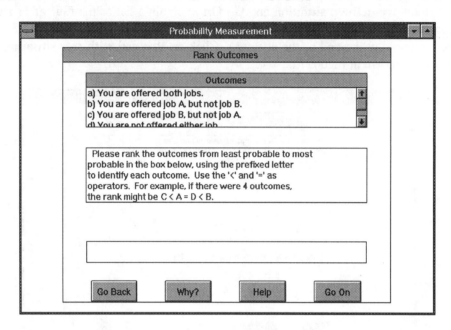

Figure 7.3 Rank Ordering the Outcomes from Least to Most Probable

particular, if you subsequently offer probability numbers that are incompatible with this ranking, the program will call attention to your inconsistency and guide you toward resolving it. (Having an initial inconsistency in your estimates of the probabilities is not a sign of stupidity; to the contrary, it simply shows that you have not yet thought the situation through as clearly as you need to in order to assign meaningful numerical probabilities to the outcomes.) You have the option of saying that two outcomes are equally probable—by entering an '=' sign between them. If you indicate that all of the outcomes are equally probable, the program jumps to a final display of the probabilities, for in this case you have implicitly specified them all to be 1 divided by the number of possible outcomes.

In the hypothetical case at hand, the person who interviewed you for Job A did not know either of the individuals who wrote recommendations for you, while you were recommended for Job B by the student who held it last summer. This gives solid reason for thinking that option *c* on the screen shown in Figure 7.3 is more probable than option *b*. Furthermore, if you are offered Job A, then you must have interviewed very well indeed, in which case your chances of being offered Job B are better than you were thinking when you assumed that you would not be offered Job A. In other words, this line of thought gives reason for saying that option *a* is more probable than option *b*. Finally, the fact that the person who interviewed you for Job B was non-committal in spite of the recommendation gives reason, beyond mere pessimism, for thinking that the most probable outcome is d. Based on this reasoning, enter $b<a<c<d$ in the box and click **Go On**. This will produce the screen shown in Figure 7.4.

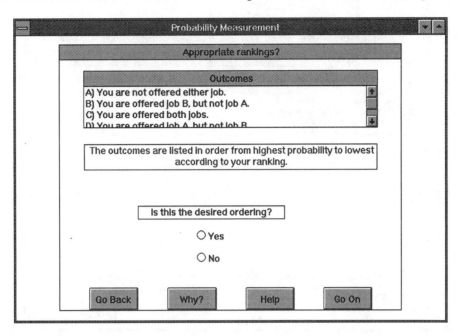

Figure 7.4 An Opportunity to Reconsider Your Ranking

The outcomes have been relabeled in the listing at the top of this screen. The outcome of not getting either job, which was previously labeled as d, is now labeled as A; the second most probable outcome, previously labeled as c, is now labeled as B. This relabeling has been done for your convenience, so that your rank ordering from the most to the least probable simply proceeds down the alphabet.

If you decide that your rank ordering is incorrect, whether because of an error in entering the ordering or because you have reconsidered, click on **No** and **Go On** to return to the prior screen. In the case of Figure 7.4, the order shown is precisely the one we reasoned our way into. So, click on **Yes** and **Go On**.

The next screen offers the option of proceeding in either of two ways in order to assign numerical estimates of the probabilities to the possible outcomes. With the second method you estimate these numbers directly. With the first, you specify them indirectly by specifying ratios among them. Which is preferable in any given situation depends on which you feel better able to do, to specify the probabilities or to specify, for example, whether one of the possible outcomes is twice as likely as another, a third is 50 percent more likely than the second, etc. Because neither choice always has clear priority over the other, we cover both of them here. Start with the indirect method, paying attention to just what it does and does not require, so that you can subsequently compare it with the direct method. Click on **Ratios of probabilities** and **Go On**.

The first screen on this pathway offers two options: specifying the minimum number of ratios needed in order to determine the probabilities, on the one hand, and specifying all the ratios of the probabilities among all the outcomes, on the other. Click on **The minimum number of ratios** and **Go On** to produce the screen shown in Figure 7.5.

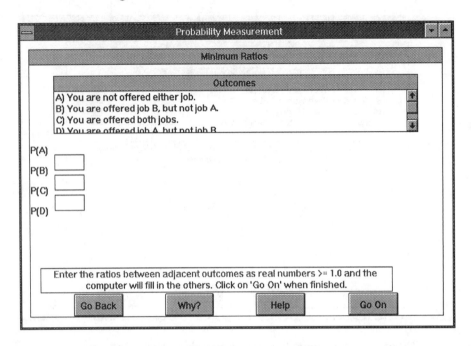

Figure 7.5 Specifying the Minimum Number of Ratios Among Probabilities Needed

The three number-entry boxes lie between the four probabilities. The idea is to enter the *ratio* between the probabilities above and below the box in each case. The instruction calls for numbers no less than 1.0 because the four probabilities have already been rank ordered from the most probable on the top to the least probable on the bottom.

In the case at hand, we decide that not being offered either job is only a little bit more probable than being offered Job B and not Job A—specifically 20 percent greater. Enter 1.2 for the ratio between $P(A)$ and $P(B)$ in the first box. We further decide that the probability of being offered only Job B was much greater than the probability of being offered both jobs—5 times greater. Enter 5 for the ratio between $P(B)$ and $P(C)$ in the second box. Finally, because we see no reason at all for being offered Job A but not Job B, we decide that the probability of being offered both jobs is much greater than the probability of being offered Job A alone—4 times greater. Enter 4 for the ratio between $P(C)$ and $P(D)$ in the third box. (If you disagree with these ratios, then return to this screen after completing the example, revise them, and proceed from there.)

Once you have entered the three ratios, click **Go On**. The screen shown in Figure 7.6 appears, listing the ratios among the non-adjacent probabilities, that is, between $P(A)$ and $P(C)$, between $P(B)$ and $P(D)$, and finally between $P(A)$ and $P(D)$. As you can readily see, these further ratios were obtained simply by multiplying the ratios you already entered. Review these further ratios to confirm that they are acceptable. If any of them seem wildly wrong, then something must not be quite right with the ratios you specified. If you conclude you need to revise them, click **Go Back**.

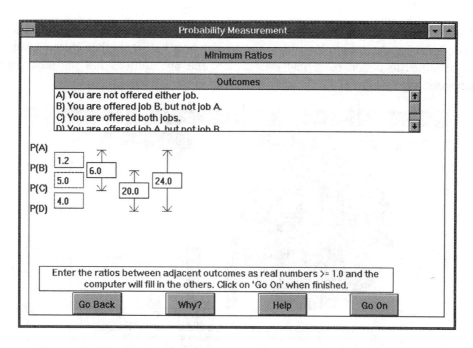

Figure 7.6 Reviewing the Full Set of Ratios Among the Probabilities

If we had selected the option of specifying *all of the ratios* instead of *the minimum number of ratios* earlier, a screen resembling the one in the figure would have appeared, with empty boxes where the numbers are displayed. We would then have had to enter the ratios between all six of these pairs of probabilities, rather than just the three ratios on the left. Why is this option available, insofar as the second group of ratios becomes arithmetically fixed once the first group is entered? The reason is that we are in the process of *estimating* probabilities. The ratios between probabilities that we entered are only estimates. We might be at least as confident about the ratios between $P(A)$ and $P(C)$ and between $P(B)$ and $P(D)$, for example, as we are about the adjacent ratios. If so, we can enter all the ratios and let the program determine whether our estimates are internally—arithmetically—consistent with one another. As before, an inconsistency is not a sign of stupidity; it simply means we have not thought the situation through to the level of clarity needed to assign meaningful numerical probabilities to the outcomes. *The-minimum-number-of-ratios* option lets us revise our ratios after we see what they imply about the other ratios. The *all-of-the-ratios* option lets us focus on what we think the ratios ought to be, ignoring questions of consistency, and then forces us to reconsider if we have violated arithmetical consistency. With both options, we are proceeding through a line of thought that should yield not just meaningful estimates of numerical probabilities, but ones that we find reasonable, too. The two options represent two ways of bringing our thoughts into focus. Each can be appropriate.

Once the ratios among the adjacent probabilities are specified, all of the probabilities have been determined. As seen from Figure 7.6, $P(A)$ is 24 times $P(D)$, $P(B)$ is 20 times $P(D)$, and $P(C)$ is 4 times $P(D)$. But the sum of the four probabilities must be 1.0. Substituting for the first three probabilities and then adding accordingly yields the equation 49 times $P(D)$ equals 1, or $P(D)$ is 1/49. In short, estimating the ratios between the probabilities of the adjacent outcomes in your rank ordering amounts to the same thing as estimating the probabilities of the individual outcomes!

77

Click **Go On** to obtain the result screen shown in Figure 7.7. The numerical probabilities are displayed in three ways: by a pie chart, by a bar chart, and by numbers below the bar chart. Using the ratios between probabilities to obtain numerical estimates of the probabilities has the advantage that the numbers automatically sum to 1.0.

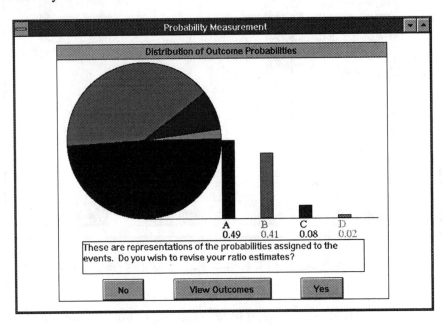

Figure 7.7 The Implied Probabilities of the Outcomes

The numerical probabilities shown in the figure are *meaningful*. That is, you have assigned numbers to all the possible, mutually exclusive outcomes in the situation, and these numbers sum to exactly 1.0. You do not have to agree with these probabilities. These probabilities reflect our earlier judgments about the rank order of likelihood of the outcomes and our estimates of the ratios between the likelihoods of the consecutive outcomes in this rank order. But now that you see the probabilities implied by these estimates, you may find them anomalous in some way or other. If so, then one or more of our ratio estimates is out of kilter with your sense of what the general relative magnitudes of some of the probabilities ought to be. Here again, then, the situation has not been thought through clearly enough to arrive at numerical probabilities that are both meaningful, on the one hand, and consistent with your general sense of the situation, on the other. By clicking on **Yes**, you can revise the ratios to obtain final estimates more in accord with your general sense of the situation.

To use the alternative, direct approach to arriving at numerical estimates of the probabilities, select **Yes** from the screen in Figure 7.7. Click **Go Back** and **Go Back**. Now select the *Probabilities directly* option earlier. The screen in Figure 7.8 appears. Enter your estimates for the probabilities of the four outcomes in the four boxes. The computer will automatically block you from going on to the next screen if the numbers you enter either violate your prior rank ordering or fail to sum to 1.0. In other words, on this pathway the computer is again forcing you to make the numerical probabilities *meaningful*. But this time the burden of coming up with numbers that sum precisely to 1.0 is on you. Click **Go On** after meaningful numbers have been entered. The results will be displayed on a screen resembling the one shown in Figure 7.7, but now presenting you with the option, *Do you wish to revise* *your probabilities?* instead of *Do you wish to revise your ratio estimates?* Why would you ever want to revise them at this point? Once you see them displayed on a pie chart and a bar chart, you may conclude that there is something not quite right about their relative magnitudes—i.e., about the *ratios* between them. This pathway too thus offers an approach that assures that your numerical probability estimates are meaningful and that also guides you toward values that are in accord with your general sense of the situation.

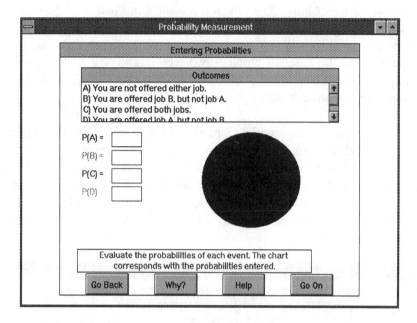

Figure 7.8 Specifying Your Probability Estimates Directly

Some Further Experiments to Consider

Using the *Probability Measurement* program once calls your attention to the requirements that have to be met for probability numbers to be meaningful. But it is not enough to make these requirements second nature to you, much less to make you skillful in satisfying them when you are estimating probabilities. Skill in bringing these requirements to bear is also important when interpreting probability claims made by others, such as the claim discussed at the beginning of this chapter that the probability of the presidential candidate's getting between 51 and 57 percent of the vote if the election were held today is 2/3. To understand this claim, you need to identify the other possible mutually exclusive outcomes comprising the situation, and then interpret this 2/3 number in relation to their probabilities (e.g., it is twice as likely that the result would be between 51 and 57 percent than that it would lie outside this range). You are then in much better position to assess where the specific number comes from, and what would have to be done to increase it.

Repeat the above example in the chapter several times, entering different ratios between the adjacent probabilities, in order to develop a feel for the sorts of probability magnitudes implied by these ratios. You can do this by clicking on **No** in the result screen shown in Figure 7.7 and then clicking on **Repeat this situation** when the options for continuing appear at the bottom of the screen. You might want to try entering all of the ratios, instead of just the adjacent ones. We also suggest you enter the probabilities directly to see how the requirement that they sum to 1.0 intrudes into the process. The goal is to envisage the probabilities when considering the ratios, and to envisage the ratios when considering the probabilities.

You can also examine some of the other situations predefined in the program. Click on **No** in the screen in Figure 7.7, then on **Try a new situation** to initiate this step. Baseball enthusiasts should consider *American League East Pennant Chase*. The situation presented in *Roulette in Southern France* is fairly simple; but unlike the example above, you can employ frequency information in thinking through it. The situation presented in *Who will get the inheritance* is the most elaborate of the predefined situations. For both it and the baseball problem, we recommend that you use only *The-minimum-number-of-ratios* option—the total number of outcomes in each case is sufficiently large that satisfying arithmetical requirements can prove frustrating.

Finally, we strongly encourage you to introduce situations of your own. Click on **Try a new situation**, as above, and then on **Define your own situation** to obtain the screen shown in Figure 7.9. The situation must involve 8 or fewer mutually exclusive outcomes. Also, the burden will now be on you to make sure that these outcomes are mutually exclusive and that they exhaust the situation, for the program will have no way of checking this for you when the situation is not predefined. To enter outcomes beyond the first, click on the + button; to delete the last one entered, click on the − button. All you have to do is to label the outcomes.

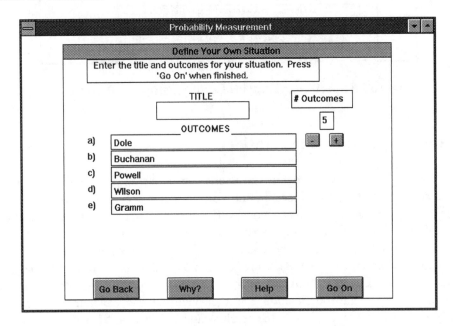

Figure 7.9 Defining Your Own Situation

Chapter 8

Probability Distributions

What May Be Investigated with the *Probability Distributions* Program:

- What it means to say that a variable has a *probability distribution*

- How the commonly occurring probability distribution functions appear graphically

- How the values of the defining parameters affect the center, spread, and shape of
  the probability distributions encountered in statistics

- How its cumulative distribution function (*CDF*) represents a probability distribution

- How the probability distributions for discrete and continuous random variables differ

Why Use This Program?

Suppose you have decided to buy a new personal computer. The purchase of a PC is a major expenditure, so you want to be careful in your choice. You want one that meets your needs for speed, memory, and ease of operation. But you are also concerned about reliability. You do not want a hard disk crash or power supply burnout the night before a deadline. Nor do you want to be faced with sending it cross-country for repair should it fail. The machine you have selected comes with a one-year guarantee on all hardware components (hard disk, floppy disk drive, CD-ROM, CPU, monitor, etc.). Since the service contract offered with the machine costs too much to be attractive, you would like a longer guarantee, but one year is all that is available from the manufacturer.

How does a manufacturer establish the guarantee period? The guarantee is meant to protect both the producer and the consumer from the costs associated with a faulty or malfunctioning product. The manufacturer wants to offer a long guarantee period to indicate the quality of the product and to develop consumer confidence in it. Nevertheless, the guarantee period cannot be too long—repair of items under guarantee can prove costly, pushing the price of the product too high to compete successfully in the market.

Is there a rational way to establish a guarantee period? One approach is to select a guarantee period over the course of which the probability of the product's failing is acceptably small. How small? That depends on a balance between many factors: costs of repair, loss of product reputation, seriousness of failure, etc. The probability must be small enough for the costs and inconvenience to be tolerable. An acceptable failure rate might be 1 in 100. Over what period of time will the probability of the product's failing be no greater than 1 in 100?

To answer this question, the manufacturer needs information about the probability of the product's failing versus time. Not all products of a given type perform identically. Some last longer than others for reasons no one can control. Typically, the longer a product is in service, the greater the probability that it will fail. But how exactly does the probability vary with time? What is the mean time to failure for the product? What is the standard deviation of the failure times? In effect, what the manufacturer needs to know in order to answer questions like these is the specific relationship between time in service and probability of failure—in other words, a curve plotting probability of failure against time in service for the entire population of products of the type in question. This curve represents the *probability distribution* for the random variable, *time in service until failure* for this product.

The *Probability Distributions* program lets you examine a variety of probability distributions, falling into 14 special theoretical "families" that can be defined mathematically. These theoretical distributions come up in important contexts in statistics. Some of them hold, at least to a high approximation, for random variables occurring in the real world. For example, the *Normal distribution*, or bell-shaped curve, applies well to baby weights; the less familiar *Weibull distribution* applies to problems in product reliability. Other probability distributions describe distributions of sample statistics. The *Normal distribution* and the *t distribution* can describe the distribution of sample means from one random sample to another, and the *Chi-square distribution*, that of sample variances. Each of these theoretical distributions consists of a family of individual distributions that share certain properties in common.

The theoretical probability distributions covered in the *Probability Distributions* program are defined by mathematical formulas that express a relationship between the values of the random variable, like baby weights, and the probability that it will assume these values. These mathematical expressions are called *probability distribution functions*. Each of the distributions defined by these functions has its own distinctive properties. Thus, to say that the *normal distribution* applies to baby weights implies a number of things about baby weights. The *Probability Distributions* program will display the mathematical functions graphically, allowing you to manipulate and compare them in order to become familiar with the distinctive properties of the distributions they describe. This familiarity will enable you to draw a number of conclusions immediately upon learning that a particular probability distribution holds for some variable of interest, and it will help you to decide whether any specific examples of the theoretical distributions apply to other variables of interest.

All of this may sound exceedingly abstract and forbidding. The fact that you will be manipulating graphs of the functions, and not the mathematical formulas defining them, should redeem the situation a little, but perhaps not as much as you would like. Limit your initial use of the *Probability Distributions* program to just two or three of the most common distributions. Once you see how to use the program to obtain a clear mental picture of the properties of these distributions, you can come back to the program to investigate the other distributions if and when you encounter them.

How to Use the *Probability Distributions* Program

To run the *Probability Distributions* program, select **Probability** from the *ConStatS* menu, then click on **Probability Distributions** and **Go On**. The initial screen offers four options: *See and select common probability distributions*, which lets you get started by choosing from four representative distributions; *Select from a list of distribution families*, which presents you with a list of 14 families of distributions that can be selected for study; *Describe data using probability*, which allows you to try your hand at fitting a probability distribution to a set of data, as well as to compare probability distributions from different families with one another; and *Exit this program.* The example that follows is confined to the first option. Click on **See and select common probability distributions** and **Go On** to obtain the screen shown in Figure 8.1.

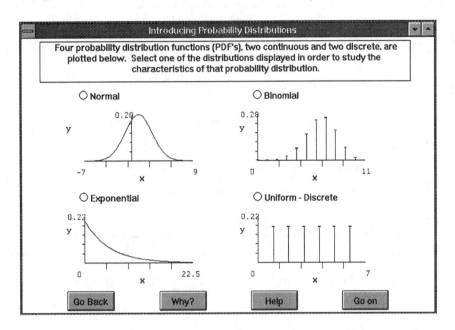

Figure 8.1 Introducing Probability Distributions

The screen displays an example of each of four common probability distributions: two *continuous* distributions, the *normal* and the *exponential*; and two *discrete* distributions, the *binomial* and the *uniform*. Two of the specific distributions shown are symmetric (the *normal* and the *uniform*), and two are skewed (the *exponential* and the *binomial*), the former positively and the latter negatively. Normal and uniform probability distributions are always symmetric, and exponential distributions are always positively skewed; but some binomial distributions are symmetric.

In the case of the two continuous distributions, the random variable x, plotted on the X-axis, takes on a continuous range of values. The quantity *y* plotted on the Y-axis is called the *probability density*. The *probability* that the value of the variable on the X-axis lies within any specific interval on this axis is indicated by the *area* under the curve in this interval. With continuous variables, we are always concerned only with the probability of the value lying within some specific interval—e.g., the probability that the weight of a randomly selected newborn baby is between 7 and 9 pounds.

In the case of the two discrete distributions, the random variable plotted on the X-axis takes on only certain discrete values. An example would be the number of hurricanes that strike the U.S. coast annually—e.g., either 0 or 1 or 2, etc. The quantity *y* plotted on the Y-axis in this case is the probability that the variable has that value—e.g., the probability that exactly two hurricanes strike the coast in a single year. The contrast between discrete and continuous distributions is a source of confusion. Comparison of these four plots will help safeguard against it.

The example below focuses on the normal distribution. Click **Normal** and **Go On** to obtain the screen shown in Figure 8.2.

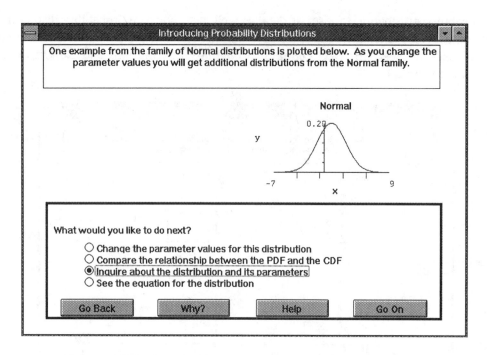

Figure 8.2 Options for Examining a Probability Distribution

The example of the normal distribution shown has a mean of 1.0 and a standard deviation of 2.0. Regardless of which family of probability distributions you select for study, you will always start from this screen, with a specific example on display. The screen offers four options for examining the distribution. The first two open pathways for manipulating the example; we will return to them shortly. The other two provide access to information about the distribution. Even though you may feel that you already know a fair amount about the normal distribution, we best start with them.

Click on **Inquire about the distribution and its parameters** and **Go On** to reach the screen shown in Figure 8.3. The small window requests you to choose what sort of information you want about the distributions: its *Parameters*, *Applications*, or *Features*. Try each one. Selecting *Parameters* will inform you that the normal distribution involves two parameters, the mean μ and the standard deviation σ. The mean determines the central point of the distribution; it is also the point of symmetry. The standard deviation represents the spread in the deviation; while this is not so easy to see, it is the distance from the mean to the inflection point in the curve on either side of the mean—i.e., the point where the curvature changes from concave to convex. Clicking on **Exit** will return you to the screen in Figure 8.3.

Selecting *Applications* provides you with a brief text indicating kinds of data that are commonly described by normal distributions. The normal distribution is often used for variables that are unimodal and symmetric, as well as for variables that can be viewed as the sum of several other random variables. Most importantly, it is the limiting probability distribution for sample means. Selecting *Features* gives you a summary of other statistical aspects of the distribution, such as the median and mode (both of which are always coincident with the mean in every normal distribution). Click on **Exit** to return to the screen shown in Figure 8.2.

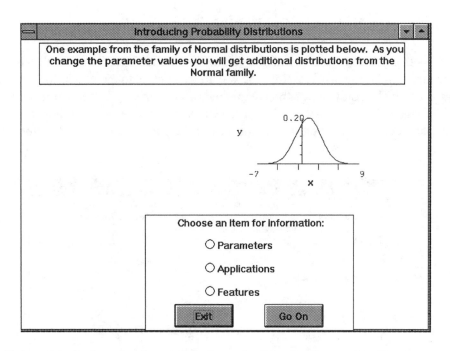

One example from the family of Normal distributions is plotted below. As you change the parameter values you will get additional distributions from the Normal family.

0.20

y

−7   9

x

Choose an Item for Information:

○ Parameters

○ Applications

○ Features

Exit   Go On

Figure 8.3 Options for Inquiring about the Distribution and its Parameters

Click on **See the equation for the distribution** and **Go On.** A window appears that presents the algebraic equation for this distribution, singling out the defining parameters and showing how they enter into this formula. Unless you are an exception to the rule, you will find the algebraic formula for the normal distribution less edifying than the bell-shaped curve depicting it on the screen. Note two things in the *Equation* window. First, there is an infinity of normal distributions, one for every combination of values of the mean μ and the standard deviation σ. The natural question, which we will turn to next, is, what sorts of graphs correspond to different sorts of combinations of these values? Second, the random variable ranges from $-\infty$ to $+\infty$. On the graph the range appears to be -7 to $+9$, but this is because the y values of the curve fall so near the X-axis outside this interval that they cannot be seen on the graph, and hence are not worth drawing on it. Equations sometimes do supply information about a distribution that graphical displays hide. When you are finished looking at the equation, click on **Exit** to return to the screen shown in Figure 8.2.

The next option we want to explore is *Change the parameter values for this distribution.* Before turning to it, however, we should review the distribution plotted on the screen. As we said before, it is the normal distribution for the combination of the mean $\mu=1.0$ and the standard deviation $\sigma=2.0$. The plotted curve is unimodal and symmetric. Its peak occurs at a value of the random variable x of 1.0. In other words, its peak locates the mean, median, and mode of the distribution. The curve has inflection points on either side of its peak. Specifically, the curve changes from concave (at the peak) to convex (in the tails) at x=−1 and x=3. These values of x are one standard deviation below and above the mean, i.e., $\mu-\sigma=1-2=-1$, and $\mu+\sigma=1+2=3$.

Once you are comfortable with the graphical display of the normal distribution, and how the values of the parameters show up in the display, you are ready to examine what happens when these values are changed.

Varying Parameter Values in Probability Distributions

Regardless of whether you are working with the normal distribution your first time through the program or with some other distribution at a later time, the way to gain entree to the option for varying the values of the parameters is to click on **Change the parameter values for this distribution** and **Go On** on the screen shown in Figure 8.2. This will produce a screen like the one in Figure 8.4, in which an example of the distribution is displayed, along with the values of the parameters for this example that you are invited to change.

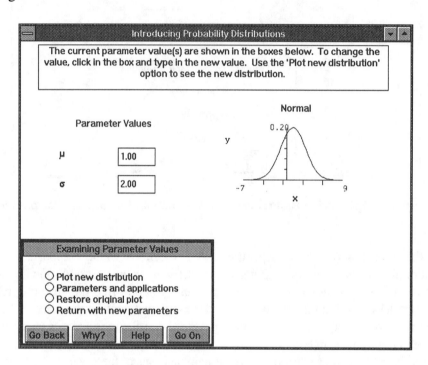

Figure 8.4 Changing the Values of the Parameters

The *Examining Parameter Values* window offers four options. The *Plot new distribution* option generates a plot after you have changed the parameter values. This is the option you will be using most of the time. The *Parameters and applications* option provides access to the text describing the distribution (the same text reached via the *Inquire about the distribution and its parameters* option from the screen shown in Figure 8.2). The *Restore original plot* option wipes the graphical display clean, leaving the plot you began with. And the *Return with new parameters* option returns you to the screen shown in Figure 8.2, but with the example of the distribution on display now one that you have selected by your choice of values of the parameters.

Parameter values are changed by entering new values in the number boxes on the left of the screen in Figure 8.4. Let us see what happens when we change the parameters of the normal distribution to a mean $\mu = 3$ and a standard deviation $\sigma = 1$. Click on the top box and enter **3**. Click on the bottom box and enter **1**. Click on **Plot new distribution** and **Go On**. The result is shown on the screen in Figure 8.5, in which the new distribution is plotted as an overlay on the old one, in a different color.

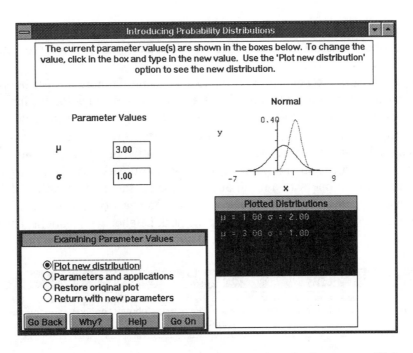

Figure 8.5 Investigating the Effects of Changing the Parameter Values

Notice first, by comparing the plots in Figures 8.4 and 8.5, that the program has altered the scale of the Y-axis to accommodate the modified distribution. Reducing the standard deviation from 2.0 to 1.0 has reduced the spread of the distribution. But the area under both curves must be the same, namely 1.0, the sum of all the probabilities. Consequently, the new distribution has a taller peak, around 0.4 rather than 0.2, and the scale on the Y-axis has been altered to accommodate it. This is a general feature of the normal distribution: the greater the standard deviation, the greater the spread, and the lower the peak.

Next notice that the peak has been shifted from x=1 to x=3. This is the only effect the value of the mean of the normal distribution has: it fixes the location of the peak of the bell-shaped curve on the X-axis. To verify this, change the value of μ back to 1.0, leaving the value of σ at 1.0, and click **Go On**. A third graph will appear in the display, in a third color, with the same peak as the second, but now located at x=1.

In short, as complicated as the formula for the normal distribution appears to be, the values of the two parameters have very simple effects on the graph, and hence on the probability distribution itself. The value of the standard deviation σ controls the height and breadth of the peak, and the mean μ controls the location of the peak on the X-axis. The graph of the normal distribution always has the general form of a bell-shaped curve, although the shape of the bell can become rather extreme. You should try other combinations of values for the parameters until you have verified this claim.

Try some values corresponding to real world examples. For instance, suppose you want to see how the standard deviation on SAT tests affects the distribution. The mean score on SAT tests is designed to be 500. (If you enter 500 you will be informed that this program restricts values of the mean to no more than 20 and values of the standard deviation to no more than 10. Simply represent the mean as 5.0, in effect changing the X-axis to units of 100. To enter an SAT standard deviation of 100, then, enter 1.0.)

You can display as many as four plots on the graph at any one time. If your graph is full and you want to try other combinations of parameter values, click on **Restore original plot** and **Go On**.

In our example, we became preoccupied with the idea of using the normal distribution to represent the probability distribution of time to failure of PCs, the problem raised at the beginning of the chapter. For this we began interpreting the variable x on the X-axis as the time in service before failure. Interpreting the graph shown in Figure 8.5, with μ=3 and σ=1, means that our manufacturer's PCs fail, on average, after 3 years in service, with a standard deviation of 1 year. Because we found these numbers not very appealing from the point of view of consumers, we then tried two additional combinations of parameters: one with a mean of 5 years and a standard deviation of 1 year, and the other with a mean of 4 years and a standard deviation of 0.75 years (i.e., 9 months). These plots are shown in Figure 8.6. Note the relationships among the peak heights, the locations, and the spreads of the four distributions.

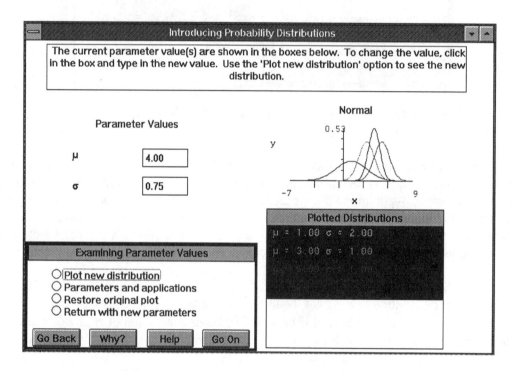

Figure 8.6 A Comparison of Four Normal Distributions

Based on the review of the figure, we decided that the distribution with a mean of 3 years and a standard deviation of 1 year was a plausible enough candidate for representing the probability distribution of time to failure of PCs that it was worthy of further investigation. The alternatives to this normal distribution were even less reasonable than it. We then decided to return to the main screen with these as the working values of the parameters. For you to get the same result, click on **Return with new parameters** and **Go On**. A window will appear asking you which combination of parameters you want. Click on μ=**3.00** σ=**1.00** in the window with the heading, *Plotted Distributions*. This will restore you to the screen shown in Figure 8.2, but with the new instance of the normal distribution displayed on the screen.

Working with the Cumulative Distribution Function

To use the option for relating the probability density function (the *PDF*) and the cumulative distribution function (the *CDF*), click on **Compare the relationship between the PDF and the CDF** and **Go On** on the screen shown in Figure 8.2. This will produce the working screen for this option, shown in Figure 8.7.

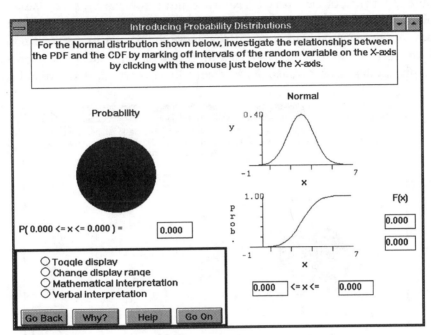

Figure 8.7 Comparing the PDF and the CDF for a Probability Distribution

The options in the window on the lower left play a lesser role here, so we will come back to them later. The blank pie chart and the *0.000*'s in the number boxes await our taking action on the screen. Our normal distribution is now displayed graphically in two ways: by the graph of the *probability density function (PDF)* at the top, which is the same as we have been working with, and by a graph of the *cumulative distribution function (CDF)* on the bottom. These are two distinct, yet equivalent ways of representing probability distributions. Notice that the X-axis has the same scale in both plots. The Y-axes are different, however. The quantity plotted on the Y-axis of the CDF is *probability*! Recall that the quantity *y* plotted on the Y-axis of the PDF is not probability, but *probability density*. Areas under the PDF curve give probabilities on it, with the total area summing to 1.

The difference in their Y-axes provides the clue to understanding how these two very different looking plots are representing the same probability distribution. The probability defined by the CDF graph is not the probability of x having a certain value, but the *probability of x being less than or equal to that value*. For example, the value on the CDF plot for x=3, the mean of our distribution, is 0.5, indicating that the probability of x being *less than or equal to* 3 is 0.5. The CDF is telling us that x=3 is the median of our distribution. This amounts to the same thing as the half of the total area under the PDF to the left of the peak. In short, the CDF is plotting the *area* under the PDF curve to the left of whatever value x takes on! The CDF is *cumulative* because this area keeps increasing as the value of x increases, until both it and the value of the CDF curve reach 1.0. Finally, notice that the slope of the CDF curve is steep at the peak of the PDF curve and flat where the value of the PDF curve is low. The *slope* of the CDF curve indicates the value of the PDF! The fact that the CDF plots the area under the PDF and the PDF plots the slope of the CDF is why these two very different looking curves can represent the same probability distribution.

We can make these abstractions concrete by clicking on either of the X-axes. Move the pointer between 1 and 1.5, a little to the right of the leftmost hash mark, just below the X-axis of the PDF display, and click. The value of x at which you clicked will replace some of the 0.000's on the screen, and vertical lines will appear at this value on both graphs. Now move the pointer to a second position on the X-axis—say, between 3 and 4, at the third hash mark over from the left—and click. Some of the number boxes will now display this value of x, and the pie chart will be activated, as shown in Figure 8.8 below.

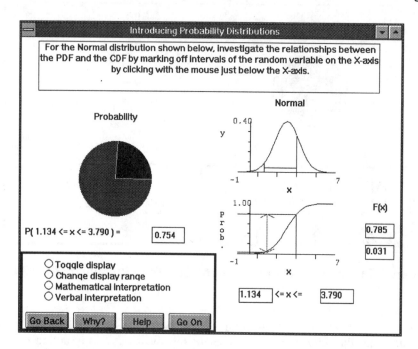

Figure 8.8 Relating Intervals on the PDF and the CDF

The two values for x in the figure are 1.134 and 3.790. The probability values on the CDF are tabulated to the right of it: the probability that x is less than or equal to 1.134 is *0.031*, and the probability that x is less than or equal to 3.790 is *0.785*. The difference between these two numbers, marked on the vertical axis of the CDF, is the probability that x will fall in the interval defined by x=1.134 and x=3.790. This probability is displayed on the pie chart, and indicated to be *0.754* underneath it. In other words, the probability of x being in the interval between x=1.134 and x=3.790 in the case of the specific normal distribution we are considering is 0.754. This is the area under the curve in the sector marked off in the PDF.

Accordingly, by clicking on this screen, we can find the probability of the value of x being in any interval whatever. Since this probability is represented by the area under the PDF curve in this interval, this amounts to the same thing as finding the area in this sector. In other words, with this screen we can shift from the *probability densities* plotted on the PDF to *probabilities* on the CDF. To move the vertical lines, all you have to do is to click on either of the X-axes. (To control which of the two lines you are moving, you may have to proceed incrementally, moving the one you want in a series of smaller steps.) Move the lines around, and see what happens on the pie chart.

Two of the options in the window on the lower left, *Mathematical interpretation* and *Verbal interpretation*, provide more or less the same information provided above. Double-click on each in turn to review this information. Click on **Toggle display** to change the screen to where only one of the two plots appears at a time. (It is sometimes helpful to focus on either the PDF or the CDF alone instead of having both in view.) Finally, the *Change display range* option lets you change the range of values displayed on the X-axis. (We will return to it in a moment.)

This facility for relating the PDF and the CDF representations of probability distributions is helpful for discovering their distinctive properties. For example, suppose we want to know what the probability is that x will lie within 1 standard deviation of the mean in the case of our normal distribution, with its mean $\mu=3$ and its standard deviation $\sigma=1$. Move the vertical line on the right until it lines up with the peak of the PDF plot, at x=3. Then move the left line to the inflection point to the left of the peak on the PDF. If, like us, you find this not so easy, you can accomplish the same thing by moving the left line on the CDF to x=3−1=2. You may not be able to get the lines exactly where you want them, but you can come as close as we did, as shown in Figure 8.9.

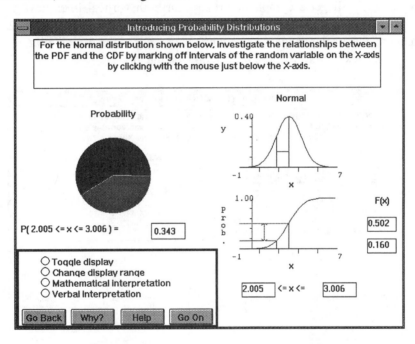

Figure 8.9 The Probability of x Being Within 1 Standard Deviation of the Mean

The pie chart shows that the probability that x lies between 2.005 and 3.006 is *0.343*. Thus, the probability that the value of x is between the mean and one standard deviation below it in the case of our normal distribution is approximately 1/3. Since our distribution is symmetric, the probability that the value of x falls within one standard deviation of the mean (on either side of it) in our distribution is accordingly around 2/3. You can confirm this by moving the right vertical line as near as you can to x=4. Finally, notice that the probability that the value of x lies below 2—i.e., to the left of the sector marked off on the PDF—is around 1/6.

Needless to say, these are distinctive numbers. The question they naturally raise is whether the same thing is true in the case of *every* normal distribution. But there are other questions too. For example, what is the probability that the value of x falls within *two* standard deviations of the mean in our distribution? Also, is this always the same in every normal distribution?

Rather than pursue these questions here, let us return to the PC guarantee problem we posed earlier, interpreting our normal distribution as the probability distribution for the variable *time to failure*. As the results displayed in Figure 8.9 indicate, what this means is that the probability the PCs in question will fail within the first three years is 0.5 (.502 on the screen), and within the first two years, about 0.160. The manufacturer is offering a one-year guarantee. The question (at least from the point of view of the manufacturer) is, what is the probability of failure within the first year?

The easiest way to answer this is to use the CDF plot. Move the left vertical line over to x=1. You will likely find that the screen resolution is too coarse to get closer than x=0.979 or x= 1.027. This situation is one where the *Change display range* option is useful, for it will allow us to zoom in on the section of the plot of interest. Click on **Change display range** and **Go On**. A window will appear on the left, as shown in Figure 8.10, asking you to specify the display range you want. Enter values of **0.0** for the minimum and **2.0** for the maximum in the boxes, then click on **Plot**. (If the right vertical line lies outside this range, you will get a complaint saying that both vertical lines have to lie in the new range. If this happens, click on **Exit**, move the right vertical line over to the left of x=2, and then repeat the steps for changing the display range.) Once you have produced the desired plot, resembling the one shown in Figure 8.11, click on **Exit** to close the window on the left.

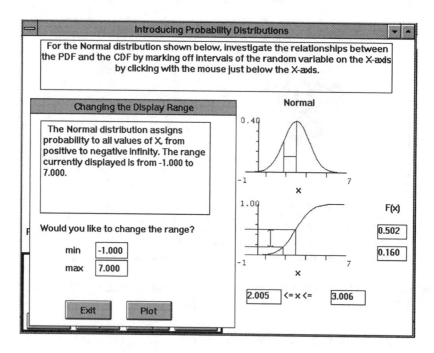

Figure 8.10 Changing the Display Range

Now, move the left vertical line as near to 1 as you can get it (1.006 on our screen) and the right vertical line as near to 2. The result is shown in Figure 8.11.

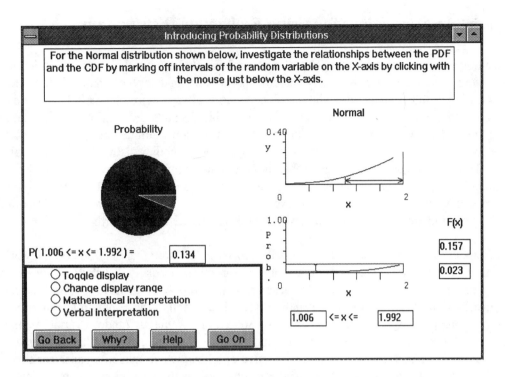

Figure 8.11 The Probability of "PC Failure" During the 1st Year

From the bottom number to the right of the CDF, we see that the probability that a normally distributed variable with mean μ=3 and standard deviation σ=1 will be less than or equal to 1.0 is about *0.023*, or 2.3 percent. In the context of the PC guarantee problem, this means that 2.3 percent of the PCs are expected to fail within one year after purchase. (The pie chart indicates that an additional 13.4 percent of them are expected to fail in the second year.)

Suppose our normal distribution really does represent the time to failure for the manufacturer's PCs. Suppose further that the manufacturer does not want to repair more than 1 percent of the PCs under guarantee. How long would the guarantee period have to be to meet this goal? We can find this by finding the value of x where the CDF plot reaches 0.01—i.e., the bottom number to the right of the CDF is 0.010. Click along the axis until you get as close as you can to this. We managed to get 0.010 exactly. We found the corresponding value of x to be 0.664, or roughly eight months.

The manufacturer is not likely to be happy with these numbers. What can be done about them? If the probability distribution for the variable *time to failure* of PC's really is a normal distribution, then the only parameters that can be changed are the mean value of *time to failure* and the standard deviation. Raising the average time to failure from three to, say, five years will help. But the added reliability is undoubtedly going to cost something. The only alternative, however, is to lower the standard deviation, reducing the variability of the *time to failure*. This will have the desired effect of increasing the peak of the normal distribution and flattening the tail. The trouble is that the standard deviation of the *time to failure* is not something the manufacturer has much control over. It depends too much on the environment in which the PCs are used, as well as the way in which they are used.

Some Further Suggestions for Using *Probability Distributions*

The preceding example revealed a lot about the *normal distribution*, but there is more to learn. For instance, it would be interesting to verify that the probability of every normally distributed random variable's falling within 1 standard deviation of the mean is always more or less 2/3. There is also the question about the probability of the variable's falling within 2 standard deviations, or for that matter 3. What are these probabilities in the case of the normal distribution examined above, and do they remain the same for all normal distributions? If so, we have exposed another distinctive property of this distribution. To have full command of any probability distribution involves knowing not just how changes in the values of its parameters affect matters, but also which properties remain the same as the values of the parameters vary. So, one suggestion, even if you plan to do little more with *Probability Distributions* at this juncture, is to go back and explore the normal distribution further.

One hears about the normal distribution and bell-shaped curves more than any others. Nevertheless, it is by no means the case that every continuous random variable is normally distributed. For example, the theoretical limiting distribution for sample variances is the *chi-square distribution*, and the theoretical limiting distribution for sample means when the standard deviation of the population is unknown is the *t distribution*. Sampling, moreover, is not the only source of continuous random variables that are not normally distributed. Real world examples abound. A likely example, close to hand, is *time to failure* of PC's. The normal distribution extends to negative numbers, which make no sense for this variable. You might want to try a *Weibull distribution*, which is often used in reliability problems, or a *log normal* or *exponential distribution*, all of which have a lower bound of 0.

Regardless of whether you want to examine other continuous probability distributions now or postpone that until you have a pressing need to know more about them, you should probably put some time now into one of the discrete variables. As Figure 8.12 shows, discrete random variables are different in some important respects from continuous ones. For one thing, the CDF for a discrete random variable is not a

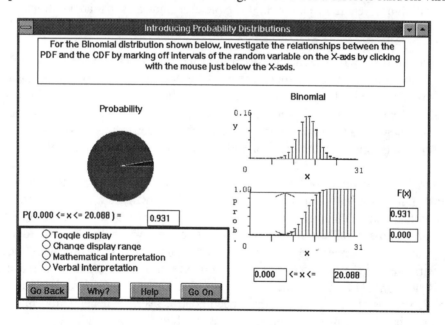

Figure 8.12 The PDF and CDF for a Binomial Distribution

94

continuous curve, for the variable takes on only discrete values. The figure shows this. The individual spikes in the CDF represent the accumulation of the spikes in the PDF, starting from the left. The example shown is a *binomial distribution*. The spikes shown on the PDF give the probability of x *heads* appearing in 30 flips of a coin that has a 55 percent bias in favor of heads; and the spikes shown on the CDF give the probability of x or fewer *heads* in 30 flips. The *Sampling Problem* program in *ConStatS* involves biased coins of this sort.

Something to notice about the binomial distribution plotted in Figure 8.12 is that smooth curves connecting the tips of the spikes in either the PDF or the CDF plots resemble the corresponding PDF or CDF curve for the normal distribution. Textbooks in statistics explain how the normal distribution approximates the binomial well enough, when the number of trials (e.g., coin flips) is large, that it can be used to calculate CDF values for the binomial. We can examine how good this approximation is by turning to an option in *Probability Distributions* that we have ignored so far, *Describe data using probability*. In addition to allowing probability distributions to be compared with data distributions, this option allows probability distributions in different families to be compared with one another. Figure 8.13, for example, shows a comparison of the binomial distribution in Figure 8.12 and a normal distribution with a mean μ=16.5 and a standard deviation σ=2.75.

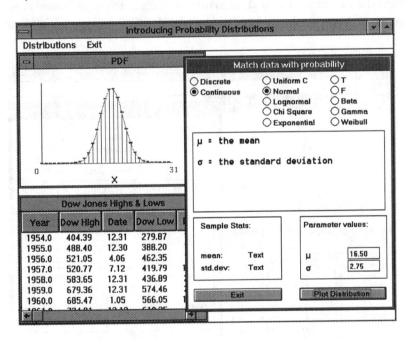

Figure 8.13 Comparing a Binomial With a Normal Distribution

The screen in the figure was reached by selecting *Describe data using probability* on the opening screen of the program, then by selecting an arbitrary data set to activate the option, followed by clicking on **Distributions** on the menu bar and **PDF** in the window that appeared. We then selected each distribution in turn and entered values for its parameters. This option can be used to explore many questions of interest once you become familiar with the probability distributions you want to compare. For instance, we could reduce the number of trials in the binomial distribution in the figure from 30 to 20 to 10, etc., to see where the normal ceases to approximate the binomial.

Another example arises in *Sampling* and *Inference*. You may recall remarks made in passing in this chapter to the effect that the normal distribution is the limiting probability distribution for sample means when the standard deviation of the population is known, and the t distribution is the limiting distribution for sample means when it is not known. This option can be used to compare normal and t distributions with a view to seeing just what the effect is of using a sample standard deviation as a surrogate for the population standard deviation.

Of course, the primary purpose of *Describe data using probability* is to compare probability distributions with data. Which, if any, of the standard theoretical probability distributions describes any given real world variable is generally an open question. The usual way of addressing this question is to see how well the different theoretical probability distributions can be made to fit a substantial body of data by varying their parameters. This option lets you explore this for any one of the data sets in *ConStatS*, or any data set you elect to add to it. This is an advanced option. It is nonetheless useful for learning about the ways in which the distinctive properties of any probability distribution restrict its capacity for describing data. The example shown in Figure 8.14 attempts to fit a normal distribution to the annual highest closing values of the Dow Jones Average (for the New York Stock Exchange) from 1954 to 1987 (in units of 100, which we obtained by dividing the data by 100). Specifically, we tried a normal distribution with the same mean and standard deviation as the transformed data. As you can see, the fit is not so good. Perhaps we should have tried a probability distribution other than the normal.

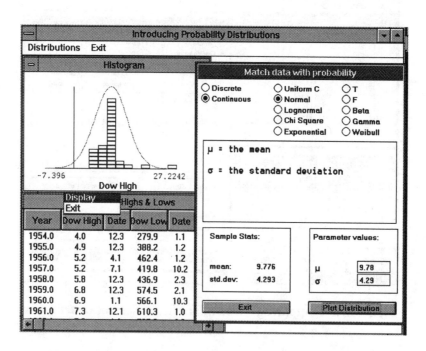

Figure 8.14 Trying to Fit a Normal Distribution to Dow Jones Highs

PART THREE

SAMPLING

We said earlier that statistics is the science of extracting useful information from data. Most of the time this means extracting reliable conclusions about populations from data obtained by sampling. Acquiring data for an entire population is usually impracticable; in the case of populations that are open-ended—e.g., all humans past, present, and future, or all possible tosses of a coin—it is impossible. Because samples differ from one another, not all of them are equally representative of the population, and few, if any, are entirely representative. Relying on a sample to answer a question about a population thus always involves some risk of being misled. The issues raised by sampling concern this risk. Some of these issues pertain to qualitative variations from sample to sample. How much do samples differ from one another, and how radically can they depart from the population? Also, since statistics like the mean and median differ from sample to sample, sample statistics are themselves random variables. How are they distributed? Other issues focus on quantifying and controlling the risk. What is the probability of a sample statistic departing from the population value by more than a given amount? What can be done to reduce this probability?

ConStatS includes three programs on sampling. *Sampling Distributions* and *Sampling Errors* are sister programs, the former concentrating on the qualitative and the latter on the quantitative issues raised by sampling. Both allow experiments to be carried out in which multiple samples are drawn from a population and compared with one another. *Sampling Distributions* allows the process of drawing samples from populations to be followed step by step. The values of the sample statistics are plotted on a histogram, and the sample corresponding to each entry can then be reviewed. This program covers all the usual statistics for center and spread. *Sampling Errors*, by contrast, covers only the mean, variance, and standard deviation. The experiments in it contrast collections of samples of three different sizes in order to explore how sample size affects the frequency with which the value of the sample statistic is misleading. In the case of the mean, these frequencies can be compared with the theoretical probabilities of unacceptable sampling error, and the distributions of the sample means can be compared with the normal probability distributions that in theory they reflect. Unless students are already acquainted with sampling, they should start with *Sampling Distributions*.

The third sampling program, *A Sampling Problem*, presents the challenge of trying to decide whether a coin is fair, is 55 or 60 percent biased in favor of heads, or is 55 or 60 percent biased in favor of tails—this on the basis of a series of tosses of the coin. Once the choice is made, the correct answer is given, and an analysis is available of what the specific series of tosses provided in the way of evidence. The fact that this program is listed last under *Sampling* suggests that it should be used last. In truth, it makes just as much sense, if not more, to use it first, as an introduction to sampling and its risks, and then perhaps return to it at the end.

Chapter 9

Sampling Distributions

What May Be Investigated with the *Sampling Distributions* Program:

- How samples drawn from the same populations vary

- How closely samples resemble population distributions

- How sample statistics, like the mean and standard deviation, are distributed

- How the distributions of sample statistics are related to population distributions

Why Use This Program?

Suppose you want to know how much money, on average, students at a large university earn per week while school is in session. You generally would also want to know what the variance in these earnings is across the student body. Asking every student is out of the question. Instead, you take a random sample of students and use the mean and the variance of the weekly earnings in this sample to approximate the mean and variance of the weekly earnings of the entire student-body population. Then you learn that someone else with the same interests has recently conducted their own sample and obtained somewhat different values. You understand that values of sample statistics will vary from one random sample to another drawn from the same population. But is this the sole reason for the difference between your values and those of the other person? Perhaps something else is going on. Perhaps one of the two samples did not represent the distribution of earnings across the entire population at all well.

Concerns of this sort raise some general questions. How much are samples drawn from the same population likely to differ from one another? They will surely differ. How are sample statistics themselves—in this case, the sample means and variances—distributed across the entire collection of samples that can be drawn from the population? The sample means and the sample variances need not be distributed in the same way. How do the distributions of these and other sample statistics change from one type of population distribution to another? Sample size is also bound to make some difference. How does it affect the distributions of the sample statistics, especially the center and spread of these distributions? The *Sampling Distributions* program allows experiments to be carried out that will help answer questions like these.

In the case of student earnings, you might take some additional random samples from the student-body population and compare them and their means and variances with one another. Alternatively, you might postulate that the weekly earnings of the students at the university are distributed in some specific way and then produce samples at your desk with the help of a random number generator or, if need be, dice.

The distribution of the earnings is surely skewed, for the higher the amount, the lower the probability. So, you might postulate that the earnings have an exponential probability distribution. This way of obtaining additional samples involves turning your original questions about samples of weekly earnings into pure mathematical questions about samples from a generic exponential distribution. It is nevertheless fully analogous to taking additional samples from the student body, yet without the associated inconvenience. Whichever approach you adopt, what you are doing in response to your concerns is to obtain a *sample of samples*. This is precisely what the *Sampling Distributions* program does. It allows you to answer questions about sampling by formulating and carrying out experiments involving samples of samples.

Taking samples of samples is not something you will ever be inclined to do in practical situations—in the field, so to speak. There you will take a single sample and draw your conclusions. Taking samples of samples is a theoretical exercise, something to do in studying statistics. Its goal is to help you think of any sample that you draw in a practical situation in the context of all possible samples that you might have drawn in the situation.

How to Run Experiments with the *Sampling Distributions* Program

To run the *Sampling Distributions* program, select **Sampling** from the *ConStatS* menu. Click once on **Sampling Distributions** and then click **Go On**. The screen in Figure 9.1 will appear.

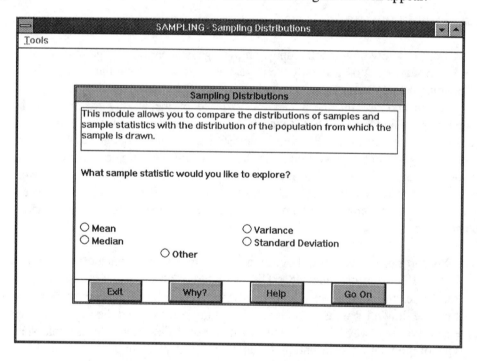

Figure 9.1 Choosing a Sample Statistic to Explore

Four items must be specified in order to perform a sampling distribution experiment: (1) the sample statistic to be investigated, (2) the population from which samples are to be drawn, (3) the size of the samples, and (4) the number of samples to draw.

The first choice you need to make is which sample statistic you want to investigate. Any time you draw repeated samples of the same size from the same population you may calculate a sample statistic from each sample and see how the values vary from sample to sample. You may do this with any sample statistic—mean, standard deviation, range, etc. For this example, select the mean by clicking on **Mean** to highlight it and then clicking **Go On**.

The next choice involves specifying a population. This choice really involves three separate choices: the *Population*, *Random Variable*, and *Population Distribution*. This trio defines the source of the samples. The *Population* may be anything: all males over 15 years of age, all brown bears in Alaska, or, if you want to get abstract, simply a generic population whose characteristics are unknown. Figure 9.2 shows the population as being *Generic*.

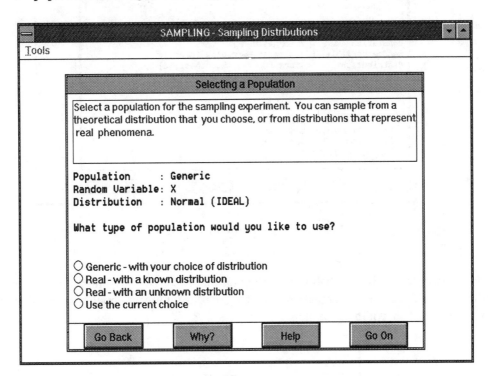

Figure 9.2 Generic Screen Setup for *Selecting a Population*

The *Random Variable* defines some property of the population you want to examine through sampling. For the population of males over 15 years, you might choose to examine the number of words in their vocabulary. For the brown bears, the number of salmon eaten every summer would be an appropriate random variable. For the *Generic* population with no known characteristics, the random variable could be *X*, as in Figure 9.2.

We will make this example a bit more concrete. Click on **Real - with a known distribution**, click **Go On**, and you will be presented with a list of random variables from which to choose. Choose the random variable *Lifetime of Barnacles* for the following experiment. Read the description of this variable by clicking on the **Description** button. Then click **Go On**.

101

As illustrated in Figure 9.3, the screen reflects the new selection. *Population* now appears as *All Barnacles*.[1] The *Random Variable* is *Lifetime*, and the third part of the population description, the *Population Distribution* is labeled *Uniform - continuous (hypothesized)*. (It is hypothesized because this is the best guess available about the probable life-expectancies of barnacles.)

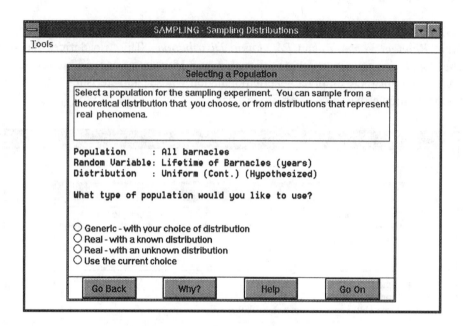

Figure 9.3 Selecting a Population

The population distribution is a probability distribution that describes how the random variable under consideration is distributed in the population. The hypothesized uniform population distribution for the lifetime of barnacles is shown in Figure 9.4.

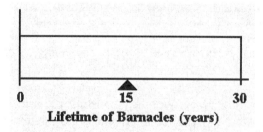

Figure 9.4 Population Distribution for Lifetime of Barnacles

According to the distribution, all barnacles live between 0 and 30 years. The probability of living to any age in between—13.3 years, 8.7 years, or 26.9 years—is the same. According to this, then, a barnacle is just as likely to live to 5 years as to 25 years. The average lifetime is 15 years.

---

[1] Barnacles are small sea creatures (crustaceans) that attach themselves to rocks or boats when they become adults.

Now that the population and sample statistic have been specified, it is time to consider the sample size and the number of samples. Click **Use the current choice** and then **Go On**. The top of the next window will say *Sample Size*. The sample size is the number of observations in each sample to be taken. It will be the same for each sample in any one sampling distribution experiment. If you are unsure about what sample size to specify, try the **Why** or **Help** buttons. When you have chosen a sample size, enter the number in the box and click **Go On**.

You now need to select the *Number of Samples*. This choice is what makes the experiment a sampling distributions experiment—i.e., an experiment involving a sample of samples—rather than a sampling experiment. A number of samples will be taken in the experiment, namely the number you specify. Each of these will have its own mean. Hence, when you specify the *Number of Samples*, you are also specifying the number of sample means the experiment will generate. These will comprise a sample in their own right, a sample of the mean values of lifetimes found in samples drawn from the population of barnacles; the size of this sample is the number you select. Use **Why** or **Help** if you are uncertain about what you want this number to be. Once you decide, enter the number in the box and click **Go On**. You will then see a summary of the experiment you have defined. If this is the experiment you want to run, click **Go On**. Otherwise, click **Go Back** and reset the items you want to change. After you click **Go On**, the program will take a short time to set up the sampling experiment. When the setup is done, you will see the screen below.

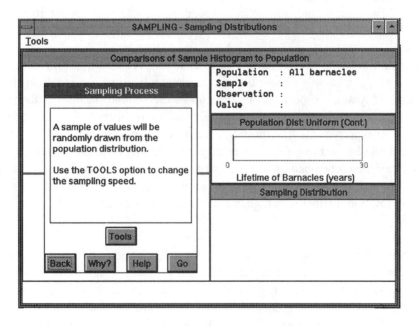

Figure 9.5 Setup for Running the Experiment

This screen illustrates the process of drawing samples from a population. The population distribution appears in the middle right. To start the process, click **Go On**. A menu labeled *Sampling Step #1* appears in the lower left. The first step in the process is *Take new sample*. During this step individual observations (i.e., the lifetime in years for individual barnacles) will be drawn from the population distribution. An *X* indicates the observation. Each observation is represented by a single sample data point plotted on a histogram that will appear in the upper left corner. Click **Go** to take the first sample. When the first sample is complete, the menu returns with *Calculate sample statistic* highlighted. Click **Go On** to obtain the mean of this sample. *Plot sample statistic* will then become highlighted. Click **Go On** again and a new histogram, labeled *Sampling Distribution*, appears under the *population distribution*. This histogram will display all the sample means (i.e., the sampling distribution of the mean). Click **Go On** to take the next sample. You can accelerate the process (and eliminate the need to click **Go On** following each step) by clicking on **Speed** in the menu that appears after each step is complete. Select **Fast**, and the remainder of the experiment will be completed at high speed.

How to Analyze the Results of the Experiment

When the experiment is finished running, two outcomes are available for you to examine: a collection of samples and a distribution of sample means. The function of *Sampling Distributions* is to help you explore the relationships between the items under your control (i.e., the sample statistic, the population distribution, the sample size, and the number of samples) and these two outcomes. For the most part you will find yourself comparing distributions. Remember, all distributions have three properties: center, spread, and shape. When you compare distributions, the comparisons will typically be based on these three properties.

The individual samples in the collection of samples are indicated as separate entries in the histogram that displays the sample means in the lower right hand corner. When you click on any one of these sample means, a histogram displaying the corresponding sample will appear in the upper left hand corner.

What questions can the two outcomes help you to answer? A good question is, how widely do the sample means vary? Each sample mean has claim to being a legitimate estimate of the true population mean, in this case 15 years. Inspect the distribution of the sample means. Is there a large distance between the smallest and the largest sample mean recorded in the histogram? Are some of the means so far removed as to misrepresent the true mean? You can get a feel for how and why the sample means differ from one another by recalling the samples they came from. To do this, click on a sample mean to obtain the display of the corresponding sample. Try clicking on the sample means at the extreme low end, and then at the extreme high end. Can you see any pattern of contrast between the samples that have distinctively low and distinctively high means that might account for why these sample means are exceptional?

Each sample is also an estimate of the overall population distribution. In this example we can examine how well samples of the chosen size approximate the population distribution, since the population distribution is known—that is, we are given that it is uniform continuous and ranges from 0 to 30. Click on a sample mean in the histogram and inspect the sample from which it came. Does the sample look like the population distribution? Would the sample by itself incline you to predict that the population distribution is uniform continuous and ranges from 0 to 30? Examine several samples and estimate what fraction of them would incline you to predict all three aspects of the population distribution—center, spread, and shape. To help you make the comparison, double click on **Compare this sample to the population**. The population distribution will be shown by a line on the display of the sample. If you think that the number of intervals used in the histogram displaying the sample is distorting the comparison, double click on **Change this sample's # of intervals**, enter a different number, and click **OK**. If you are not sure why the number of intervals might be having an effect on the comparison, highlight the option of changing the number and click on **Why** or **Help**.

104

You can also compare the sampling distribution—that is, the distribution of the sample means—and the population distribution. A good way to make this comparison is by making the range in the histogram displaying the sample means the same as the range in the plot of the population distribution. Click on **Pop. Range** in the middle of the bottom of the screen, and the histogram will be re-plotted to have the same range as the population distribution. Figure 9.6 shows the sampling distribution on the same range as the population distribution. The sampling distribution in the figure is based on 75 samples of size 25.

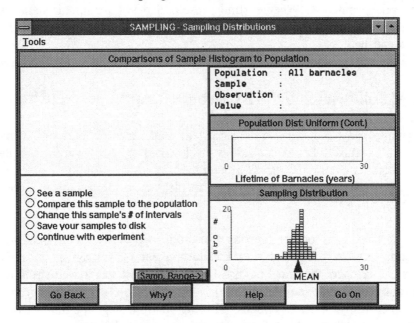

Figure 9.6 Comparing the Sampling and Population Distributions

How do the centers, spreads, and shapes of these two distributions compare? They have similar centers, but they differ markedly in spread and shape. The sampling distribution has a much smaller spread, and it looks much more like a normal distribution than a uniform continuous distribution.

Both of these differences are of real benefit. Consider spread first. Although the individual sample means differ from one another, there is less variation among them than among individual data points in the population. Individual data points selected from the population, which are equally likely to be anywhere between 0 and 30, also have some claim to being legitimate estimates of the average lifetime. But the variation among them is so large that any one individual data point is likely to be far removed from the true mean. By contrast, the variation in the distribution of the sample means is much smaller. Each individual sample mean is much less likely to be at a far remove from the true mean.

The difference in shape is also of real benefit. Trying to estimate the true mean with an individual data point from the uniformly distributed population involves a significant risk. The point is equally likely to fall anywhere between 0 and 30. By contrast, the sample means, at least in the outcome of the experiment shown in Figure 9.6, cluster in the middle, with extreme highs and lows balanced on either side. While there is still risk of a misrepresentative sample and hence a misleading sample mean, the risk is greatly reduced. Moreover, a normal probability distribution fitted to the distribution of the sample means can be used to determine the likelihood of a sample mean falling misleadingly far from the true mean.

These two features—the reduced spread among the sample means and their being distributed normally—comprise the Central Limit Theorem. In substance, this theorem says that the sampling distribution of the means is a normal distribution, regardless of the distribution of the population from which the samples are drawn, and the variance of the sample means is less than the variance of the population. The extent to which these features emerge in any one *Sampling Distributions* experiment focusing on the mean will depend on several things, including the number of samples, the sample size, and the variation in the population. Whether similar results also hold for sample statistics other than the mean is an interesting question. One way to answer it is to carry out experiments like this one, but with a different sample statistic.

Some Ways of Following Up the Experiment

Whether other sample statistics behave in the same way as the mean is only one of many interesting questions the experiment raises. For example, how much would an increase in the sample size cause the sampling means to cluster even more tightly around the true mean? And how much would a greater number of samples cause the distribution of the sample means to look even more like a normal probability distribution?

You can investigate these questions by clicking **Continue with experiment**, **Go On**, and **Compare distribution of sample MEAN to population distribution**, and **Go On** again. This will take you to a screen where you can compare the sampling distribution with the population distribution more closely by clicking on **Plot histogram of sample statistic**, followed by **Go On**. The histogram will be plotted. You will be presented with a series of options, allowing you to change the number of intervals in the histogram (by clicking on **Change Hist. Intervals**, and entering a different number) and its range (by clicking on **Change Hist. Range**, and entering whatever numbers you want). The third of these options, **Update Experiment**, allows you to set up and run direct variations on this experiment. Click on it and then **Go On**. As Figure 9.7 shows, you will be presented with a menu that allows you to alter any of the items that you originally selected for this experiment except the population distribution.

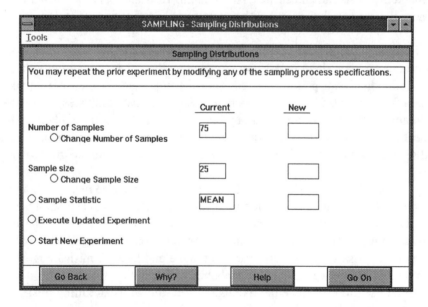

Figure 9.7 Running Variations of the Experiment

You can easily change the number of samples or the sample size to see what effect each of them has on the outcome, or you can shift to a different sample statistic to see how its behavior compares with the mean.

It is wise to make only one change at a time because a single change can have more than one effect. For example, a change in sample size may affect how closely the individual samples resemble the population as well as features of the sampling distribution. Changing the sample size or the number of samples allows you to explore how these two affect the outcome of the original experiment. Shifting to a different sample statistic, while moving you away from the original experiment, allows you to explore whether different sample statistics behave in the same way as the mean. The median is a natural alternative for comparison in the present case, but then so too is the standard deviation.

If you want to change the population distribution, select *Start New Experiment*. An obvious alternative experiment in the present case is to replace the uniform continuous distribution of *Lifetime of Barnacles* with, say, a normal population distribution in order to see how the population distribution tends to affect the sampling distribution in the case of the mean. One way to do this is by selecting the *Generic - with your choice of distribution* option. This option presents you with a screen that allows you to specify any population distribution you might want. A comparison that might prove to be an instructive variant of the above experiment is a normal distribution with a mean of 15 and a standard deviation of 4.

Once you turn to normally distributed populations, you should explore the effect of the population standard deviation on the spread of the sample means. Intuitively, an increase in the sample size should tend to decrease the spread of the sample means. So too should a decrease in the variability, and hence in the standard deviation, of the population from which the samples are drawn. Assuming both of these expected effects occur, how do they compare? You can explore this by comparing a doubling of the sample size with, say, a halving of the population standard deviation—from 4 to 2 in the example proposed at the end of the preceding paragraph.

An interesting follow-up experiment of an entirely different sort is trying a random variable with an unknown population distribution. You can conduct such an experiment by clicking on **Real - with an unknown distribution** on the screen where you specify the population (see Figure 9.3). Try the random variable, *Personal weekly income*, and do your best to estimate the population distribution.

The *Sampling Distributions* program allows you to examine the center, spread, and shape of the distributions of sample statistics, as well as how these are affected by sample size and population distribution. As such, it helps you answer *qualitative* questions about how the values of sample statistics vary from one random sample to another. The more you see of these variations, however, the more you may want answers to some *quantitative* questions—questions like, what is the probability that the value of the sample statistic will deviate from the population value by more than a given amount? The *Sampling Distributions* program leaves much of the burden of extracting such quantitative information on you. If you find yourself becoming more preoccupied with questions of this sort, turn to this programs's sister, *Sampling Errors*, which is covered in the next chapter.

Chapter 10

Sampling Errors

What May Be Investigated with the *Sampling Errors* Program:

- How sample size affects the distributions, especially the spreads, of sample statistics

- How and when the value of a sample statistic may be considered misleading

- How probability distributions serve to represent distributions of sample statistics

- What the relation is between sample size and the probability of large sampling error

- How this relation can be exploited to decide on sample sizes in practice

Why Use This Program?

Suppose the Student Senate deadlocks on the size on next year's Student Activities Fee. You and one other student are assigned the task of surveying the students to see what they think. The issue is not merely the average of the opinions about what the fee should be, but also their standard deviation. If the standard deviation is large, setting the fee at the average may produce a lot of complaints among the substantial body of students who think it should not be so high. You and your colleague decide to carry out separate random samples among the students, with the expectation of combining them at the end. When you compare the results of your sample of 100 students with her sample of 125, however, you are both astounded to see how different they are. A review of one another's approaches convinces the two of you that the samples are both random. Nevertheless, at least one of them must not be representative of the entire student body. Under these circumstances you are reluctant to combine the two insofar as, if only one of them is misrepresentative, you are better off not combining them. Her sample has some claim to being the more reliable because it is larger; but it is not that much larger. If only there were some way to tell from looking at each sample whether it is drastically misleading.

The wish for some fail-safe way of sampling opinions is probably as old as sampling itself. We have good news here and bad news. The bad news is that there is no guaranteed way of designing a sample to yield truly representative results, nor of telling whether a given sample is representative just from examining it. The good news is that the risk of being seriously misled by a sample can nevertheless usually be quantified. Specifically, the *probability* that the value of a sample statistic differs from the population value by more than a given amount can generally be calculated, or at least estimated. Moreover, this ability to quantify the risk can then be used to assure that the level of risk you are taking when relying on a sample is appropriate to the situation at hand. Quantifying and controlling the risks of being misled by samples is what the *Sampling Errors* program is all about.

Three factors influence how far a sample statistic is likely to depart from the population value. First, the greater the variance in the population, the more variance there is likely to be in the samples drawn from it and hence in the sample statistics. Unfortunately population variance is usually not easy to manipulate or control. Second, natural randomness causes each sample to be a little bit—or sometimes a lot—different from others. While techniques like stratified samples can sometimes help reduce its unwanted effects, natural randomness is intrinsic to random sampling.

The third factor influencing the likelihood of a sample's being misleading is sample size. This factor is easiest to control. The trouble with increasing the sample size in order to reduce the likelihood of being misled is that larger samples cost more, in time as well as money. The obvious question is whether there are ways of balancing the costs of increasing the sample size against the risks of being misled—i.e., ways of trading one off against the other. This in turn raises questions about just what the relationship is between sample size and the probability of sample statistics deviating from population values by different amounts. How sensitive is this probability to sample size? Does this sensitivity change with the amount of discrepancy that is regarded as tolerable? And how does the population affect the relationship? The *Sampling Errors* program allows experiments in sampling to be carried out that help to answer questions like these.

Like those in the *Sampling Distributions* program, the experiments in *Sampling Errors* allow you to compare many samples drawn from the same population. In other words, the experiments here too involve samples of samples, with the goal of investigating sampling itself. The focus in *Sampling Errors*, however, is on the *frequency* with which the value of a sample statistic deviates unacceptably far from the population value. The experiments in this program always involve three separate collections of samples, with the sample size differing from one collection to the next. This allows the frequency of unacceptable error to be plotted against sample size. Finally, the program offers options for comparing the observed distribution of the sample mean with the theoretical limiting probability distribution for it, and also the observed frequencies of error with the theoretical probabilities of error.

This talk of error and deviation presupposes that the true population value is known. In the *Sampling Errors* program you will be in a position of omniscience concerning the population distribution from which the samples are being drawn. This luxury is almost unheard of when sampling from real world populations. It is nonetheless appropriate in the *Sampling Errors* program precisely because the questions it is designed to let you investigate are not about real world populations, but about sampling.

How to Run Experiments with the *Sampling Errors* Program

To run the *Sampling Errors* program, select **Sampling** from the *ConStatS* menu. Click on **Sampling Errors** and **Go On**. The screen shown in Figure 10.1 will appear.

Five items have to be specified in order to perform a sampling errors experiment: (1) the sample statistic to be investigated; (2) the population from which samples are to be drawn; (3) three sample sizes to be examined; (4) the number of samples to be drawn; and (5) boundaries on either side of the population value outside which you regard the value of the sample statistic to be misleading. The screen shown in Figure 10.1 covers the first of these items.

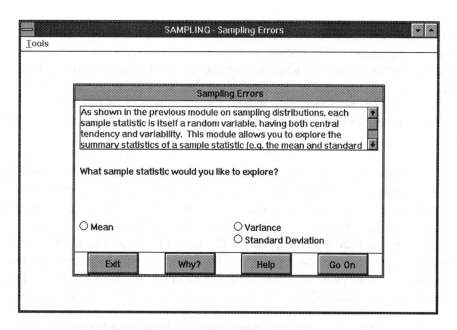

Figure 10.1 Choosing a Sample Statistic to Explore

The choices of sample statistics are more limited than in the *Sampling Distributions* program because the focus here is not on how different sample statistics are distributed, but on how to deal with the risk of being misled, regardless of the sample statistic. To proceed with the example below, click on **Mean** and **Go On**. This will produce the screen, shown in Figure 10.2, for selecting the population from which the samples are to be drawn. Technically, this selection involves three choices: a population, a random variable across this population, and the distribution of this random variable.

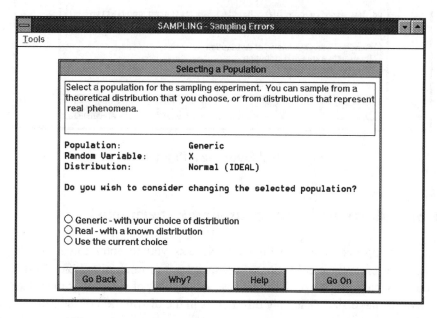

Figure 10.2 Generic Screen for Selecting a Population

In our example in the *Sampling Distributions* program, we chose the *Real — with a known distribution* option to select *All Barnacles* as the population and their *Lifetime* as the random variable, a variable which someone has hypothesized has a *uniform* distribution over the range from 0 to 30 years. (In other words, barnacles were hypothesized to have the same chance of dying at all times from birth to 30 years, after which none survive.) In point of fact, the only thing from this selection that made any difference at all in the experiment presented in the *Sampling Distributions* chapter was the uniform distribution.

The fact this distribution was being taken to describe the lifetimes of barnacles did nothing more than lend a little concreteness to the discussion. We gain from using the same population in the example here. This time, however, we use the same uniform distribution in the abstract. Click on **Generic — with your choice of distribution** and **Go On**, followed by **Uniform** under *Continuous* and **Go On**. Enter **0.0** in the *a=* box and **30.0** in the *b=* box. Click on **Plot new distribution,** and the uniform distribution will be displayed over the default distribution. Now click on **Use current parameter values** and **Go On**. This will yield the screen shown in Figure 10.3. After reviewing the choice, click on **Use the current choice** and **Go On** to proceed to the specifics of the sampling errors experiment.

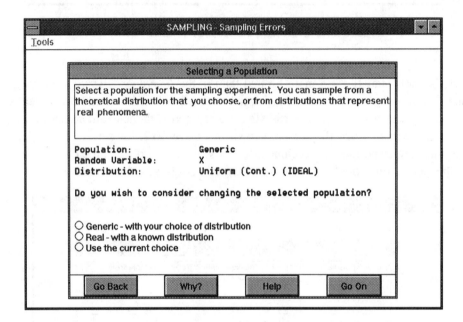

Figure 10.3 Selecting a Population

Setting the Specifications for the Sampling Experiment

The screen that next appears, shown in Figure 10.4, asks you to enter three *sampling sizes*. The program is going to generate three collections—i.e. samples—of random samples from the population: one collection consisting of samples of the small size; the second, of samples of the middle size; and the third, of samples of the large size. The only differences in the distribution of the sample statistic across each of these collections come from the natural randomness involved in random samples and from the sample size. The idea, accordingly, is to choose three sizes that will bring out the effect of sample size.

In the example below we have chosen 10, 25, and 50. Enter these sizes in the three boxes on the screen, then click **Go On**. (Repeat the experiment later with different sample sizes within the indicated ranges.)

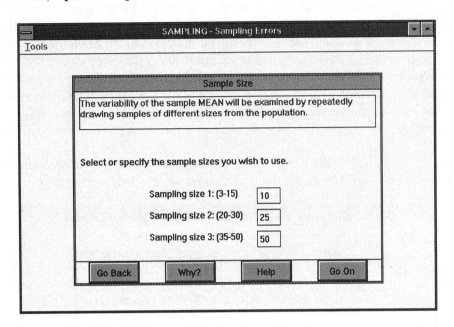

Figure 10.4 Entering Three Sample Sizes to Obtain Three Distributions

The next screen asks you to choose the number of samples to be drawn. The same number of samples will be drawn for each of the three sizes. Thus, the number you choose here will dictate the number of observations comprising each of the three distributions of the sample statistic under study, in the present case the *mean*. In the example we chose 40, so that the experiment will involve first the generation of 40 samples of size 10, then 40 samples of size 25, and finally 40 samples of size 50. Enter **40** and click **Go On**.

Up to this point the process of specifying a *sampling errors* experiment is just like the one for a *sampling distributions* experiment save for the fact that three distributions of the sample statistic are going to be generated, one for each sample size, rather than just one. From here on, however, the two types of experiment differ. *Sampling error* refers to the difference between the value of the statistic in the sample and the value in the population—in the example, the difference between the sample mean in each sample and 15, the mean for the population. The central issue, however, is not just with sampling error, for small sampling errors are usually of little concern and eliminating sampling error completely is impossible unless one abandons sampling entirely and takes data for the entire population. The central issue is with *unacceptable amounts of sampling error*—i.e., amounts so large that the sample can legitimately said to be *misleading*.

What makes a sampling error of a given amount *unacceptable* or *misleading*? There is no general answer to this question! It depends entirely on the situation, or more precisely on the question for which you are obtaining information by means of sampling. Consider for example the question of the

Student Activities Fee raised at the beginning of the chapter. Suppose the fee was $75 last year, and the issue over which the Student Senate deadlocked was whether to leave it there, to raise it to $100, or to raise it to $125. A sampling error of $10 in the average obtained from a survey of student opinion would not be all that bad. But a sampling error of $25 would vitiate the whole point of the survey. If, for instance, the average value from the opinion survey sample is $110, while the true average across the entire student body is $85, then every student senator would legitimately regard the sample average as seriously misleading. This sample average would be misleading even if all but a handful of students were in fact indifferent between a fee of $75 and a fee of $125. It would still be misleading because the original question that the sample was intended to answer concerned a choice between $75, $100, and $125. A sampling error is *unacceptable* or *misleading* only in relation to a specific question.

With this in mind, let us turn to the third and last choice in specifying a *sampling errors* experiment, presented by the screen shown in Figure 10.5. The example involves a generic, and hence abstract,

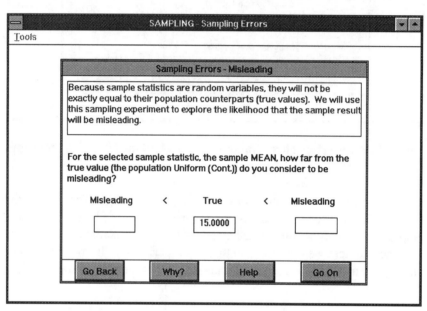

Figure 10.5 Specifying the Boundaries Defining Misleading Sampling Errors

population distribution. Consequently, there is no concrete, practical basis for saying what amount of error is unacceptable or misleading here. Our goal in using the program, however, is not to deal with some specific concrete problem at hand. Rather, it is to explore what is involved in assessing and controlling the risks of being misled when relying on samples. The best thing to do for this purpose is to set the boundary between acceptable and unacceptable sampling error at different points in a series of experiments in order to see how the boundary affects matters.

In this example, we decide that a discrepancy in excess of 2 between the sample mean and the population value of 15 is unacceptable. Choosing boundaries much farther away from 15 than this risked having too few misleading samples in the example, and boundaries much closer risked having too many. Enter **13** in the left box and **17** in the right box and click **Go On** to continue with the example. A screen appears that summarizes the specifications for the experiment. Review it; if you want to change anything, just click on **Go Back** however many times you need to in order to return to the screen where the choice you want to change was made. Otherwise, click **Go On**. After a short time the screen for executing the experiment, shown in Figure 10.6, will appear.

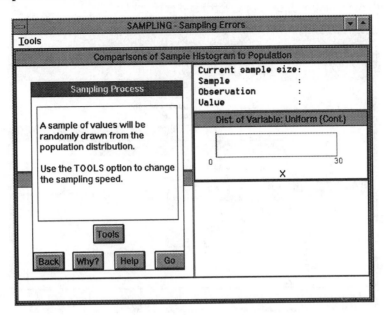

Figure 10.6 Initiating the Experiment

Carrying Out the Sampling Error Experiment

The population distribution from which the samples will be drawn is shown in the middle on the right in Figure 10.6. Click on **Tools**. The first three speeds require you to take action when each major step in the experiment is completed; with the *Results* option, the only action you have to take is to acknowledge the fraction of misleading samples in each of the three collections of samples. Keep the option at *Step*, at least to begin with. (In this program, unlike the *Sampling Distributions* program, the *Step* option does not require you to restart the experiment each time a sample is complete, but only when each collection of samples has been completed.)

Click on **Go** to start the experiment. A window appears leading you through the subsequent steps. Click on **Take new sample and calculate sample statistic** and **Go On**. The program will proceed to draw 40 samples of size 10 from the population. The value of each data point drawn is marked on the X-axis of the population distribution by a cross and listed in the window above it. A histogram displaying each sample in turn is shown at the top left, and the calculated values of the sample statistic, in this case the mean, are displayed in a histogram at the bottom left.

When all 40 samples of size 10 are complete, an options window appears with *Calculate frequency of non-representative statistics* highlighted. Click **Go On**, and the fraction of the 40 that are misleading is shown. After you click on **Exit**, the options window will reappear, with *Plot frequency of non-representative statistics* highlighted. Click **Go On**, and the percentage of misleading samples will be indicated in a graph on the lower right, and the computer will begin drawing the next collection of samples. The entire sequence will be repeated for the collection of samples of size 25, and then for the collection of size 50. Figure 10.7 displays the experiment screen after the samples of size 10 have been drawn. When all the samples have been drawn, a screen resembling the one in Figure 10.8 appears, though initially with the window in the upper left hand corner blank.

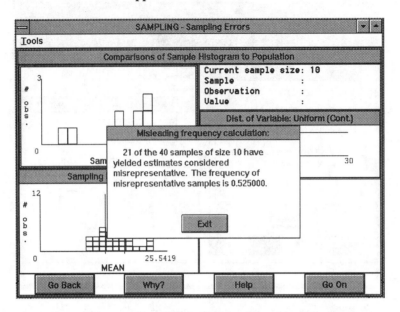

Figure 10.7 After the First 40 Samples, of Size 10, Have Been Drawn

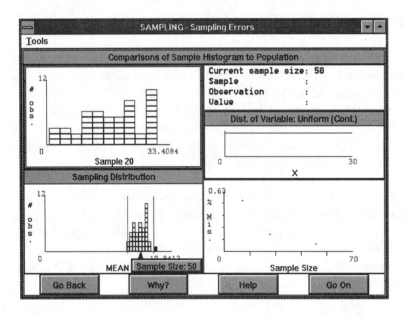

Figure 10.8 The Sampling Distributions for the Three Sample Sizes

The screen shown in Figure 10.8 allows you to review the results of the experiment. You can click on any data point in the sampling distribution histogram, and the corresponding sample will appear in the window at the top left. Click on *Sample Size* to toggle among the three distributions. In the example in the figure, we have clicked on the sample of size 50 that lies furthest outside the acceptable range (marked by the vertical lines) in order to see what looks peculiar about it. You should review the results before proceeding to the analysis of what they are indicating.

Analyzing the Results of the Experiment

Click **Go On** when you are ready to analyze the experiment. A window appears at the top left offering four options: *Compare Distributions*; *Distributions and Probability*; *Describing Misleading Frequencies*; and *Update Experiment*. The first three of these provide separate ways of analyzing the results. We shall review each of them in turn.

Click on **Compare Distributions** and **Go On**. A screen resembling the one shown in Figure 10.9 will appear, initially without the display of the summary statistics. Click on **See Summary Stats** and **Go On** to obtain these as well.

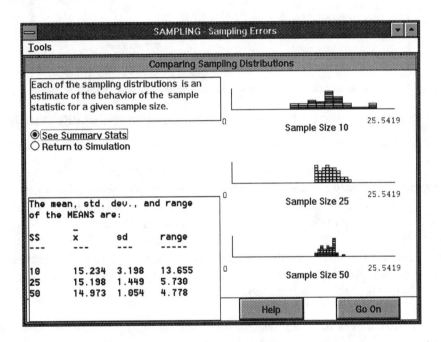

Figure 10.9 Comparing Sampling Distributions for the Three Sample Sizes

The centers of all three sampling distributions are in more or less the same location, as the numbers for their means confirm. (Indeed, although this is of no significance at all, the mean value of the means for the samples of size 10 happens to come closest to the population mean of 15.) By contrast, the spreads of the three sampling distributions differ markedly: the standard deviations of the sampling distributions become progressively smaller as the sample size increases. This, however, does not mean that all the samples of size 50 were at least as reliable as any of size 10. To the contrary, some of the samples of size 10 yielded estimates closer to the true population mean of 15 than some of the samples of size 50. Increased sample size does not guarantee an improved estimate!

117

Next, click on **Return to Simulation** and **Go On**, followed by **Distributions and Probability** and **Go On**. A screen resembling the one shown in Figure 10.10 will appear, but initially without the display of the parameters in the window on the left and without any curves superimposed on the three sampling distribution histograms.

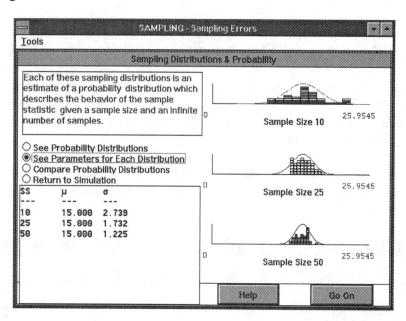

Figure 10.10 Comparing the Sampling Distributions with Probability Distributions

Each of the three distributions of the sample means generated in the experiment represents an approximation to the *theoretical limiting probability distribution* for sample means of samples of the indicated sizes drawn from the population distribution in question. The *limiting probability distribution* is the distribution that is defined by the infinity of sample means from all the samples of the indicated size drawn from the population. To display the three limiting probability distributions for the three sample sizes in this experiment, click on **See Probability Distributions** and **Go On**. The curves superimposed on the three histograms in the figure will then appear. Because the sample statistic we are examining is the mean, these limiting probability distributions are normal distributions.

Click next on **See Parameters for Each Distribution** and **Go On** for the display of the values of the parameters—the mean μ and the standard deviation σ—of these normal distributions. The standard deviations of the probability distributions decrease as the sample size increases, implying that the probability of obtaining sample means close to the population value increases with increasing sample size. You can confirm this graphically by clicking on **Compare Probability Distributions** and **Go On**. The three probability distributions will be displayed superimposed on one another in a window overlaid on the parameter window. The decreasing probability of sample means lying far from the population mean as the sample size increases is especially clear from the decreasing spreads and increasing peaks of the curves in this graph.

Finally, click on **Return to Simulation** and **Go On**, followed by **Describing Misleading Frequencies** and **Go On**. A screen resembling the one shown in Figure 10.11 will appear. To complete the screen as shown, first click on **See Frequency of Misleading Estimates** and **Go On**, and then on **See Probability of Misleading Estimates** and **Go On**. The top table on the left displays the percentage of

118

samples with a sample mean below the boundary of acceptable error, the percentage with a sample mean above the boundary of acceptable error, and the percentage with a sample mean outside the acceptable range. The table on the bottom left displays the theoretical probabilities for the same three

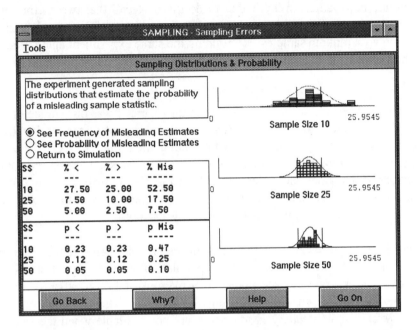

Figure 10.11 Comparing the Frequencies and Probabilities of the Misleading Samples

categories, based on the limiting probability distribution. While the percentages do not match the probabilities of misleading estimates exactly, they are reasonably close. The difference between them arises because the collections of samples yield a sampling distribution that is only an approximation to the limiting probability distribution.

The results displayed in Figure 10.11 let us see what sort of reasoning goes into selecting a sample size that strikes an appropriate trade-off or balance between the costs of sampling and the risks of being misled. Needless to say, one does not examine samples of samples. Rather, one uses the theoretical limiting probability distributions. Being misled by a sample involves a cost in its own right. Given any sample size, the limiting probability distribution defines the probability of the sample statistic differing from the population value by any given amount. The product of this probability and the cost of being misled represents the "expected costs" from relying on sampling. So long as these expected costs are greater than the cost of a sample of the size in question, it makes sense to increase the sample size further. But once the costs of a still greater sample size exceed the expected costs from being misled, it no longer makes sense to consider a still larger sample size.

Some Ways to Follow Up the Experiment

Once you have reviewed the results, click on *Return to Simulation* and *Update Experiment* to change any of the specifications of the preceding experiment, including the sample statistic. A screen will appear presenting you with the current specifications and number boxes for new specifications. The only thing you cannot change by means of this screen is the population. For this, you need to select *Start New Experiment* on the *Update Experiment* screen.

For starters, we suggest that you repeat the very same experiment again, with no changes at all in its specifications. Click on **Execute Updated Experiment** and **Go On** on the *Update Experiment* screen without entering any new values. Why bother to do this? Recall that two factors contributed to the differences in the three sampling distributions obtained in the example: sample size and the natural randomness arising with random samples. By running the same experiment again, you may begin to get some feel for how much the contrasts in the results reflected natural randomness rather than sample size.

The most arbitrary specification for the experiment in the example was our choice of the boundaries of acceptable sampling error, referred to as the *Misrepresentative Range* on the *Update Experiment* screen. We chose margins of error of 2 on either side of the population value to see what would happen. To complete the process of seeing what the effect of this range is, we suggest you try both a larger margin of acceptable error and a smaller one. What should emerge clearly from carrying out such alternatives can be summarized in a truism: the larger the margin of acceptable error, the lower the probability of, and hence the less reason to worry about, being misled by a sample.

Another variant of the experiment is to switch from the sample *mean* as the *sample statistic* to the sample *variance* or the *standard deviation*. The population standard deviation for the uniform distribution in the example is 8.66. Try acceptable error margins of 1.0 on either side of this value. (You will find that two of the options for analyzing the results of the experiment, *Distributions and Probability* and *Describing Misleading Frequencies*, are not available when the sample statistic is the variance or standard deviation. The limiting probability distribution in these cases is not the normal distribution. Because the sample sizes permitted in the *Sampling Errors* program are small—to avoid wasting your time while waiting for samples to be drawn—comparisons between the sampling distributions generated for these statistics by the program and the limiting probability distributions are likely to be more a source of confusion than one of edification. You can still compare the sampling distributions for these sample statistics with one another and draw conclusions from the frequencies of misleading samples.)

The third factor affecting sampling error, the variability of the population, was ignored in the above example. You can change the variability of the uniform distribution used in the above experiment by changing its range. Select *Start New Experiment* on the *Update Experiment* screen, keep the *mean* as the sample statistic, but change the uniform distribution by changing its range from the former *0 to 30* interval to *5 to 25*. This will reduce the population standard deviation from 8.66 to 5.77. Keep all the other specifications just as they were in the experiment in the example, and see what the effect is on the frequencies and probabilities of misleading samples.

Finally, you should recognize that a *uniform distribution* was chosen for the example to keep matters as simple as possible. At some point you should surely carry out experiments parallel to the one in the example and the variants suggested above, but with a *normal distribution*. To avoid complicating the situation, you might begin with a standardized normal distribution—i.e. one with a mean of 0 and a standard deviation of 1.0. You could then vary the standard deviation to explore the effects of population variability. It is also worth the bother to examine at least one discrete population distribution. We suggest that you consider the *binomial distribution* in conjunction with the biased coins in the *Sampling Problem* program.

Chapter 11

A Sampling Problem

What May Be Investigated with *A Sampling Problem*:

- How sampling is used to reach conclusions about populations
- How sample size affects the reliability of conclusions drawn from samples
- What the limitations are when relying on sampling
- How to design experiments involving a binomial probability distribution

Why Use This Program?

We have always been told that the probability of getting any specific number when individual dice are tossed is 1/6, and the probability of getting "heads" on a coin is 1/2—at least it is if the coin is tossed high, it tumbles rapidly while in the air, and it is allowed to land on the floor. But we have also heard of loaded dice that favor certain numbers and trick coins weighted or beveled to favor "heads." To verify that a particular coin is fair, you might toss it a number of times and see if it is showing any signs of bias toward either heads or tails. How confident can you be from doing this? Can you readily detect a coin that is biased, say 60% to 40% in favor of heads, in this way? The program, *A Sampling Problem*, lets you explore such questions in the unusual situation in which the truth is known about whether and how much the coin you are considering is biased.

What does this have to do with sampling? Outside the realm of statistics, we speak of cooks as sampling when they test a small portion, or sample, of a dish before serving it. Within the realm of statistics, the examples of sampling that typically come to mind are when 1,500 citizens are polled in order to predict what will happen in an election, or when the marketing department of a firm surveys a group of people in an effort to determine whether a new product is going to sell well. The feature that coin tossing has in common with these examples—the feature that makes all of them instances of sampling, in the technical sense—is that a small portion of a larger group is examined in order to reach a conclusion about the larger group. The larger group, or *population*, involved when we say that a coin is biased 60% in favor of heads is the collection of *all possible* tosses of the coin in question. In the case of an election, pollsters rely on a sample because asking everyone is impractical. In the case of a coin, we rely on a sample of tosses because checking all possible tosses is impossible. Most scientific experiments involve sampling in this way—they rely on a comparative handful of results to reach conclusions about what would happen if the experiment were repeated an indefinite number of times.

Sampling involves a risk. Suppose we want to find out whether a particular movie is good. We could ask 10 or 20 people coming out of the theater what they thought of it. If we approach only individuals who are laughing or smiling as they come out, we could easily be misled; our sample could be biased to the point where it consists only of the people who actually enjoyed an otherwise dreadful movie. At the very least, we have to approach individuals at random. In the case of *A Sampling Problem*, coin tossing will be simulated by the computer, using what is known as a random number generator. How can you be sure that the samples are truly random? You will have to trust the program.

Even if you choose the people you ask coming out of the theater at random, however, you are still faced with at least the possibility of a sample that consists of the only people who enjoyed the movie. The risk may be very small, but it still exists. The most you can be confident of is that on the average a random sample will tend to be representative of the overall population. The key phrase here is "on the average." Of course, the larger the sample size, the lower the risk of being misled by it. Thus, the more times you toss a coin in *A Sampling Problem*, the less likely the conclusion you reach about whether it is biased will be mistaken. Nevertheless, tossing a coin—even simulated tossing of a coin on a computer—involves a cost. It takes time.

In general, whenever one takes a random sample, one would like the sample size to be appropriate. What is an appropriate number of tosses when deciding whether a coin is fair or is biased a little—say, 55% in favor of heads? *A Sampling Problem* will allow you to investigate this question. You can select a number of tosses; review the result so far and add some further tosses if you wish; reach your conclusion; evaluate your conclusion not only on the chance of its being wrong, but also in the light of the truth about the coin; then start all over again with a new coin. Think of the problem as if it were a game at a carnival and see how quickly you can learn to tell whether a coin is biased.

How to Carry Out Experiments with *A Sampling Problem*

To run the *Sampling Problem* program, select **Sampling** from the *ConStatS* menu. Click once on **A Sampling Problem**, followed by **Go On**. The first screen offers you the choice of continuing or exiting this program. Click on **begin the coin flipping experiment** and **Go On.** The screen shown in Figure 11.1 appears, displaying five pennies.

These coins differ from one another in a peculiar way. Four of them have been certified to be systematically biased: the probability of *heads* in the case of *Coin 1* is only 40%; in the case of *Coin 2*, it is 45%; in the case of *Coin 4,* it is 55%; and in the case of *Coin 5*, it is 60%. Only *Coin 3* is fair—that is, has equal 50% probability for both *heads* and *tails*. Click on the appropriate **examine coin** button and **Go On**; each coin has a different year stamped on it, so that it can be identified later.

Click on **Begin the experiment** and **Go On**. The screen in Figure 11.2 will appear. At the top is a coin that has been chosen at random from the five shown on the prior screen. The program challenges you to figure out which of the five coins it has chosen. You are no longer allowed to examine it—you cannot tell which coin it is by checking the year stamped on it. The only thing you can do is to have the program carry out an experiment with the coin at your direction, tossing it a specified number of times and recording the frequency with which it comes up *heads*. Figuring out which coin it is would be easy if the difference in the biases from one coin to the next were large, but the biases differ from one another only a little. This is where the challenge lies. You could guess right away and have a 20% chance of being right. The interesting question is how much you can improve your chances over 20% by having the coin tossed some number of times.

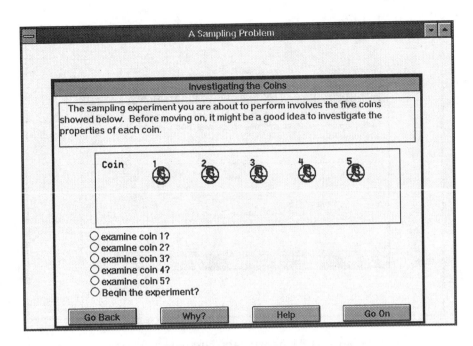

Figure 11.1 Five Coins

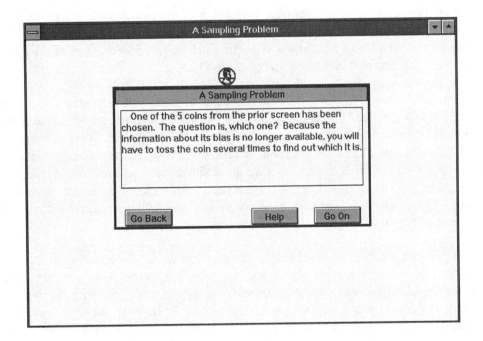

Figure 11.2 The Challenge: Which Coin Is It?

Click on **Go On** and the screen in Figure 11.3 will appear, asking you how many times you want to toss the coin. You can choose any number you wish. (Keep in mind, however, that each toss of the coin takes time, and as you sit and wait for all the requested tosses to be completed, you will be getting increasingly bored.)

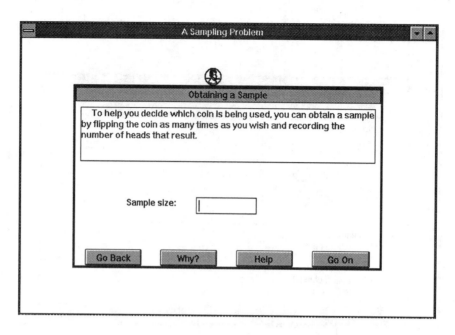

Figure 11.3 Choosing the Number of Tosses

The ultimate challenge might be to determine the number of tosses that will increase your chances of being right about which coin it is to, say, 80%. Let's think about that later, however. At this point choose a number of tosses that you would consider sensible if this were a carnival game. In this example we chose 20. Enter **20** in the box, and click **Go On**.

The next screen shows the coin being tossed the number of times you requested. As the experiment proceeds, the frequency of the two possible outcomes, *heads* or *tails*, is recorded in the window below the coin, as well as the number of tosses and the percentage of *heads* so far. This sampling process can become tedious to watch. Click on **medium** or **fast,** presented on the screen while the tossing is occurring, to speed it up. This is a special advantage of simulated experiments on a computer—in real experiments there is no faster speed option. Each data point requires time, and in most cases time means money. This is why most sampling experiments use the smallest sample size consistent with the question at hand and the reliability needed in the answer.

Once the computer has finished tossing the coin, a screen similar to the one in Figure 11.4 will appear. The final results of the experiment are shown just below the coin in the *Sample Results* window. You now have three options: you can request additional tosses; you can review the problem; or you can indicate which of the five coins you believe was being tossed. Review the results to decide whether you have an adequate basis for making your decision. If you think not, click on **increase the number of flips** and **Go On**, and enter the number of additional tosses you want. You can repeat this process as many times as you wish, but sooner or later you will have to indicate which coin you think it is. When you are ready, click on **specify the P[heads] for the coin above** and **Go On**. The decision screen shown in Figure 11.5 will appear.

In our example, the number of heads after 20 tosses, as shown in Figure 11.4, was 8—exactly 40% (your screen may show a different number). This seemed compelling enough evidence to conclude that the coin

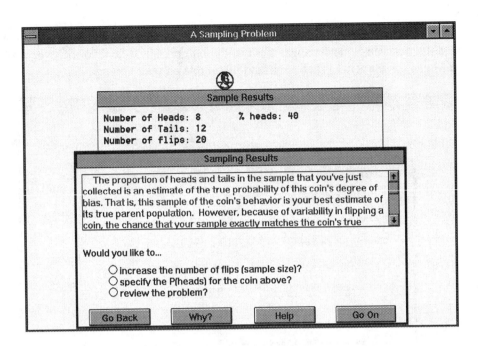

Figure 11.4 Deciding How to Proceed

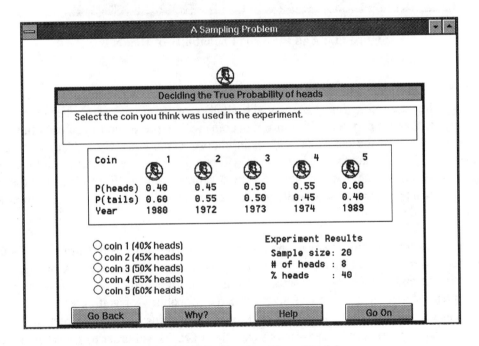

Figure 11.5 Indicating Your Decision

in question was the one biased for 40% *heads* and 60% *tails*, namely *Coin 1*. We did not request more tosses after the first 20. We clicked on **Coin 1** and **Go On**, leading to the rather disappointing screen shown in Figure 11.6. Even though the 20 tosses resulted in exactly 40% *heads*, the coin that the computer had in fact chosen at random was *Coin 4*, the one biased in favor of 55% *heads*. You may have the good fortune of not getting such a misleading sample on your first try.

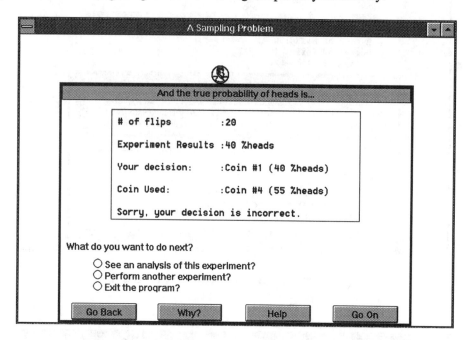

Figure 11.6 And the True Probability of Heads Is ...

The screen shown in Figure 11.6 presents you with three options. We strongly recommend that you repeat the experiment several times, keeping the number of tosses the same, before you turn to a technical analysis of any experiment. Five different coins will be presented to you each time you do the experiment, one of which the computer will again choose at random. By repeating the experiment several times with the same number of tosses, you will begin to see how much the samples of this size vary from one another, whether the coin has the same or a different bias. Repeating the experiment will also give you a chance to see how frequently you can come up with the right answer using the number of tosses you chose the first time.

For purposes of illustration here, however, and also because we are anxious to learn more about how we could have been so misled, we turn directly to an analysis of the experiment. Click on **See an analysis of this experiment** and then **Go On**. A screen appears that offers a choice of two ways of examining the just completed experiment. You can investigate the probability of getting exactly the result you got—in our case 8 heads in 20 tosses—from each of the five coins; or you can plot the frequency of *heads* as the number of tosses increased—in our case from 1 to 20—in order to see whether any telltale pattern emerged as the experiment unfolded.

Click on **Probability of getting the observed results from each coin** and **Go On** first. In our case this action produced the screen shown in Figure 11.7. The column on the right gives the probabilities of getting the result just obtained from each of the five coins. Thus, the probability of getting exactly 8 heads when *Coin 1* in the example is tossed 20 times is just below 0.18, while the probability of getting

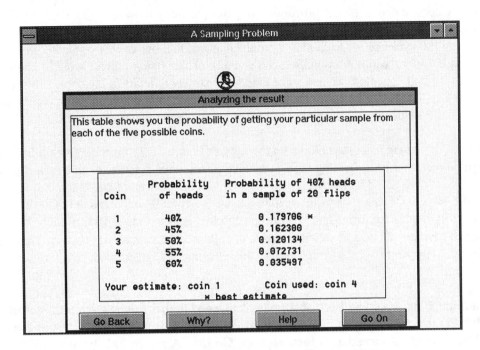

**Figure 11.7 Analyzing the Experiment: Which
Coin Was Most Likely to Have Produced the Result?**

this result when *Coin 4* is tossed 20 times is slightly above 0.07. In other words, for a coin biased to come up *heads* 40% of the time, you would expect 8 *heads* out of 20 tosses 18% of the time if you were to repeat the 20 tosses again and again; for the coin the computer actually chose in our example, biased for *heads* to come up 55% of the time, you would expect 8 *heads* out of 20 tosses only 7% of the time. However, 7% of the time is not 0. We were unlucky, but not all that unlucky.

(We should pause to comment on where the probabilities in Figure 11.7 come from. The numbers were calculated using the *binomial probability distribution*. 'Binomial' here refers to the fact that there are only two possible outcomes when flipping a coin. The *binomial probability distribution* gives the probability of getting k instances of one of these outcomes in n trials if the probability of getting that outcome on any one trial is p. For instance, the second number in the column on the right is the probability of getting 8 *heads* in 20 tosses if the probability of getting *heads* on any one toss is 0.45. You can see how each of the numbers was generated, and what the probabilities are for different numbers of outcomes besides 8 in 20 trials with each coin, by clicking on **Probability** in the *ConStatS* main menu and running the *Probability Distributions* program at this point. Simply select the *Binomial Distribution*, enter 20 for n and the probability of *heads* for the coin you wish to examine for p. The *Probability Distributions* program will even graph the probabilities of getting all the different numbers of *heads* in 20 tosses with different coins, letting you compare one coin with another. Once you feel comfortable with the probability numbers, you can close *Probability Distributions*, and the screen in Figure 11.7 will reappear.)

The asterisk on the far right in Figure 11.7 tells us that, given the result of 8 *heads* in 20 tosses, *Coin 1* was the best guess to make. Our guess was wrong. Given the evidence, however, it was the most reasonable choice. We really were misled by the evidence.

127

We can now see that the result of 8 *heads* in 20 tosses is not so strong evidence for *Coin 1* as we may have thought when we chose it. The probability of getting exactly 8 *heads* in 20 tosses of *Coin 1* is not that much greater than the probabilities of getting this result with some of the other coins. This raises a question: given the evidence we had, what were the chances that our choice of *Coin 1* was correct? If we had guessed *Coin 1* without any tosses, the chances of our being correct would have been 1/5 or 0.20. When we finally guessed, we had some evidence, namely 8 *heads* in 20 tosses. Insofar as *Coin 1* was the most reasonable choice under these circumstances, yet it was wrong, we have good reason to ask how much this evidence increased our chances of being correct when we chose *Coin 1*?

The answer is easy to see from the column on the right in Figure 11.7. Sum the five probabilities in the column roughly in your head (getting 0.58), and then check what fraction of this total the probability listed for *Coin 1* (0.18) is. The fraction is less than 1/3. The chances of our being wrong in choosing *Coin 1* on the basis that 8 *heads* came up in 20 tosses were greater than 2 times out of 3. In other words, if you repeatedly request 20 tosses and you always choose the coin biased 40% in favor of *heads* when *heads* comes up exactly 8 times, then—reasonable though this choice may be—you will nevertheless be wrong more than two-thirds of the time. Perhaps 20 tosses are simply not enough if we want to be right most of the time.

There is not much more we can learn about what happened in this example from the screen shown in Figure 11.7. Turn to the other way of analyzing the result in this program. Click **Go Back** and then click on **The %heads observed as N increases** and **Go On**. A screen like the one in Figure 11.8 will appear.

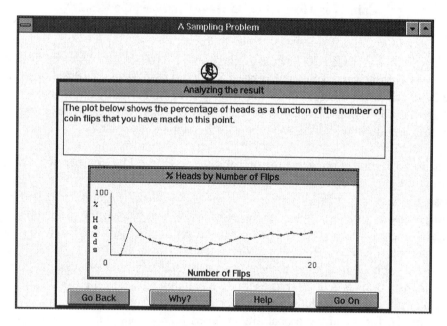

Figure 11.8 Analyzing the Experiment:
Had the *% heads* converged on a value?

The advantage in plotting how the percentage of *heads* changed as the experiment progressed lies in a principle called *the law of large numbers*. This law has many applications. For the case at hand, it says: usually[!], the percentage of *heads* will tend to converge toward the true number for the coin as the number of tosses increases. (How usually it will do so within 20 tosses, however, is a matter we leave for you to determine.) Accordingly, if the percentage of *heads* is still changing a good deal at the end of an experiment, one has reasons for caution in taking the result at face value. The first few tosses may have produced a misrepresentative trend at the beginning, and the number of subsequent tosses may not have been great enough to have recovered from this. This is illustrated in the example shown in Figure 11.8. Remember, this coin was biased 55% in favor of heads. Nevertheless, after the first few tosses the percentage of *heads* so far was well below 30%. By the end of the 20th toss, the percentage had climbed to 40%. The curve appears, at least to some extent, to be still climbing. Regardless, the curve has not stayed tightly around a single value for a substantial number of tosses, which is a prerequisite for its having converged. To see how often the curve does tend to converge within 20 tosses, you can repeat the experiment many times, each time examining this plot when you analyze the result.

Your example of 20 tosses most likely came out less misleading than ours. Ours is by no means typical. You should keep it in mind, however, not just as you continue to use *A Sampling Problem*, but generally. Because of the chance element in sampling, the results of a sampling experiment can be systematically misleading.

Some Ways of Following Up the Experiment

Given the systematically misleading result in our example, a natural question is, how often are the results of 20 tosses going to be so misleading? You can begin finding out by repeating the experiment many times, holding the number of tosses at 20. In the process, keep track of how often you guess correctly, as well as how often your guess is the same as the "best estimate." You might think about what odds you would want if you were placing a bet on your choice after 20 tosses.

Another obvious experiment is to change the number of tosses in order to see the effect on your chances of guessing correctly. How many tosses do you need before you can legitimately be said to be making an educated guess? Will as few as 10 tosses raise the frequency of your being correct substantially above 20%? How many tosses are needed for the conclusion you reach to be correct at least 50% of the time? And how many for it to be correct 80% or more of the time?

A Sampling Problem allows you to explore the answers to such questions by going back to the screen shown in Figure 11.6 and clicking on **Perform another experiment** and **Go On**. Do not lose sight of another alternative, however. At any juncture you can examine the *binomial probability distributions* arising with the coins in this program by turning to the *Probability Distributions* program as indicated in the discussion following Figure 11.7. This may be especially productive when you are trying to decide how many tosses to make to achieve any specific probability of your answer being correct. Being able to pause when a question comes up and turn to one of the other programs for an answer is a more useful feature of *ConStatS* than it may first have appeared.

PART FOUR

INFERENCE

Using statistical methods to extract information from data is not an end unto itself. The goal is usually one of reaching conclusions. Sometimes the goal is to reach a conclusion about a population from a sample drawn from it. For instance, given that 1.2 percent suffered side-effects from a new medication during a trial run, what conclusion is it appropriate to draw about the rate of side-effects if the medication is made available to the population at large? At other times the goal is to decide whether to accept a hypothesis on the basis of data. For instance, given that a group of people who took 1000 mg of Vitamin C a day suffered 20 percent fewer colds during 1995 than a control group, is it appropriate to accept the hypothesis that 1000 mg of Vitamin C a day substantially reduces the incidence of common colds?

There is no way to guarantee that the conclusions reached on the basis of statistical methods will always be correct. As we have emphasized repeatedly, some risk always exists that a sample is systematically mis-leading. Risk in drawing conclusions from data is like death and taxes—it is inevitable. The methods of statistical inference, however, do allow the risk of mistaken conclusions to be assessed. These methods exploit ways in which probability can be joined with sampling to weigh this risk. The logic that joins these two is subtle and often complex, making inference one of the more difficult topics in statistics.

ConStatS includes two programs on statistical inference. *Beginning Confidence Intervals* deals with *estimating* population statistics on the basis of sample statistics. There is virtually no chance of the mean value for a sample being exactly the same as the mean of the population. But given a sample and its mean, there is an *interval* around this mean within which the population mean is likely to lie to a specified *level* of confidence. The greater *confidence level* you insist on, the larger this *confidence interval* is. *Beginning Confidence Intervals* provides two pathways for exploring the relationship between sample size, confidence intervals, and confidence levels. An initial pathway offers exercises in informally estimating intervals in which a certain fraction of values will fall. In the main pathway, formally calculated confidence intervals for estimates of the mean can be explored in examples for which the population value is known.

The other program on inference in *ConStatS* is *Beginning Hypothesis Testing*. It too contains two pathways, both of which are example-driven. Each pathway emphasizes the way in which assigning a burden of proof enters into the logic of statistical hypothesis testing. The first pathway presents examples in which the hypothesis to be tested involves a claim about the mean of a population. The second pathway presents examples in which the hypothesis involves a claim about the difference between the means of two populations. The program takes the user through the steps needed to turn these claims into ones amenable to test, then through the process of assigning a specific burden of proof, and finally through the test itself.

Chapter 12

Beginning Confidence Intervals

What May Be Investigated with *Beginning Confidence Intervals*:

• How a 68% interval for a random variable compares to a 68% interval for its mean

• How the width of a confidence interval relates to the confidence level

• How different samples produce different confidence interval estimates

• How the confidence level of an interval estimate is determined by repeated sampling

Why Use This Program?

Suppose that you are deciding whether to invest your life's savings in one of five different stocks that have been recommended to you by your friends. You want to collect and analyze data on the past prices of these five stocks. Before you begin your research, you need to be aware of the possible pitfalls. First, you realize that collecting price data on every stock trade is simply not feasible—there are hundreds of trades every day, and these stocks have been traded for decades. What *is* feasible is collecting a sample of the prices of each stock over the last few years.

Once you collect the price data, you still have to decide how to draw conclusions. For example, suppose you find that over the last few years the price of the computer company stock has increased an average of 10% per year, while the price of the electric company stock has increased an average of 6% per year. Should you choose the computer company? Your answer depends on whether the average price increase for the sample is an adequate representation of the range of possible outcomes. The 10% average increase could result from some years where the increase for the computer company was 50% and other years where the stock price *dropped* by 30%. You might decide that you prefer the electric company stock with annual increases that vary over a much smaller range, say between 5% and 7%.

Comparisons of average price increase can be made by using an *interval estimator* of the annual stock price increases, that is, a formula that can be applied to calculate a range of values for the true annual stock price increase. Applying this formula to a sample of data produces a *confidence interval*. If you imagine applying this formula to many different samples, each sample will produce a different interval. Some proportion of these intervals, however, will contain the true annual stock price increase. This proportion is the *confidence level*.

Confidence interval estimates for population characteristics, like the mean or variance, are useful for assessing the precision with which that characteristic can be estimated from experimental data.

Consider the stock performance example. If a stock's confidence interval is large, say from −30% to +50%, the stock performs more variably than if the interval is small, say +5% to +7%. These two intervals imply very different stock price behavior. The first interval includes a 0% annual increase, or no long-term growth in the price of this stock. The second interval suggests real growth in the annual stock price.

The *Beginning Confidence Intervals* program provides an introduction to *interval estimation*—i.e., to using samples and the values of their statistics to estimate intervals within which the corresponding population values generally lie. The program contains two pathways. The first, *an example using sampling and intervals*, lets you try your hand at estimating intervals informally before turning to the formal approach to determining confidence intervals. In this pathway you are first asked to guess the endpoints of an interval that contains the values of a city's daily high or low temperatures for 68% of the days in a given month over the years. You can then evaluate your guess by conducting a sampling experiment to see what fraction of the daily temperature values falls in your interval. You are then asked to guess the endpoints of an interval that contains that same month's *average* temperature for 68% of all possible years. Once again you will be able to run a sampling experiment to evaluate how good your estimate is. The two exercises together emphasize the difference between the probability distribution of a variable and the probability distribution of an *average* calculated from the values of that variable. As you develop a knack for estimating the intervals for the daily and monthly average temperatures, you will see why the specific variable for which you are making estimates makes such a difference in interval estimation.

The main pathway in *Beginning Confidence Intervals*, *the confidence interval for a population mean*, shows how to take the guesswork out of estimating confidence intervals. It allows you to compute intervals with different theoretical confidence levels for covering the population mean. You can choose a specific problem context and set up your confidence interval. While doing the latter, you can investigate how different choices in the confidence level affect the sizes of the confidence intervals. Finally, you can investigate what the confidence level signifies by drawing repeated samples from the population and seeing what proportion of those samples produce confidence intervals that contain the population mean.

How to Run Experiments with *Beginning Confidence Intervals*

To run the *Beginning Confidence Intervals* program, select **Inference** from the *ConStatS* menu. Click on **Beginning Confidence Intervals** and **Go On**. The screen that appears, shown in Figure 12.1, presents you with two options: *an example using sampling and intervals* and *the confidence interval for a population mean*. The first of these pathways offers background and preparation for the second.

Using Sampling and Intervals

From the opening screen in Figure 12.1, click **an example using sampling and intervals** and then **Go On**. The screen in Figure 12.2 will appear. This example involves guessing a range of values to represent the *typical* daily high or low temperature for a given city for a given month of the year. Click on your choice of city, the month, and whether you want to use the daily low or high temperature. Then click **Go On**. For this example, click on **Atlanta**, **August**, **High**, and **Go On**.

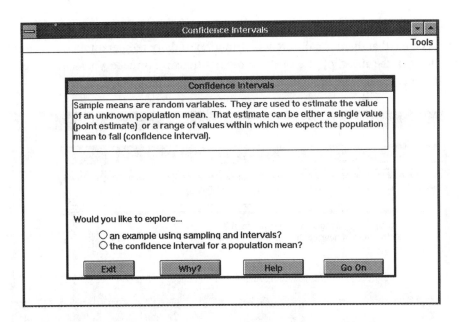

Figure 12.1 Choosing the Type of Intervals to Explore

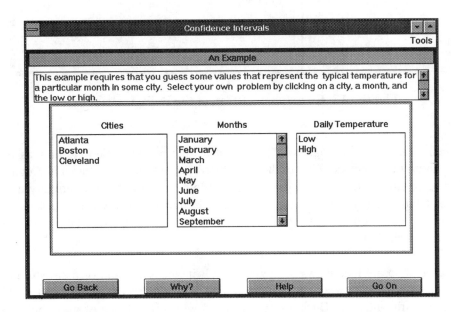

Figure 12.2 Choosing a City, Month, and High or Low

On the next screen specify how close you expect to come to the true values of the range of temperatures. The properties of distributions can be used to determine the difference in the width of the interval that you would guess for a daily high or low temperature as compared to the width of the interval that you would guess for a monthly average. But these properties cannot help you decide on a particular center and spread. Without some data you must simply make an educated guess. If you think that guessing these temperatures will be hard, you might choose an average standard of accuracy. If you are confident about your meteorological ability, choose a tougher standard. For this example, click on **Average** and **Go On**.

The next screen, shown in Figure 12.3, requests your best guess about the mean of the daily temperatures. Assume that there is a different distribution of daily temperatures for each month and that you are trying to pick the mean of one of these distributions. To make your choice for our example, click on the entry box, enter your best guess value as **89**, and click **Go On**.

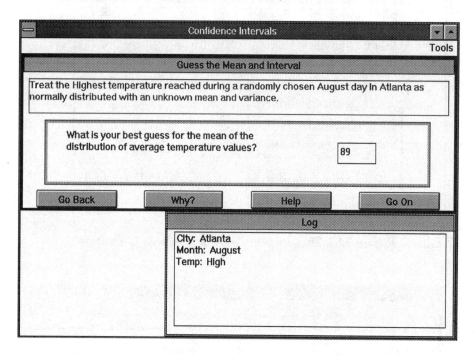

Figure 12.3 Guessing the Mean of the Daily Distribution

The next screen looks similar to Figure 12.3 but changes the request. You are now asked to enter a range of temperatures that includes 68% of the daily high temperatures for Atlanta in August. Since we might think it reasonable to assume that daily high and low temperatures are normally distributed, we are looking for temperature values that are one standard deviation below and one standard deviation above the mean. To enter your best guess values for this example, click on the entry boxes, enter values of **84** and **94**, and click **Go On**.

A summary screen appears that shows your guesses. It includes a graph of the distribution of daily temperatures that is implied by your choices. If you do not find this distribution reasonable, you can change the mean or the interval. Once you are satisfied with your choice of mean and interval, click **Yes**, and the screen shown in Figure 12.4 will appear. Before proceeding, take a close look at the information on this screen. The *Log* box in the lower right of the screen shows the choices that you have made. The *Best Guess* box in the lower left shows the distribution of daily temperatures based on a normal distribution with your choices of mean and standard deviation (one-half the width of the 68% interval).

So far, you have only made a guess about the mean and the 68% interval for the distribution of temperatures. Although you will never know the true mean and standard deviation of the underlying distri-

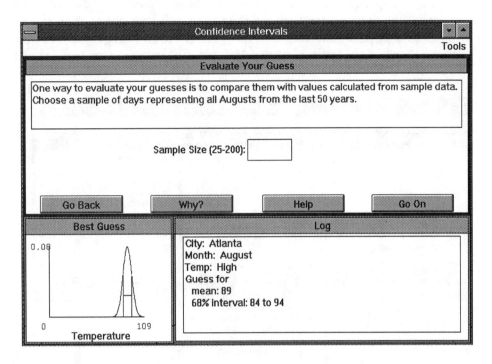

Figure 12.4 Evaluating Your Guess

bution, you can evaluate your guess by examining a sample of data from the unknown distribution. If your guesses are correct, approximately 68% of a random sample of daily temperatures will fall in the range you specified. To begin the sampling experiment, select the size of the sample that will be drawn—our example uses 50. Click on the entry box, enter **50**, and click on **Go On**.

For a sample size of 50, you will see a simulation of 50 daily high temperatures for Atlanta in August. Each of these values represents a random draw from a distribution that represents all August days for all years. As the first temperature is displayed, you will see its entry in the histogram in the lower right corner of the screen. Click **Next**, and a second temperature value will be drawn, displayed, and plotted.

Each individual temperature value either will fall within the 68% interval that you have specified or will fall outside of the interval. This will be true for any value that is drawn. It highlights the fact that our assignment of a probability to an interval depends on the concept of repeated sampling. Imagine a thought-experiment in which we make an infinite number of random draws from a distribution. The probability that a random draw falls in an interval will ideally be the proportion of drawn values that fall in that interval. When we actually conduct simulations with a finite number of random draws, we will get an approximation to the true probability.

Continue to click **Next** to see how individual values compare to your interval. Once you get a feel for the proportion of values that fall in the interval, click **Finish** to move to the next screen.

The screen in Figure 12.5 presents the results of the sampling experiment. The box labeled *Your Performance* compares the sample mean from the simulation with your guess. You can see whether 68% of the sample values fell within your interval. Select either **change your estimate of the population mean** or **change your estimate of the 68% interval** to refine your guesses and click **Go On.**

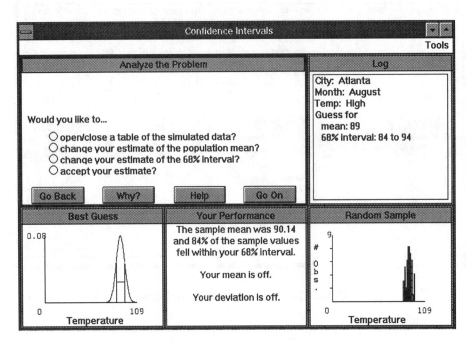

Figure 12.5 Analyzing Your Performance

After each revision, you will be returned to a screen similar to Figure 12.5. Once you are satisfied with your revised values, click **accept your estimate**. The program checks your accuracy and a message box will appear. If you did not meet the standards that you set at the beginning of the program, click on **OK** to return to the screen in Figure 12.5 to try again. If you did meet the standards, click **OK.**

You can now begin the second experiment. The screens that appear with this new situation are similar to the prior screens, but the problem is different. You are now asked to guess the mean and 68% interval for the distribution of *average* monthly temperatures. Imagine that you are randomly choosing years and calculating the average temperature for the same month each year. The distribution of average monthly temperatures will differ from a distribution of the temperatures of individual days. As you move through this new problem, keep in mind the difference between the distribution of a random variable and the distribution of the mean of a sample of random variables. Click on **OK** after you read the description of the experiment.

The first screen (similar to the screen in Figure 12.3) requests your guess for the mean. Recall the relationship between the mean of a random variable and the mean of an average of independent draws of the same random variable. By using this relationship, you can use the earlier simulations to make a very good guess. (If you cannot recall, look for the relationship as you evaluate your guess.) Enter a guess, and click **Go On** to move to the 68% interval request (similar to the screen in Figure 12.4).

Knowing the relationship between the variance of a random variable and the variance of an average allows you to use the earlier simulations to make a very good guess for the 68% interval. Remember that you are trying to estimate the spread of a distribution for the average of the daily temperatures over a month. Would you expect the monthly average temperature to vary more or less than the daily temperature? Enter your guess and click **Go On**.

As before, a summary screen will appear and show your guesses. Once you are satisfied with your choices click **Yes**. The next screen requests both the *sample size* and the *number of samples* that you want to use for your simulation. In this problem, we are examining monthly average temperatures so the *sample size* represents the number of days in the month. The entry for August would be **31**. The *number of samples* represents the number of years that we want to include. For example, enter **50** to generate fifty years of August temperatures. Click **Go On** to start the simulation and **Finish** to conclude it.

The next screen is similar to the screen in Figure 12.5. The results of the simulation are presented. You can *change your estimate of the population mean, change your estimate of the 68% interval,* or *accept your estimate*. If you accept your estimate when it does not measure up to your standard of accuracy, you will be returned to this screen to revise your guess. Once you have made an accurate guess, you will be alerted by the message box and allowed to move to the screen shown in Figure 12.6.

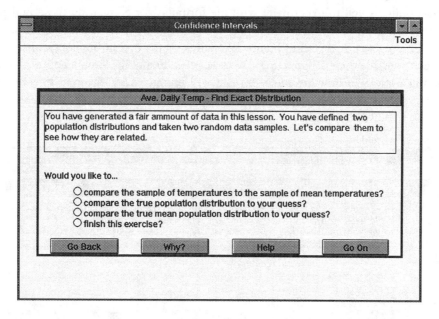

Figure 12.6 Comparing Daily and Monthly Average Results

The options on this screen allow a series of comparisons. For a direct comparison of the sample mean and standard deviation for the two problems, click **compare the sample of temperatures to the sample of mean temperatures** and **Go On**. Look carefully at the differences between the two sample means and the two sample standard deviations. Unless your samples are unusual, these should mirror the theoretical relationships.

To compare your guesses to the true values, click on **compare the true population distribution to your guess**, or **compare the true mean population distribution to your guess**, and **Go On**. A table showing the means and standard deviations will be displayed, along with graphs of the two distributions. Since your final guesses were based on the sample data, these values should be close to the true values. Click on **finish this exercise** and **Go On** when you are done.

Confidence Interval for a Population Mean

The pathway for *an example using sampling and intervals* illustrates how repeated sampling is used to assign probability to intervals and how intervals for random variables differ from intervals for means of random variables. Although these ideas are used for the construction and interpretation of confidence intervals, probability intervals are *not* confidence intervals. Confidence intervals and probability intervals have different interpretations. Probability intervals are ranges over which the value of a random variable (e.g., the sample mean) will fall with the stated probability. Confidence intervals are ranges of values that are likely to contain the unknown value of a population characteristic (e.g. the population mean) with the stated level of confidence. Unlike the end points of a probability interval, the end points of a confidence interval are not chosen directly. The end points of confidence intervals are given by formulas that use the sample statistics (typically the mean and standard deviation) to calculate particular end points for any specificied level of confidence. These end-point formulas represent random variables with their own probability distributions.

The next pathway allows you to experiment with the formulas for computing these end points and to conduct an experiment to see how the formulas perform over many independent samples. To begin the pathway, start with the opening screen in Figure 12.1, click on the option **the confidence interval for a population mean**, and then click **Go On**. The screen in Figure 12.7 will appear. Each example provides vivid illustrations of how the same formula will produce very different intervals for different samples. It also shows how the proportion of these intervals that contain the true mean may be interpreted as a probability known as the confidence level.

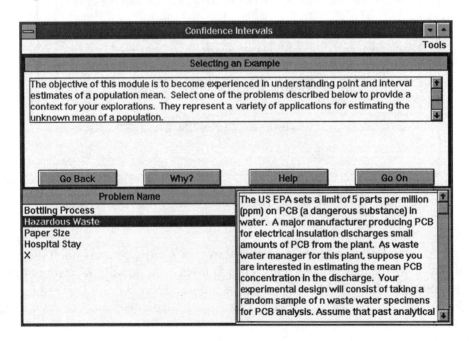

Figure 12.7 Selecting an Example

The concepts of estimation can be illustrated in the context of a particular problem, or with a generic random variable X. Click on *Hazardous Waste* to see one example of a problem. The background information about this problem tells you that you are interested in estimating the true mean of PCB concentration in waste water by taking a random sample of measurements. It also tells you that you can assume a standard deviation of 0.5 ppm based on past data. To use this example, click **Go On**.

The next screen allows you to take two small samples in order to conduct a preliminary analysis. To draw two samples of size 10, click on **enter a sample size, n** and **Go On**. Enter **10** and click **Accept**. Move to the screen shown in Figure 12.8 by clicking on **continue with selected sample size** and **Go On**.

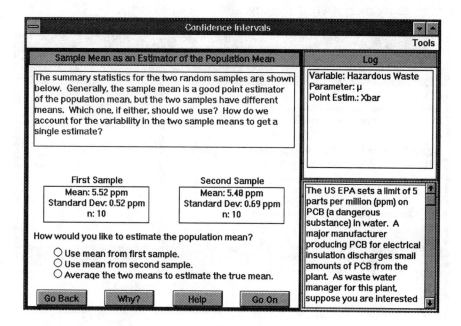

Figure 12.8 Sample Mean as an Estimator of the Population Mean

The summary statistics for the two samples are shown on this screen. Each is the result of random sampling, and each is produced independently. It is important to notice the differences in the sample statistics for these two samples. They will virtually always be different, since the individual sample values are almost certain to be different.

After drawing the two samples and noting their differences, you are asked to make a choice about how to use these data to estimate the unknown population mean PCB concentration. You have the unusual luxury of having two sample means that could be used to estimate the population mean. Either of the two could be used, or they could be combined to produce a single sample mean.

Click on **Use mean from first sample**, **Use mean from second sample**, or **Average the two means to estimate the true measure** and **Go On** to see an evaluation of your choice. The information box that appears on the screen will explain whether your choice is appropriate. Click **OK** to close the box and continue. Once you make the correct selection, reflect on why it is the best one. Statisticians are always reluctant to throw away sample data. There will always be some way that it can be used to improve estimation of the unknown population parameter.

The next screen presents two options. Click on **Repeat this experiment with two new random samples** and **Go On** to draw two new random samples and repeat the comparisons just shown. Click on **Develop an interval estimate of the population mean** and **Go On** to see the confidence intervals that can be generated from the preliminary samples.

You will now see the screen shown in Figure 12.9. Begin exploring the intervals by choosing a confidence level from among the four levels shown in the lower left window. For example, click on **50%** to display the width of the confidence interval implied by this confidence level. As you try other levels, the width of the interval changes. Remember that the confidence level represents the proportion of the time that the confidence interval formula produces an interval that covers the population mean. The wider the interval, the more likely it is to cover the population mean.

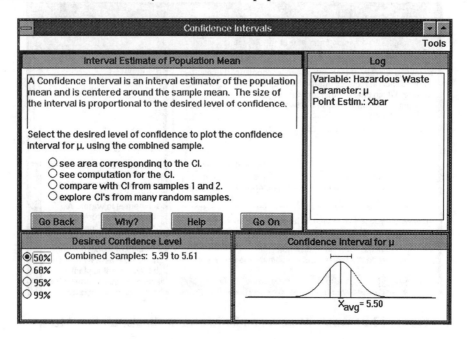

Figure 12.9 Interval Estimate of Population Means

The first three options on this screen provide additional ways of viewing the interval. Click on **see area corresponding to the CI** and **Go On** to highlight the area under the distribution that lies between the end points of the interval. As you try different confidence levels, you will see how the area changes.

Click on **see computations for the CI** and **Go On** to display the formula used to calculate the end points of the confidence interval. The formula for each end point yields a statistic, so that each is a random variable with outcomes that can be described by a probability distribution. Each sample is used to calculate one particular pair of end points for the confidence interval. That interval may or may not cover the population mean.

Click on **compare with CI from samples 1 and 2** and **Go On** to see the widths of the confidence intervals that would be generated by each of the two half samples and the combined sample. You will find that the interval for the combined sample is never as wide. To see why this holds, look at how the sample size enters the formula for the end points of the confidence interval.

Each of the ideas presented above can be visualized by constructing an interval and simulating its performance. Click on **explore CI's from many random samples** and **Go On** to begin setting up this simulation experiment. The screen shown in Figure 12.10 will appear.

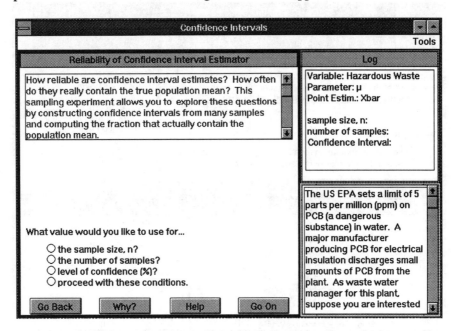

Figure 12.10 Setting Up the Sampling Experiment

You can evaluate the performance of the confidence interval computations by conducting a sampling experiment and constructing a new confidence interval for each sample. First you must define the confidence interval by setting the sample size and confidence level. Click on **the sample size, n** and **Go On**, enter a sample size in the entry box, and click **Accept** to use this value. Click on **level of confidence (%)** and **Go On**. Enter a confidence level in the entry box, and click **Accept** to use this value.

Suppose that you select a sample size of 40 and a confidence level of 95%. Your interval will be centered on the mean of a sample of size 40. The standard deviation of the PCB concentration distribution is known to be 0.5, so the standard deviation of the sample mean will be 0.5 divided by the square root of 40. Setting a confidence level of 95% implies that if you repeated this experiment an indefinitely large number of times, 95% of the intervals can be expected to cover the true mean of the PCB distribution.

Even though you cannot draw an infinite number of samples, you can perform a simulation. Click on **the number of samples** and **Go On**. Enter a number in the entry box and click **Accept** to use this value. For example, you might use 50 samples for your first experiment. Keep in mind that the larger the number of samples, the more likely it is that your results will be close to the 95% coverage suggested by theory. When you are satisfied with the experiment that you have set up, click on **proceed with these conditions** and **Go On.**

The next screen gives you a chance to see the mean of the population used to generate the data for this simulation. Click on **Reveal the population mean** and **Go On**. According to the statistical theory used to construct confidence intervals, 95% of all intervals will cover this mean. To see whether this result holds for your sampling experiment, click on **collect 50 samples of size 40** and **Go On**.

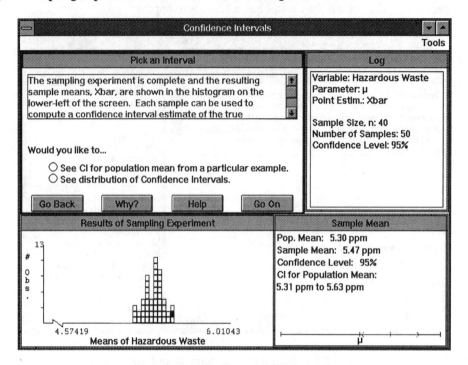

Figure 12.11 Sampling Experiment Results

The results of your experiment are shown on the screen in Figure 12.11. The histogram in the lower left corner is a plot of the 50 sample means. Each of the 50 samples can be used to construct a 95% confidence interval, and these intervals can be individually displayed by clicking on the blocks in the histogram. As you do this, look for two characteristics of these intervals: the width remains the same while the center changes, and not all intervals cover the population mean!

Although you could count the number of intervals that do not cover the population mean, a dramatic display of all intervals is available. Click on **see distribution of confidence intervals** and **Go On** to produce the screen shown in Figure 12.12.

The horizontal line in the graph represents the mean of the population. The vertical lines represent the 50 confidence intervals. Notice that the confidence intervals for these 50 samples are all of the same size, but they are not all centered in the same way with respect to the population mean. The two colors show whether a confidence interval covers the mean. To see how close the actual percentage that cover the mean is to the 95% ideal, click on **see computation of percent in range** and **Go On.**

The percent-in-range is shown as a pie chart in the lower right window. For our example, the difference between the 95% ideal and the actual percentage is due to sampling error associated with the small number of samples that we took. Click on **Repeat this experiment using different sample size, number of samples, and CI** and **Go On** to rerun the experiment with a larger number of samples.

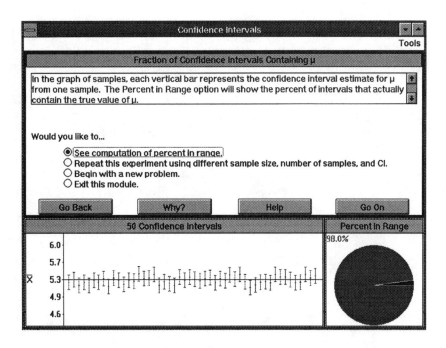

Figure 12.12 Confidence Intervals Covering μ

The primary difference between these experiments and real estimation problems is that we do not know the population mean in a real problem. Real problems require that we estimate the population mean. The benefit of the experiments in the program is that they can be used to verify and understand the theoretical properties of the confidence interval estimator. Once the properties of a confidence interval formula have been established, those results can be applied to any problem based on the same underlying population distribution.

Some Ways of Following Up the Experiment

This program contains two different pathways. The first requires that you make guesses about the mean and 68% interval for a daily temperature and a monthly average temperature. As you repeat this experiment, your guesses should improve. Once you understand the relationship between the two distributions, you should be able to make accurate guesses for new scenarios. To test your understanding, repeat this experiment using different combinations of city, month, and high or low temperature. As you do so, vary the accuracy standard that you are trying to meet.

The second pathway illustrates how a confidence interval is constructed and interpreted. Since each example comes from an underlying population with a different mean and standard deviation, the different examples will produce different intervals. To see whether your initial results were typical, try some of the other examples. As you do so, vary the number of samples that you draw. Then, see if you can find a relationship between the number of samples and the difference between the simulated confidence level and the actual confidence level.

Chapter 13

Beginning Hypothesis Testing

What May Be Investigated with *Beginning Hypothesis Testing*:

- What enters into the process of testing a hypothesis or claim *statistically*
- How to formulate a set of hypotheses suitable for statistical testing
- Why general claims must be turned into precise hypotheses for purposes of testing
- How sample size and sampling error affect decisions about the validity of hypotheses

Why Use This Program?

The course description brochure put out by the Math Department at a certain college once claimed, "College graduates who have had two years of calculus in college have substantially higher incomes 10 years after graduating than those who have not." When a student was overheard making a remark about truth in advertising, the head of the department said, "We're completely confident that this statistic is true. The burden is on you, if you doubt it, to show that it isn't." How might you go about doing so? You can find out the average income of college graduates 10 years after graduation from statistics on income put out by the government. If you are lucky, you might also find the standard deviation in the same place. But what about the subset of graduates who have taken two years of calculus in college? You are scarcely going to find their average income 10 years after graduation in any standard source. Instead, you are going to have to rely on a sample of college graduates that you carry out yourself.

Obtaining this sample raises a host of issues. Some of them are merely practical. How are you going to locate a reasonable number of people 10 years out of college who had 2 years of calculus while in college? How can you be confident that your sample is truly random? There are technical issues, too. What if the average income for your sample is less than 2 percent greater than the average for college graduates in general listed by the government. Is this sufficient evidence to show that the claim made by the Math Department is false? The head of the Math Department may say, "But look, even though your sample average is only a little bit greater, it *is* greater. So, it actually tends to support our claim. The burden is still on you to show otherwise." How can you demonstrate that, at the very least, your evidence shifts the burden of proof onto the Math Department? More specifically, how can you go about showing that this small difference is almost certainly due to chance alone, and that if those who took two years of calculus really did have substantially higher incomes, your sample average would almost certainly have come out much higher than it did? The *Beginning Hypothesis Testing* program allows experiments to be carried out that will help answer questions of this sort.

One reason why *hypothesis testing* is an important topic in statistics is that so many claims can only be tested statistically, such as claims about the effectiveness and side effects of prescription drugs, the costs of maintenance for different makes of automobiles, environmental phenomena like global warming, or the gains from eating broccoli on a regular basis. Even when a claim can in principle be verified by identifying a specific causal mechanism that makes it true, we often have to rely on statistical evidence, at least for the time being. That smoking causes cancer is an example of this. Or, consider the suggestion that some disease is inherited. One could, in principle, show that this is true by isolating a gene and determining how it causes the disease. Searching for such a gene, however, could be a complete wild goose chase. Before embarking on such a search, one would normally insist on having statistical evidence that the disease does in fact occur significantly more often among descendants of those who suffered from it than it does in the general population.

Another reason why *hypothesis testing* is important is that, even if you are far removed from the technical world of statistics, you will still have to make many decisions in life in which the information you are relying on consists of some sort of statistical evidence presented in a newspaper or elsewhere in the media. The newspaper statements of statistical evidence are often accompanied by a quotation from an expert announcing that this evidence finally establishes or refutes some hypothesis or other. Your decisions will be better informed if you understand how one goes about testing a hypothesis statistically and you know where the potential pitfalls and loose ends lie.

The phrase *hypothesis testing* is used in statistics to refer to an intricate procedure that, because of its technical underpinnings, often requires patience and effort to understand. The procedure involves three steps. First, the claim or hypothesis that is to be tested is transformed into a precise hypothesis about some measurable characteristic of the population or populations the claim is about. Second, an experiment is carried out to obtain a sample of data concerning this characteristic. Finally, the truth of the precisely formulated hypothesis is assessed in the light of these data, taking into account the fact that the sample is subject to sampling error. Choices have to be made at each of these three steps. The choices that are made can have a significant effect on the overall outcome of the assessment.

To understand hypothesis testing is to understand why choices have to be made at each of the three steps and what effects these choices can have. *Beginning Hypothesis Testing* allows you to go through the procedure for some elementary examples, reach initial assessments, and then change some of your choices in order to see the effect they can have on these assessments.

Hypothesis testing is one of the more advanced topics in statistics—*Beginning Hypothesis Testing* is only an introduction to it. Even so, it will enable you to see the two great virtues of the technical procedure involved. First, this procedure makes the process of assessing claims *orderly*. Second, it makes the process *transparent* in the sense that each choice is explicit and can be returned to and its effects evaluated when appropriate. Thanks to these two virtues, you can always be clear on just what has and what has not been accomplished in any statistical test of a hypothesis.

How to Run Experiments with *Beginning Hypothesis Testing*

To run the *Beginning Hypothesis Testing* program, select **Inference** from the *ConStatS* menu. Click on **Beginning Hypothesis Testing** and **Go On**. The screen shown in Figure 13.1 appears. You have two options: *a claim about the mean of a single population* and *a claim about the differences between the* *means of two populations.* Because our example involves only one population, click on **a claim about the mean of a single population** and **Go On.**

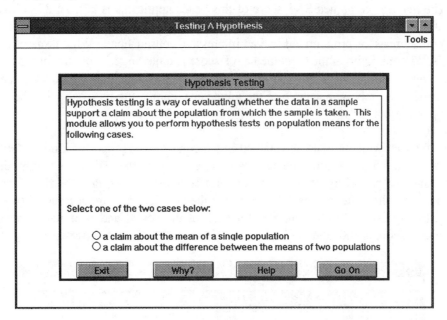

Figure 13.1 Choosing the Type of Hypothesis to Test

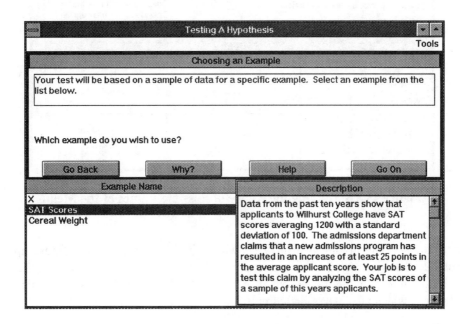

Figure 13.2 The Problem in the SAT Example

Several example situations are available. Click on **SAT scores**, and read the description of the problem in the window on the lower right, as shown in Figure 13.2.

The first step is always to understand what claim is being made and what issue of proof it is raising. What population is the claim about? This year's applicants to Wilhurst College. What is the nature of the claim? The *average* combined SAT score of this year's applicants is at least 25 points higher than the average of 1200 over the last 10 years. Why is the claim being made? The Admissions Department says that its new admissions program has had an impressive consequence. What issue of proof does the claim raise? A 25 point jump in the combined SAT score is quite large. How might we test this claim? We could survey—take a census of—the entire applicant pool, but that would be excessively time consuming. Instead we rely on a sample of the applicants, comparing its mean with the mean claimed for the entire population.

Once you feel familiar with the issue, the context in which it is arising, and the kind of data that we will be using to address it, click **Go On**. The next two screens prepare the way for replacing the claim with a precisely formulated pair of hypotheses for purposes of statistical testing. The first screen, shown in Figure 13.3, requests the range of *possible* values for the population mean at issue. Since SAT scores lie between a low of 200 and a high of 800 for each of the verbal and quantitative tests, the *lowest possible* combined score is 400, and the *highest possible* is 1600. Click on **Between _____ and ____**.

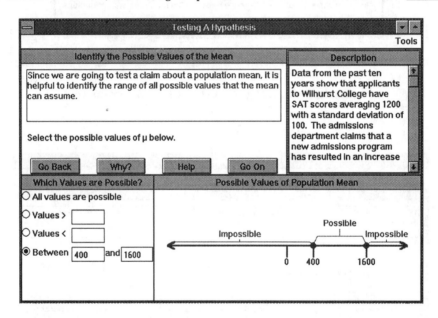

Figure 13.3 Specifying the Range of Possible Values of the Mean

Enter **400** and **1600**. The graphical display shown in the lower right of the figure appears. (It is extremely unlikely that the mean SAT score of any moderate to large population of college applicants will lie near the extremes of this range, but it is possible. The point here is to eliminate from consideration all values which are categorically impossible.)

Click **Go On**. The next screen requests the range of values for the population mean that are consistent with the claim under scrutiny. The Admissions Department says that its new policy has resulted in an average combined SAT score *at least* 25 points higher than the prior 10-year-average of 1200. Thus, any value of the population mean greater than 1225 supports the claim. Click on **Values > ____** and enter **1225**. As shown in Figure 13.4, a graphical display in the lower right of the screen appears that indicates just what the claim is being taken to amount to.

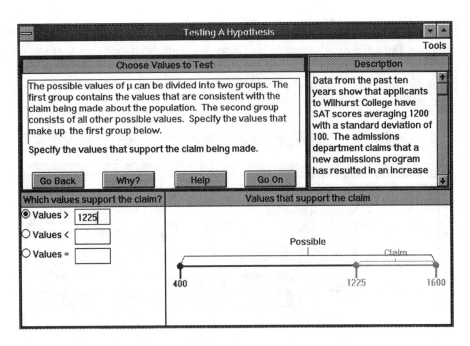

Figure 13.4 Which Values of the Mean Support the Claim

At this point we have made the issue fully explicit and precise, but we have not yet begun to transform the claim into a *statistical* hypothesis. As you will see, the choices made so far will have some effect on the overall outcome of the test. None made so far, however, enter directly into the testing process. This will change with the next screen, which you can obtain when you are ready by clicking **Go On**.

The Alternative and Null Hypotheses

Statistical hypothesis testing requires the claim to be replaced by two mutually exclusive hypotheses, called the *null* and the *alternative*. The need for two hypotheses in place of a single claim stems from the fact that statistical evidence can be inconclusive. The *null hypothesis* is the hypothesis that continues to stand when the evidence is inconclusive. It is the one that does not call for special new evidence. The *alternative hypothesis*, by contrast, is the one on which the *burden of proof* lies. Compelling evidence is required before it is to be accepted and the null hypothesis rejected. The statistical test itself will be of the null hypothesis. The question will be whether the statistical evidence provides adequate grounds for rejecting it. If the evidence falls short of providing adequate grounds for rejecting the null hypothesis, then the burden of proof on the alternative hypothesis has not been met. Looked at in this way, the process of replacing a claim by a set of statistical hypotheses suitable for testing requires a choice first about where the burden of proof lies and second how great this burden is. The next few screens will lead you through these two steps.

Where should the burden of proof lie in the case of Wilhurst College's claim that their average applicant SAT score has jumped to at least 1225? One can argue either way. On the one hand, a 25-point jump in a single year is quite large. From this point of view, the burden of proof lies on the college—i.e., on the hypothesis that the true population mean falls among the values supporting the claim. On the other hand, the Admissions Department of Wilhurst College has been consistently accurate in the past in its statements about applicants. From this point of view, the burden of proof lies on anyone who is saying that the Admissions Department is wrong in its claim—i.e., on the hypothesis that the true population mean falls among the values that do not support the claim. It is up to you to decide where you want the burden of proof to lie. The screen shown in Figure 13.5 allows you to indicate your choice by identifying what you want the *alternative hypothesis*, called Ha, to be.

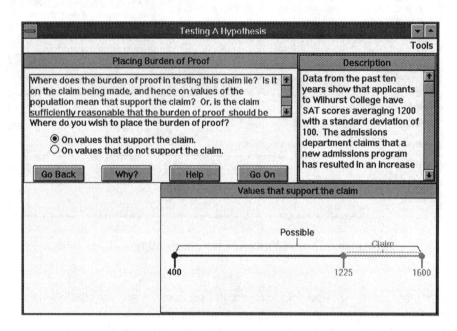

Figure 13.5 Identifying the Alternative Hypothesis

In the example that follows, we place the burden of proof on Wilhurst College. To follow us, click on **Values that support the claim** and **Go On**. Keep in mind that a substantive choice has been made that can have a significant effect on any decision about whether the Wilhurst College claim is true. If we had instead given it the benefit of the doubt and put the burden of proof on anyone who was going to challenge its claim, the very same evidence obtained during our subsequent test might have very different implications.

Because the choice of the *alternative hypothesis*, Ha, and the *null hypothesis*, called Ho, can make such a difference, the next screen, shown in Figure 13.6, gives you an opportunity to reconsider it. The window in the lower left allows you to display each hypothesis on the graph in the lower right. Click on **Display Ho** and the null hypothesis will be indicated on the graph and stated as an assertion, namely μ < *1225*. Click on **Display Ha** and the alternative hypothesis will be indicated and stated as an assertion, μ > *1225*, as shown in Figure 13.6. You can *Change Ho and Ha* or *Proceed with this Ho and Ha*. Selecting the former will take you back to the earlier screen shown in Figure 13.4. Keep in mind that the statistical test will be of the *null hypothesis*, Ho, and the issue will be whether the statistical evidence is sufficiently strong to *reject* it. To continue with the example below, click on **Proceed with this Ho and Ha** and **Go On**.

The next screen, shown in Figure 13.7, covers the final step in formulating the precise hypothesis that is to be tested. The statistical test must be of an assertion about some specific value for the population

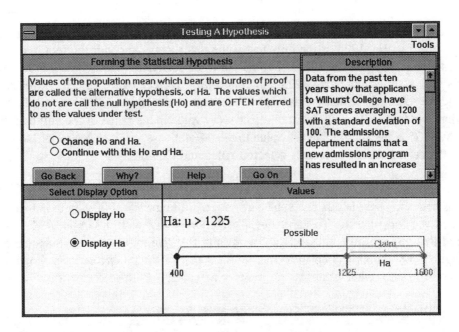

Figure 13.6 A Chance to Reconsider the Choice of Ho and Ha

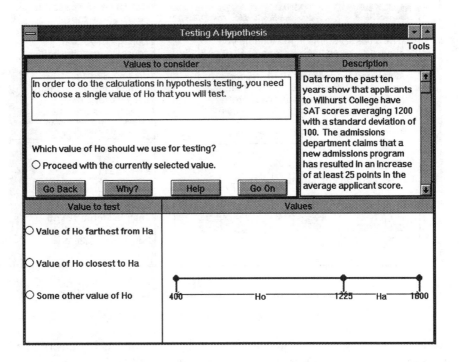

Figure 13.7 Identifying the Test Value for Ho

mean. When the null hypothesis involves a range of values, as it does here, one needs to choose a single value in that range to test. We want to choose a test value in such a way that, if the evidence calls for the null hypothesis to be rejected for that value, then the same evidence would call for it to be rejected for every other value in that range. You can see the alternatives by clicking on the three options in the window in the lower left corner of this screen. Examine all three alternatives by clicking on them. The *value of Ho closest to Ha*, 1225, is the only test value that meets the condition required for testing the null hypothesis. For, suppose the evidence turns out to be sufficient to conclude that the average SAT score of this year's applicants is not 1225, *but some value greater than 1225*; then the same evidence will be sufficient to conclude that the average SAT score is not 1224, 1223, etc., all the way down to 400—i.e., that evidence will be sufficient to reject every value in the range of the null hypothesis. Once it is clear why 1225 is the appropriate test value in the present case, click on **Value of Ho closest to Ha**, followed by **Proceed with the currently selected value** and **Go On**.

You can now proceed with the formal test by clicking on **Proceed to formal test** and **Go On**. Often, however, it is better to pause at this point and carry out a preliminary test, if only to help anticipate what can happen in the formal test. To carry out a preliminary test with a sample of 5, click on **Take advantage of this opportunity** and **Go On**. The result of the preliminary test will appear on the screen shown in Figure 13.8. In our example, the mean SAT score for the sample of 5, as shown in the figure, is 1217.8. You are asked whether this result points in any clear way toward a final decision.

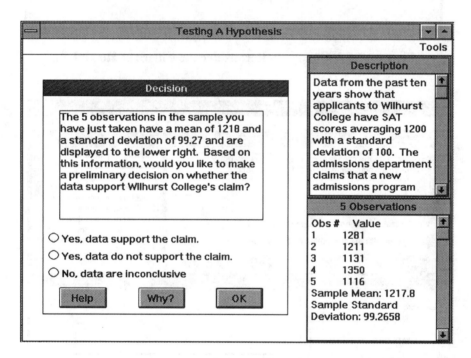

Figure 13.8 Assessing the Results of the Preliminary Test

Think about which of the three views of the preliminary test, presented as options on the left hand side of the screen, seems most correct. Once you decide, click on it and **OK**. The program will then give you its own view of the preliminary test. When you are ready to continue, click on **OK**.

If the preliminary test has made you uncomfortable with any choices you made earlier, you can click on **Go Back** however many times you need to in order to return to the screen where you want to reconsider a choice. In particular, the sample mean of 1217.8 obtained in the preliminary test above calls attention to the distinct possibility that the result of the full test will not provide adequate grounds for rejecting the null hypothesis, yet equally will scarcely provide grounds for thinking that Wilhurst College's claim is flatly false. Maybe you want to reconsider where the burden of proof ought to lie.

Data for Testing the Hypothesis

Two steps remain before the formal test is fully specified. First, a sample size has to be chosen. When the screen shown in Figure 13.9 first appears, the bottom half will be blank, as will the box to the right of *n=*. Enter a value in this box, say **20**, and click on **Enter n**. The bottom half will be filled in.

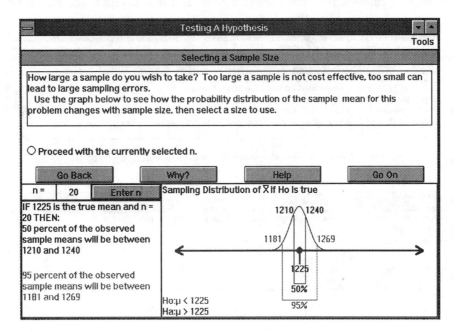

Figure 13.9 Selecting a Sample Size

The bottom half of the screen indicates how the mean of sample sizes of **20** will vary from one sample to the next if the population mean is 1225. This variability is based on the population standard deviation of 100 from the previous 10 years. With a sample size of 20, 50 percent of samples will have a mean between 1210 and 1240 if the true population mean is 1225. In other words, the chance element in sampling is as likely as not to lead to a sample mean more than 15 points away from 1225 if this is the true value; and the chances are 1 in 20 of a sample mean more than 44 points away from 1225. The *Sampling Errors* program showed us that the variability in the sample means decreases as the sample size increases. Enter a larger number in the box, such as 40, to see how much the variability is reduced.

Try several numbers before deciding on a sample size. The larger your sample, the more time it will take you at the next stage in the test to collect the data. The smaller your sample, the greater the chances that any difference you obtain between the mean of your sample and 1225 is due only to chance. You need to decide what the appropriate trade-off between these two considerations is here.

To continue with the example, enter **20** as the sample size, then click on **Proceed with the currently selected n** and **Go On**. The next screen that appears is shown in Figure 13.10. This screen asks you for

155

a *Decision Rule*. In the present case what this amounts to is the mean value of the SAT scores, in the sample you are about to take, that you are going to regard as sufficiently high to reject the null hypothesis—that is, to reject the hypothesis that the mean for all the applicants is 1225 (or less). The screen offers three ways of specifying this rule: (1) You can click along the axis in the graph on the right to indicate the lowest sample mean for which you are going to reject Ho. (2) You can enter the amount the sample mean has to be above 1225 for you to reject it. (3) You can enter a probability value indicating the level of risk you are willing to accept that you will reject Ho on the basis of a sample mean that is much higher than 1225, purely on the basis of chance. However you specify the decision rule, the other two ways will immediately be indicated on the screen. Assuming this is the first time you select a decision rule, click along the axis at a few different points, noting how the two

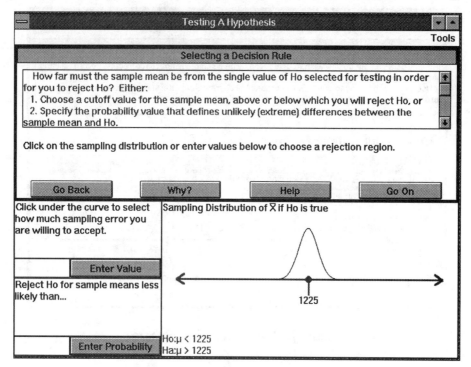

Figure 13.10 Selecting a Decision Rule

numbers in the lower left change. As Figure 13.11 shows, the probability value in the box on the lower left shows up as a highlighted region on the graph. This region indicates the probability that chance alone will produce a sample mean this far above a true value of 1225 with the sample size you have chosen.

The preferred way of selecting the decision rule in hypothesis testing is by specifying the risk of rejecting the null hypothesis when it is true—that is, by the probability in the lower left hand corner. In the case of Figure 13.11 the value for this risk is 0.05; this means being prepared to live with 1 chance in 20 of rejecting the null hypothesis even though it is true. Is this an acceptable level of risk? It depends on the consequences of making a wrong decision. Falsely rejecting a claim about mean SAT scores is undoubtedly of far less consequence than declaring a hazardous waste not hazardous. Some risk of falsely rejecting the null hypothesis is unavoidable regardless of the situation. What level of risk is appropriate must depend on the situation.

With a risk of 0.05, shown in Figure 13.11, the null hypothesis will be rejected with a sample size of 20 only if the sample mean is 1262 or greater. This is a high value, far removed from 1225. Because it is so high, there is quite a significant risk of samples that will not provide adequate grounds for rejecting the null hypothesis even when it is false. This is the other form of unavoidable risk involved in statistical hypothesis testing. Enter some probability values other than 0.05—say, 0.01, 0.10, and 0.20—to see what you have to do to lower the critical value of 1262 and thereby reduce the risk of not rejecting the null hypothesis even though it is false. Clearly, there is a trade-off between these two risks, and a proper balance needs to be struck between them.

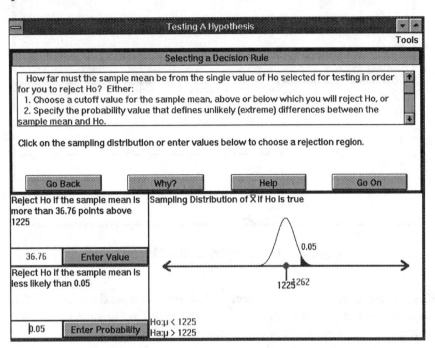

Figure 13.11 The Decision Rule Selected

Earlier we said that the *burden of proof* is on the alternative hypothesis. What this means is that we are not prepared to reject the null hypothesis and accept the alternative unless the evidence is decisive. How decisive? With the risk specified as 0.05, the sample mean for a sample size of 20 must exceed 1262 in order for the evidence to be sufficiently decisive for us to conclude that the population mean is above 1225. This is the burden of proof we have placed on the alternative hypothesis with the decision rule shown in Figure 13.11.

Because this burden of proof is so substantial, consider what factors contributed to it. One way of lowering it, as you have already seen, is by accepting a greater risk of falsely rejecting the null hypothesis. But what about the sample size? Would using a sample size larger than 20 lower the critical value of 1262? Click on **Go Back**, change the sample size, and return to the screen shown above, re-entering the probability of 0.05. How much does increasing the sample size reduce the burden of proof on the alternative hypothesis without increasing the risk of falsely rejecting the null?

When you are ready to continue with the example, restore the sample size to 20 in the preceding screen, enter 0.05 for the probability (re-creating the screen shown above), and click **Go On**. The next screen, shown in Figure 13.12, summarizes the test as you have defined it. Review it carefully before turning to the experiment that will generate the data needed to carry through the test.

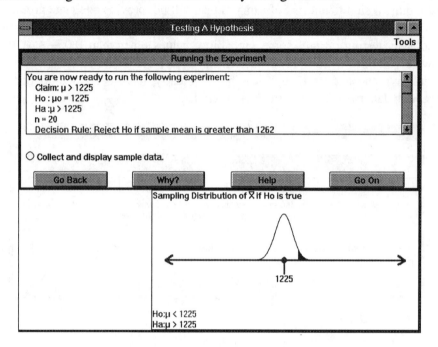

Figure 13.12 Summary of the Planned Test

Once you are ready to collect data, click **Collect and display sample data** and **Go On.** You can step your way through the process of obtaining the data by clicking **Go On** each time you are ready for the next datum, or you can click **Finish** and have the process completed for you. Once the sample of 20 has been obtained, the results will be displayed and summarized as shown in Figure 13.13.

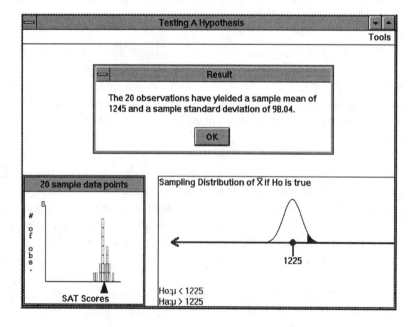

Figure 13.13 The Result of the Experiment

In the case of the sample of 20 shown in the figure, the result is a sample mean of 1245 and a sample standard deviation of 98.04. Because the samples are random, the result you obtain from your sample of 20 will be somewhat different. Regardless, the statistical evidence is now in. The question is, what does it show?

Has the Burden of Proof Been Met?

To complete the hypothesis test, click **OK**. A screen will appear offering you three options: *Make a decision about Ho*; *See a z-value analysis*; and *Do a new experiment*. The last option is discussed in the section on further experiments. The *z-value analysis* will take you through the steps of restating the result of the experiment on a standardized *z-scale*. Specifically, the difference between the sample mean (1245 in the example) and the population mean assumed in the null hypothesis (1225) will instead be expressed as a certain number of standard deviations, as will the rejection value (1262). One advantage of transforming the result onto a *z-scale* is that this example of a hypothesis test can then be compared with others involving topics and numbers totally different from SAT scores. Also, it will make clear just how big the gap is between the sample mean and the rejection value. If you wish to go through this analysis before continuing, click on **See a z-value analysis** and **Go On**, repeating the latter following each step.

When you are ready, click on **Make a decision about Ho** and **Go On** to obtain the *decision* window shown on the left of Figure 13.14 below. For the moment, consider the sample mean of 1245 obtained in the example, and forget the value you obtained. Does 1245 persuade you that the null hypothesis is false, i.e., that the mean SAT for the entire set of applicants is 1225 or greater, just as the Admissions Department claimed? Should you let the null hypothesis stand on the grounds that 1245 is not in the rejection region? Has the result left you uncertain what you should do? Click on each of the three options to see *ConStatS's* opinions.

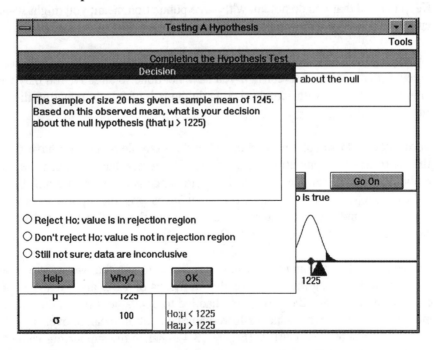

Figure 13.14 Making a Decision About the Null Hypothesis

159

The opinion of *ConStatS* reflects nothing but an insistence on abiding by the decision rule selected earlier. According to it, to reject the null hypothesis when the mean of a sample of 20 is less than 1262 is to take a greater than 1 in 20 risk of falsely rejecting this hypothesis. To see how much greater a risk, click **OK**, then **No** when you are presented with the option of trying a new sample of 20. Then click **Go Back** until you reach the screen shown in Figure 13.11. Click along the axis until you find 1245, and the risk of falsely rejecting the null hypothesis on the basis of this sample mean will then be indicated.

Suppose we decide to abide by the decision rule and not reject the null hypothesis on the basis of the 1245 result obtained in the sample. Have we decided that the alternative hypothesis, and hence the Admissions Department's claim, is false? Not at all. We have only decided that the evidence obtained from the sample does not meet the burden of proof we elected to place on the Admissions Department's claim. Indeed, suppose we had reversed our null and alternative hypotheses when the screen shown in Figure 13.6 presented us with the opportunity to do so. Then the burden of proof would have been on the claim that the mean SAT score is less than 1225, and we would have tested to see whether the claim that it is greater than 1225 ought to be rejected. Had we made these choices and obtained the very same sample, with mean of 1245, we would have had no reason for even thinking about rejecting the Admissions Department's claim. *Hypothesis testing* does not offer an infallible way of making decisions. There is no way of doing this. What *hypothesis testing* does is to make the risk of any decision clear.

Some Ways of Following Up the Experiment

Much more can be learned from the SAT example. Once you have made your decision and received the opinion of *ConStatS*, you can repeat the experiment by obtaining another sample of the same size. You have already seen results from two samples, yours and the one shown in the example. Perhaps one or both of these are misleadingly atypical. Take the *new sample* option by clicking on **Yes** to explore this possibility. (Keep in mind that you do not know the true population mean; you might want to give some thought to what it likely is, after reviewing a few samples.)

Another way of varying the SAT example is to change the decision rule or the sample size. Use the **Go Back** option to return to the relevant screens. If you have not done so already, you may well want to see how the rejection value changes with sample size while the risk of falsely rejecting the null hypothesis is held constant.

As indicated above, the 1245 sample mean obtained in the example would not have provided grounds for rejecting the claim that the population mean is 1225 or greater, had this been the null hypothesis. So, the choice about where the burden of proof lies, and hence about what the null hypothesis is, can make quite a difference. Go back to the screen that gives you the option of switching the two hypotheses (Figure 13.6) and see what happens when you put the burden of proof on anyone who is going to challenge the Admissions Department's claim.

In somewhat the same spirit, our example may have suggested to you that we were a little unfair to the Admissions Department in saying that only population means of 1225 and greater support its claim. The real force of its claim was that the new policy had led to a notable jump in the average SAT score of the applicants. Perhaps we ought to have allowed any population mean above, say, 1215 to support the claim. Go back to the screen in question (Figure 13.4), change the supporting value to those above 1215, and repeat the entire hypothesis testing process with the same choices otherwise as those made above. The burden of proof will still be on the Admissions Department, but its claim is now weakened a little. How much more susceptible to rejection does this make the null hypothesis?

Finally, try the *Cereal Weight* example offered at the outset. It involves a two-tail alternative hypothesis, in contrast to the one-tail one in the SAT example.

The *SAT* and *Cereal Weight* examples both illustrate testing hypotheses concerning the mean of a single population. One can test hypotheses about a variety of statistics. *Beginning Hypothesis Testing* offers one further alternative, testing hypotheses about the difference in the means of two different populations. To pursue this alternative, click **Go Back** until you reach the opening screen in Figure 13.1. Then click **a claim about the difference between the means of two populations** and **Go On.** Several concrete examples for testing hypotheses of this sort are offered, along with a generic example. Try at least one of them.

Hypothesis testing is an intricate and difficult to grasp topic in statistics, but it is also one of the more important. Do not be discouraged if, after working your way through your first example, you find yourself uncertain about how to do it and what it can and cannot be used to accomplish. Experience is the best teacher. Even though *Beginning Hypothesis Testing* covers only the most elementary types of cases, you can still gain a good deal of experience by exploring examples with it.

PART FIVE

EXPERIMENT

Most of the data in the data sets pre-packaged in *ConStatS* did not come from experiments in the strict sense. Instead, they came from observing processes as they happened in the world. In true experiments, the experimenters manipulate variables in a systematic fashion in order to observe the effects on other variables. At the very least this requires intervention in real world processes, and it is often best done in artificial situations contrived to limit or control the influence extraneous variables have on the outcomes. Experiments have to be designed. Their design includes a statistical dimension, the aim of which is to increase the likelihood that the data will yield reliable conclusions. One reason for including a part on *Experiment* in *ConStatS* is to let students develop some experience in designing experiments and then seeing for themselves how the evidential quality of the data they obtain depends on the design.

A second reason for including a part on *Experiment* is to give students an opportunity to work with data that they themselves have generated. It is one thing for students to use statistical methods to extract information from pre-packaged data. It is quite another for them to use statistical methods to extract information from their own data. This contrast is even greater when the data the students generate pertain to themselves or their friends and the questions that the data can be used to address are ones in which they have a natural interest. Working with data that students themselves have generated also eliminates worries about whether someone has manufactured or tampered with the data in some way or other, worries that can be distracting.

The present version of *ConStatS* contains one program for carrying out experiments, *An Experiment in Mental Imagery*. This program reproduces the experimental framework of a classic experiment in cognitive psychology, the Shepard-Metzler experiment on rotating mental images. This experiment has two important virtues: first, it is typical of experiments in cognitive psychology in which the time required to perform a cognitive task is taken as a basis for drawing conclusions about the mental processes involved in performing it; and second, the data obtained by Shepard and Metzler, and by many others who subsequently replicated their experiment, have generally proved to be robust. *An Experiment in Mental Imagery* has two pathways. The first offers an already set-up version of the Shepard-Metzler experiment that students can immediately try on themselves and their friends. The second lets students design their own versions of the Shepard-Metzler experiment.

Chapter 14

An Experiment in Mental Imagery

What May Be Investigated with *An Experiment in Mental Imagery*:

- How to collect data from an experiment and put them in a usable form

- What steps need to be taken in designing experiments

- How you and others use mental imagery in answering questions

- How experiments in psychology are used to probe cognitive processes

Why Use This Program?

Several questions naturally arise when you use any pre-packaged data set in learning statistics. Have the data been "cooked"—i.e., have they simply been made up, with no relation to anything in the real world? (We do not think any of the data sets in *ConStatS* have been cooked, but we cannot be certain because we did not generate the data in them.) Have the data been touched up, for example by eliminating outliers? (The best we can do is to make educated guesses about whether the data sets in *ConStatS* have been cleaned up, guesses based on the data themselves and our knowledge of the circumstances in which they were most likely acquired.) Are any of the data sets "loaded"—i.e., have any of them been selected purely because they display some specific point dramatically? (Sometimes yes, sometimes no, but hopefully never heavy-handedly.)

You have no occasion to ask these questions when you work with a data set that you have personally generated. You know the data are real. You know whether you have cleaned them up and, if you have, exactly what you have done and why you have done it. And you know that the data set was not chosen to illustrate any special point. So, instead of being tempted to worry about what you are supposed to be learning from it, you can concentrate on the data themselves, asking whether they are telling you anything interesting.

An Experiment in Mental Imagery lets you generate your own data set by carrying out an experiment in cognitive psychology either on yourself or on your friends. The basic experiment is one that attracted a good deal of attention in the early 1970s. It is easy to carry out, and it has generally produced robust data. The program has two pathways. The first offers an example experiment that is already set and and ready to run. The second lets you design your own version of the experiment, varying the basic design in any of several ways. Because the experiment is a classic, it will give you a good idea of the type of experimentation cognitive psychologists employ in trying to fathom how our minds work. You may even discover something about your or your friends' cognitive capacities. The main point, however, is to let you generate data sets that you can use elsewhere in *ConStatS*.

The Shepard-Metzler Experiment in Mental Rotation

Many of our cognitive processes are below the level of consciousness. For example, no amount of introspection reveals to us how we go about parsing and interpreting the sounds that make up sentences in our native language. Most of us, however, are persuaded by introspection that we employ mental images when answering questions like, "Which breed of dog has longer ears, boxers or collies?" It may surprise you that the claim that we use mental images has been extremely controversial among cognitive psychologists. Those who have denied that we employ mental images grant that it feels as if we do, but suspect that what is actually going on at a level below consciousness involves nothing remotely like forming or manipulating pictorial representations.

One of the first and most famous experiments to probe whether we do use images was designed by Roger Shepard and Jacqueline Metzler of Stanford University (reported in *Science*, Vol. 171, 1971, pp. 701-703). They presented subjects with two-dimensional pictures of three-dimensional objects formed by collections of blocks of the sort shown in Figure 14.1. Each stimulus consisted of two such objects,

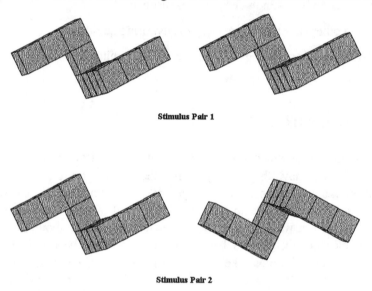

Figure 14.1 Examples of the Stimuli Used in the Experiment

sometimes the same as one another and sometimes different, at different angular orientations with respect to one another. The subjects were asked to decide whether the two objects are the same or different. (The two objects are the same in both stimulus-pair 1 and stimulus-pair 2 in Figure 14.1; they have a different angular orientation in stimulus-pair 2, and the same orientation in stimulus-pair 1.)

In the experiment Shepard and Metzler manipulated the relative angular orientation of the two objects as their principal independent variable. The *independent variable* in an experiment is the factor that is manipulated or selected by the experimenter to see what effect it has on a *dependent variable*. The dependent variable in Shepard and Metzler's experiment was the length of time it took the subject to pull a lever marked "Same" or "Different" in response to each pair of objects. This measure of the subject's response is called the *reaction time*, or RT. It is a commonly used measure in experiments investigating how humans perceive, discriminate, and remember different kinds of things.

Eight adult subjects participated in Shepard and Metzler's experiment. Each was presented with 1600 pairs of objects. Figure 14.2 shows a plot of the most important results from the experiment. The variable on the Y-axis is the mean reaction time of subjects giving the correct answer when the two objects are the same. The variable on the X-axis is the number of degrees of difference in the angular orientation of the two identical objects. The centers of the circles indicate the mean reaction time, and (when they extend far enough to show outside the circles) the vertical bars around each circle indicate an estimate of the standard error in that mean, based on the eight means for the individual subjects. The data shown are for angular differences in the picture-plane; similar results were obtained when the angular difference was into the depth of the picture-plane.

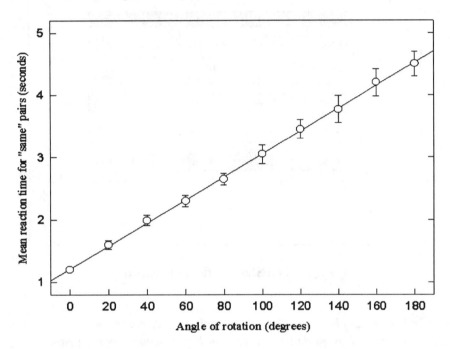

Figure 14.2 Shepard and Metzler's Reaction Time Data

The striking feature of the results plotted in Figure 14.2 is the tight linear relationship between the reaction time and the angular difference between the two identical objects. The subjects' reaction times increase linearly with the angular difference. We let Shepard and Metzler speak for themselves in giving the conclusions they drew from this result:

> These findings appear to place rather severe constraints on possible explanations of how subjects go about determining identity of shape of differently oriented objects. They are, however, consistent with an explanation suggested by the subjects themselves. Although introspective reports must be interpreted with caution, all subjects claimed (i) that to make the required comparison they first had to imagine one object as rotated into the same orientation as the other and that they could carry out this 'mental rotation' at no greater than a certain limiting rate; and (ii) that, since they perceived the two-dimensional pictures as objects in three-dimensional space, they could imagine the rotation around whichever axis was required with equal ease.

Whether your results will support these conclusions remains to be seen.

How to Preview the Mental Rotation Experiment

To run the *Experiment* program, select **Experiment** from the *ConStatS* menu. The opening screen shown in Figure 14.3 will appear.

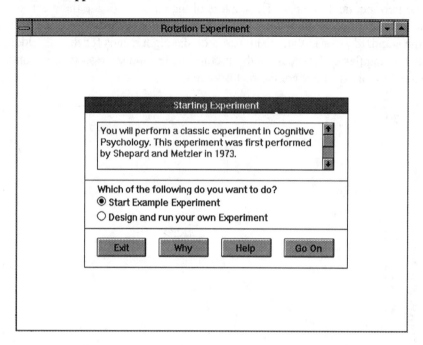

Figure 14.3 Starting the Experiment

The first option is *Start Example Experiment*. This option previews and starts a preset experiment for you. The second option is *Design and run your own Experiment*. Click on **Start Example Experiment** and **Go On**. The screen shown in Figure 14.4 will appear. It offers you three options on how to proceed.

In the first option, *Preview One Trial*, you can see and experience what one trial of the experiment is like. What exactly do the stimuli look like? How are they arranged on the screen? What kind of response will I need to make? To see an example of one trial, click on **Preview One Trial** and then **Go On**. The screen in Figure 14.5 will appear, giving you instructions on how to indicate whether the two objects shown on the screen are the same or different. To indicate that the two objects (you will soon see) are the same—except for their orientation—press the "s" key on your keyboard. If they look to be different, then you should press the "d" key instead. The computer will automatically detect and keep track of the time between the onset of the stimuli and your response. This reaction time is the dependent variable that you will be using to measure the effects of different orientations on your perceptual judgment. When you begin to collect data for real, it is generally best if you try to make your decision about the two stimuli as quickly *and* as accurately as possible. For this preview trial, however, there is no need to hurry as no data are being collected. Look carefully at the stimuli to see how they are constructed. When you are ready to start the trial, click on **OK** in the lower portion of the instruction window. At this point, there will be a *short four or five second delay* as the computer generates these complex objects. The program gives a visible 3-second countdown to tell you when the stimuli are about to appear.

168

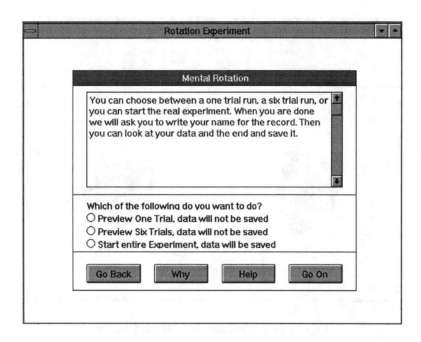

Figure 14.4 Previewing the Experiment

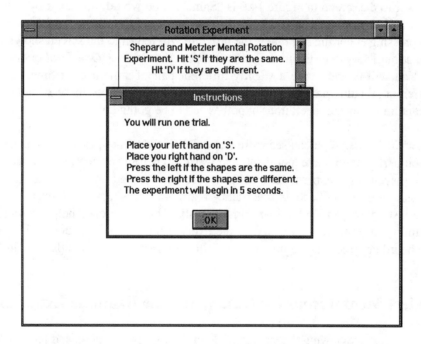

Figure 14.5 Instructions about how to indicate your choice

Because the computer randomly determines which stimuli to show each time the program is run, your next screen may not exactly match Figure 14.6. It will have two complex 3-D objects, one on the left and one on the right side of the screen. Figure 14.6 contains a pair of stimuli that are the same, though in somewhat different orientations. Your screen could show a pair of objects that are either the same or different.

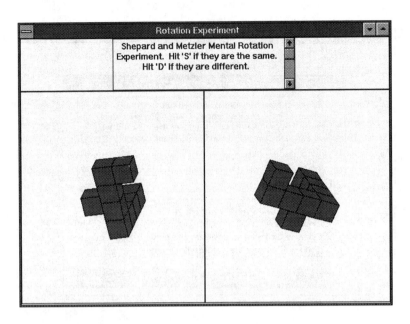

Figure 14.6 It's Time to Make a Choice

The correct answer to the screen in Figure 14.6 is "Same". You would indicate it by pressing the *s* key. The instructions will be displayed to you in the box at the top of the screen. After you have indicated your choice by pressing either the *s* or *d* key, the program will return to the screen shown in Figure 14.4. To see how the stimuli vary over the trials, you can repeat the *Preview One Trial* option as many times as you wish. You will probably see a slightly different pair of stimuli each time. If you choose to explore the different stimulus pairs in this way, think further about how these stimulus manipulations operationally capture the mental operations hypothesized to be going on.

Now try *Preview Six Trials*. You can see more examples of the stimuli, experience exactly what it will be like when you perform the real experiment, and warm-up before starting any real data collection. In many cognitive psychology experiments, subjects are encouraged to experience and practice the experimental task prior to collecting real data. Warm-up trials serve to make sure the subject understands the instructions and is familiar with the task. This experience helps to minimize data that might be contaminated by factors unrelated to the experimental question, such as locating the proper keys on the keyboard or forgetting the instructions. Click on **Preview Six Trials** and **Go On.**

How to Collect Mental Rotation Data Using the Example Experiment

After you have finished previewing the sample trials in the first two options and feel comfortable about what is going to happen on each trial, you can execute the experiment and collect data. The preset experiment lasts for 28 trials: in 14 trials the two objects are the same (except for orientation), and in 14 trials the objects are different. Equal numbers of both kinds of trials are conducted so that you will not be biased to choose one key over the other. Such a bias could contaminate the reaction time. In addition, each set of same and different stimuli will be tested 2 times at 0, 30, 60, 90, 120, 150, and 180 degree rotations. The 7 different degrees of rotation represent the different levels of our independent variable. Collecting equal numbers of observations for each level of an independent variable typically makes statistical analyses easier to carry out and interpret.

To start the preset experiment, click on **Start entire Experiment** and then **Go On**. At the instruction screen (Figure 14.5), click **OK**. The experiment will start. Unlike the preview option, this time the program will be collecting your reaction times on each trial. After completing all of the trials, the screen shown in Figure 14.7 will appear.

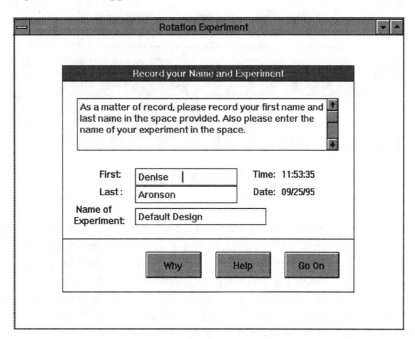

Figure 14.7 Filling Out Information about the Experiment.

Enter your first and last name and a title for your experimental data set. Click **Go On** to see the data collected during your experiment. The screen will look like the one in Figure 14.8, on the next page. Only the data in the table will be different. The screen shows the results for each trial of your experiment and offers several options.

On the bottom of the screen is a six-column data table that lists the variables in your experiment. The separate columns list the following information: (1) *Your Answer* on each trial (1= a "Same" response; 0= a "Different" response), (2) the *Right Answer*, (3) your reaction *Time(sec)* on each trial, and the difference in the angular rotation along the (4) X (*Xdeg*), (5) Y (*Ydeg*), and (6) Z (*Zdeg*) axes for the two stimuli tested on each trial. In the example experiment you need only concern yourself with *Zdeg* rotations.

What should you do next? When you click on the name of a variable in the table, you will be presented with options for sorting the data and creating histograms of individual variables. Click on **Sort** if you want to sort the table on the selected variable, and click on **Histogram** to see a graph of the variable.

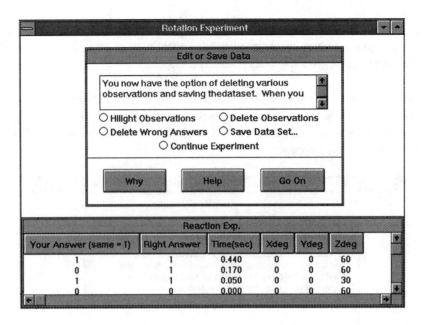

Figure 14.8 Edit or Save Your Data

Only options for sorting or graphing single variables are available. There are no options for examining bivariate relationships in these data, such as a scatterplot of reaction times for the different levels of the independent variable. You can explore the data by using other *ConStatS* programs. The *Displaying Data* program (Chapter 3) is useful for an in-depth examination of the *Time(sec)* variable. The *Describing Bivariate Data* program (Chapter 6) is useful for examining the relationship between the *Time(sec)* variable and the *Zdeg* variable. Before you switch to those programs, however, there are several important options to discuss on the screen shown in Figure 14.8.

How to Save Your Data

The most important step is saving your data set in a computer file. This step allows you to examine your data with any other *ConStatS* programs. To save your data in a file, click on the **Save Data Set** option in the *Edit or Save Data* portion of the screen and then **Go On**. A new window will appear on the screen, like that shown in Figure 14.9. This *Save Data Set* window allows you to save your data in several different ways. The first and easiest way is to accept the default file name that is provided (*rotate.dzt*) by clicking **OK** at the bottom of this window. This option will save your data using the *rotate.dzt* file each time, deleting any previous data you might have stored under that name. The second and perhaps more useful way of saving your data is to save it with a unique file name that you have chosen. This way you can collect and compare several sets of data either from yourself or from different people. To save your data this way, click in the box below **Filename:**, enter an up to 8 letter name with the suffix ".dzt" and click **Go On**.

For both of these options, it is a good idea to include a title and description describing the data set you are about to save. The *Save Data Set* window will close and you will then return to the screen shown in Figure 14.8. You have now saved your data on the disk drive. Now you can manipulate your data. For example, you can *Hilight Observations* or *Delete Observations* from the data table. The *Delete Wrong*

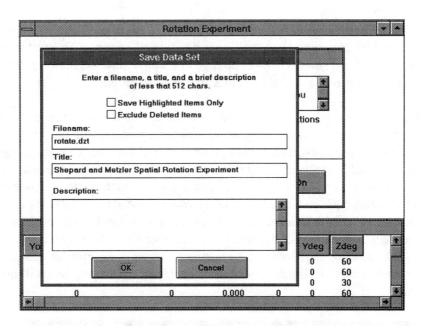

Figure 14.9 Very Important! Save your Data

Answers option is of the most interest. Click on this option and *Go On* to mark off all of the trials in which your response was incorrect. Besides demonstrating that we are not always perfect, there is a sound scientific reason for utilizing this option. Any trial on which you made an error may not truly represent your capacity to rotate the objects mentally. Whatever cognitive processes allowed you to discriminate the two stimuli on the majority of trials did not function in the same way on these incorrect trials. Something went wrong. Because we cannot know why this was, cognitive psychologists often exclude reaction times for incorrect answers from their analyses. You can examine whether this makes any difference in your data by saving your data again, with the incorrect trials excluded. To create such an errorless data set, click on **Delete Wrong Answers** and **Go On**, then click on the **Save Data Set** option and **Go On**. When the *Save Data Set* window reappears, click on **Exclude Deleted Items** and save your data to a file again—be sure to use a *different* data file name than you used before.

(Once they are saved, these files cannot be deleted from within *ConStatS*. To delete them when you are finished using them, or to copy them onto a diskette and then delete them, use the *Windows File Manager*.)

How to Analyze your Data

If this is the first *ConStatS* program you have used, click on **DataRep** in the *ConStatS* menu. Run **Displaying Data**. (See Chapter 3 for instructions on how to get started). This program will permit you to look at one variable at a time. Once you start the program, choose **change to another data set**, and select the data set you saved. Then follow the pathways through the program.

Since you have just collected observations involving relationships between two variables—an independent variable (*Zdeg*, the one we manipulated) and a dependent variable (*Time(sec)*, the one we used to measure the effects of varying the first), look at the relationship between these two variables. The most direct way to do this is to run the *Describing Bivariate Data* program. To run the program, select

173

DataRep from the *ConStatS* menu. Then click on **Describing Bivariate Data** and **Go On**. The next screen, labeled *Describing Bivariate Data*, will give you several options. To use the mental rotation data that you just collected and saved, click the **change to another data set** option and **Go On**. Choose the data file containing your results, and **Go On** to load it into the program.

You can now begin to analyze your data set. Your data will appear at the bottom of the screen. Scroll through the table and examine the data. Graph your results. To proceed with this type of analysis, click on the **Examine the data using bivariate techniques** option and **Go On**. To make a scatter plot of the data, first specify the X and Y variables. Traditionally the X variable displays the different levels of the independent variable (*Zdeg*), and the Y variable displays the dependent variable *Time(sec)*. To assign your independent variable, click on **X:** and then select your independent variable by clicking on **Zdeg**. To assign your dependent variable, click on **Y:** and then click **Time(sec)**. Now click on **Display** in the menu at the top of the screen and select the option for a **Scatter Plot**. You should see a screen like the one in Figure 14.10, showing your individual reaction times as a function of the difference in the angular rotation between the two stimuli presented on each trial. A best-fit line will automatically be drawn based on your data.

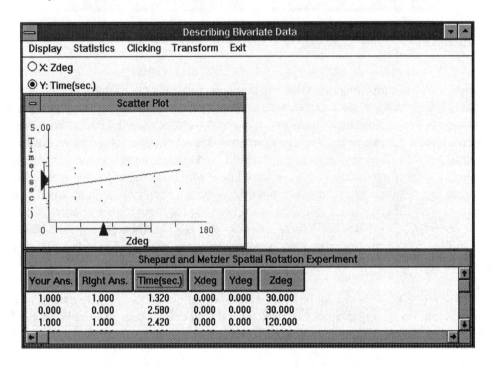

Figure 14.10 A First Look at Your Mental Rotation Data

If you are like most people, the slope of this line should increase from left to right, as it typically takes longer to respond to stimuli whose angular positions are quite different. If this is so, then you have replicated the essence, if not the precision, of Shepard and Metzler's original observations. This is just the simplest of many different analyses that you can investigate with your data. Since most of the fun in conducting an experiment is in exploring the final results, we have left these additional questions for you to pursue on your own. Some questions to guide these explorations are included at the end of this chapter.

How to Design Your Own Mental Rotation Experiment

Now that you are familiar with the experimental procedure, you can design your own experiment. The most important step in designing an experiment is to think of a question to which you would like the answer. Even within the constraints of the present testing situation, many questions remain to be explored. In the example experiment, we manipulated only one of the three axes of rotation. Do all three axes give you the same results? Can you rotate objects along some axes faster than others? Are there any differences in accuracy among the conditions? What happens if you manipulate two of the axes of rotation at the same time? Are there any tradeoffs between the speed of your response and its accuracy? As you can see, our first experiment seems to have raised more questions than it answered.

To design your own experiment, return to the *Experiment* program. (If you closed the *Experiment* program to use another *ConStatS* program to look at your results, simply start the *Experiment* program as described in the beginning of this chapter. If you left the *Experiment* program running, bring it to the foreground, click **Continue Experiment** and **Go On**. Either way should bring up the opening screen of the program as shown back in Figure 14.3.) Click on **Design and run your own Experiment** and **Go On** to open the *ConStatS* experimental design facility. This facility gives a wide array of options for reconfiguring different aspects of the basic mental rotation experiment used in the example portion of the program. A screen like the one in Figure 14.11 will appear.

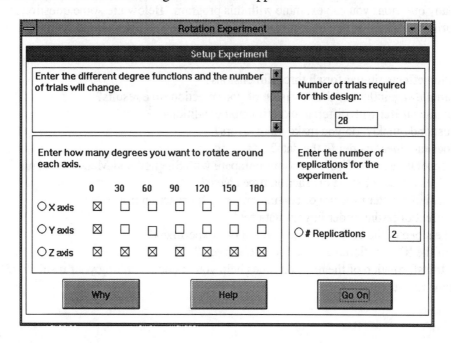

Figure 14.11 The ConStatS Facility for Designing Your Own Experiment

You first need to decide which independent variables you want to manipulate. You can control three from this screen, the angular rotation of the stimuli around the X (or horizontal) axis, the Y (or vertical) axis, and the Z (or into the plane of the screen) axis. Within each of these you can test up to seven different conditions or levels of the independent variable. Click on each box to add both a same and different trial for that particular rotation to your design. Listed in the upper right is a count of the number of trials that will be required to complete the design you have specified. As you add more levels, you will need more trials to maintain an equal number of tests for your different conditions.

Another factor that affects the number of trials in your experiment is the number of times you want to repeat each of your test conditions within the experiment. As you may have discovered in the sampling modules, increasing the size of your samples increases their precision. You can control the number of complete replications of all of your conditions by changing the number in the lower right box of this screen (click on this box and then enter the desired number with the keyboard). As you increase this number, you will again also increase the number of trials needed to complete your design. Thus, the number of trials in your experiment is jointly determined by the number of test conditions and the number of times you test each one. If your time is limited, keep this factor in mind so that you have enough time to collect all of your experimental observations. Once you have set all of these options, click on **Go On** to proceed with collecting your data in the same way as described above for the example experiment.

Some Further Experimental Questions to Consider

There are many questions you can examine with this program. Below are some questions that can guide you in exploring the data that you have already collected. They also provide ideas for new experiments.

Are the rotation effects similar for all three dimensions?
How does sample size influence the precision of your reaction time results?
Does the accuracy differ with different experimental conditions?
When you respond quickly, do you make more errors?
How well does the linear model fit the data?
How do the absolute values of your reactions compare with Shepard and Metzler's results?
What shape does the distribution of reaction times have?
Is mean or median a better measure of central tendency for reaction time?
Is there any effect of testing order in your data set?
What does the slope of the best-fit line tell you in this experiment?
Is the slope of the RT function the same for all observers?
Could some transformation of the reaction times help you in understanding your results? (*Hint*: reaction times are prone to outliers.)

Adding or Modifying Examples in *Sampling* and *Inference*

Adding New Random Variables to the *Sampling* Programs

Two of the *ConStatS* programs, *Sampling Distributions* and *Sampling Errors*, allow user-configured random variables. *ConStatS* recognizes two types of random variables: ones where the population distribution and parameter values are shown to the user, and ones where the distribution and parameter values are kept hidden from the user. Two steps are involved in adding random variables: (1) setting up a random variable definition file, and (2) adding the random variable to the appropriate list of random variables.

Step One: Random Variable Definition File

The procedure for creating a random variable definition file requires modifying an ASCII text file. The file can be prepared using any text editor, such as Windows Notepad or MS-DOS EDIT. It must conform to the following line-by-line structure.

First Line: **Random Variable Description**. Text describing the random variable to be defined. The text can be as long as 512 characters, and must occupy only the first line of the file.

Second Line: **Random Variable Information**. Four components, separated by spaces or tabs.

1. **Caption**: Alphanumeric text describing the population defined by the random variable. Limited to a maximum of 40 characters, appearing in double quotes.

2. **Type of probability distribution**: An integer code indicating the probability distribution of the random variable. A summary of probability distributions available in *ConStatS* is given in Table A.1 on the next page. The integer code for each probability distribution appears in the second column.

3. **Number of random variables**: An integer representing the number of random variables to be defined. Because each definition file can only hold one random variable, this value must equal 1.

4. **Number of parameters**: An integer representing the number of parameters needed to define the random variable probability distribution. This value is taken from the third column of Table A.1.

Table A.1 Probability Distributions Available for Random Variable Definition in *ConStatS*

Distribution	ID code	Number of Parameters	Parameter	Min	Max
NORMAL	410	2	μ	-20	20
			σ	.75	10
EXPONENTIAL	420	1	L	.1	20
LOGNORMAL	430	2	α	0.0	4.0
			β	.1	4.0
BINOMIAL	440	2	n	1	32
			p	.05	.95
POISSON	450	1	L	1.0	30
CHI SQ.	460	1	v	2	40
BETA	470	2	α	.5	50
			β	.5	50
WEIBULL	490	2	α	.5	15
			β	.5	15
UNIFORM (cont.)	510	2	a	0	100
			b	0	100
GEOMETRIC	520	1	p	.1	.9
GAMMA	550	2	α	.1	15
			β	.1	15
UNIFORM (discrete)	570	2	a	0	100
			b	0	100

<u>Third Line</u>: **Name of the random variable**. The variable name can be a maximum of 40 characters, but brief names (less than 10 characters) work best. Must be in double quotes.

<u>Fourth Line</u>: **Reserved for Future Use**. For compatibility with future editions of *ConStatS*, enter 1.

<u>Fifth Line</u>: **Reserved for Future Use**. For compatibility with future editions of *ConStatS*, enter 1.

<u>Sixth and Seventh Lines</u>: **Parameter Values**. Depending on the type of probability distribution specified in line 2, the random variable will need one (on line 6) or two (one on line 6 and one on line 7) parameter values. Values must be within the min-to-max range specified in Table A.1.

Once created, the data file must be saved as an ASCII file in the *ConStatS* directory. For compatibility with the *ConStatS* protocol for naming files according to academic discipline, the file extension must be one of the following:

.ibt = data for Biology	.ipt = data for Psychology
.iet = data for Economics	.ist = data for Sociology
.igt = data for Engineering	.izt = Generic random variable

Figure A.1 shows the file *BW.IBT*, a sample random variable definition file for a normal population distribution with a revealed mean and standard deviation. The first line is the text description of the variable. The second line contains the title of the name of the population followed by the distribution integer code (*410*, corresponding to a normal distribution), the number of variables (*1*) and then the number of parameters (*2*, corresponding to μ and σ in a normal distribution). The third line contains the name of the random variable. The fourth and fifth lines contain the required value of 1, and the last two lines give the values of μ (*7.0*) and σ (*1.0*).

> Weight of Human Babies, in lbs, hypothesized to be normally distributed: μ=7.0, σ =1.0.
> "All human babies" 410 1 2
> "Baby weights (human, in lbs.)"
> 1
> 1
> 7.0
> 1.0

Figure A.1 Example Random Variable Definition File

Step Two: Adding the Random Variable to the Random Variable List

ConStatS maintains two separate lists of random variable definition file names. These lists are contained in the two files HRV.CSS and RRV.CSS. HRV.CSS is a list of definition files for random variables whose parameters are revealed to the user in the text description of the random variable. RRV.CSS is a list of definition files for random variables whose parameters are kept hidden. These files can be edited with any text editor, such as Windows Notepad or MS-DOS EDIT. They must have the following structure.

First line: **Number of variables**: An integer value equal to the number of variables that are listed in the file.

Remaining lines: **Variable and File names**. Each line contains two entries: (1) the name of the random variable (maximum of 40 characters) and (2) the name of the random variable definition file. The two entries must be in double quotes and separated by spaces or tabs.

Once created, the data file must be saved as an ASCII file in the *ConStatS* directory. Figure A.2 is an example of an RRV.CSS file with three random variables.

> 3
> "Lifetime of Barnacles (years)"   "barn.ibt"
> "Baby Weights (human, in lbs.)"   "bw.ibt"
> "Hits Per Game (baseball)"   "hits.izt"

Figure A.2 Example Random Variable List File, RRV.CSS

Modifying the *Beginning Confidence Intervals* Problem Contexts

The *Beginning Confidence Intervals* program uses one file to store its problem contexts, CONFID.LST. Additional problem contexts may be added in subsequent groups of five lines. The procedure for adding or modifying problem contexts requires editing an ASCII text file. Once created or edited, the file must be saved as an ASCII file, in the *ConStatS* directory. The file can be prepared using any text editor, such as Windows Notepad or MS-DOS EDIT, and must conform to the following line-by-line structure.

Problem Contexts for *Beginning Confidence Intervals*: File: CONFID.LST

Beginning line: **Number of problem contexts**: An integer value equal to the number of problem contexts that are described in the file. It is important to update this number every time problem contexts are added or removed from the file.

The remaining lines describe the *Beginning Confidence Interval* problem contexts. Each problem context description consists of 5 lines, which are repeated in sets of five lines, as problem contexts are added to the file.

First Line: **Problem Context Information**: Three components, separated by spaces or tabs:

1. **Title**: Alphanumeric text describing the title of the problem context. Limited to a maximum of 40 characters, appearing in double quotes.

2. **Population mean:** Numerical value.

3. **Population standard deviation:** Numerical value.

Second Line: **Problem Context**: Text describing the problem context for the single mean hypothesis test. The text may be as long as 510 characters, and must occupy only the second line of this group.

Third Line: **Reserved:** Enter the word **Reserved**

Fourth Line: **Reserved**: Enter the word **Reserved**

Fifth Line: **Unit of measure**: Text naming the units in which the sample random variable is measured.

Comment lines: Any line beginning with the # symbol is a comment line and is disregarded by the program. The file must not contain any blank or empty lines.

Modifying the *Beginning Hypothesis Testing* Problem Contexts

The procedure for adding or modifying problem contexts requires editing an ASCII text file. Once edited, the file must be saved as an ASCII file in the *ConStatS* directory. The file can be prepared using any text editor, such as Windows Notepad or MS-DOS EDIT.

The *Beginning Hypothesis Testing* program uses two files to store its problem contexts. The first file, ONEMEAN.HYP, contains the information for the problem contexts involving a single mean. The second, TWOMEAN.HYP, contains the information for the problem contexts involving two means. The structure of these two files differs from that of the data files and random variable files, where each data set or random variable has its own file name. In the *Beginning Hypothesis Testing* program, all problem contexts of a similar kind (e.g. single mean) are grouped into a common file, one for single means and another for two means. The structure of these two files is discussed separately.

Problem Contexts for a Single Mean: File: ONEMEAN.HYP

<u>Beginning line</u>: **Number of problem contexts**: An integer value equal to the number of problem contexts that are described in the file. It is important to update this number every time problem contexts are added or removed from the file.

The remaining lines describe the single-mean hypothesis test problem contexts. Each problem context description consists of 5 lines, which are repeated in sets of five lines, as problem contexts are added to the file.

<u>First Line</u>: **Problem Context Information**: Four components, separated by spaces or tabs.

1. **Title**: Alphanumeric text describing the title of the problem context. Limited to a maximum of 40 characters, appearing in double quotes.

2. **Population mean:** Numerical value.

3. **Population standard deviation:** Numerical value.

4. **Restriction code**: An integer having the following value: 1 if the hypothesis test is to be restricted to integer values only, or 0 if there is no such restriction.

<u>Second Line</u>: **Problem Context**: Text describing the problem context for the single mean hypothesis test. The text may be as long as 510 characters, and must occupy only the second line of this group.

<u>Third Line</u>: **Name of the claimant:** Text name.

<u>Fourth Line</u>: **Sampling Process**: Text describing the process of taking a sample.

<u>Fifth Line</u>: **Unit of measure**: Text naming the units in which the sample random variable is measured.

<u>Comment lines</u>: Any line beginning with the # symbol is a comment line and is disregarded by the program. The file must not contain any blank or empty lines.

Additional problem contexts may be added in subsequent groups of five lines following the format above. Once created or edited the file must be saved as an ASCII file in the *ConStatS* directory. An example problem context for a single mean hypothesis test is shown in Figure A.3. The first line shows a problem context entitled *SAT Scores*, that samples will be drawn from a normal distribution of mean *1235* and with a standard deviation of *100*, and that all values will be rounded to the nearest integer. The problem description (most of which has been omitted for reasons of space) is on the second line. On line 3, *Wilhurst College* is identified as the claimant. The fourth line has a description of the sampling process, and the final line contains the units that SAT scores are measured in (*points*).

"SAT Scores" 1235 100 1
Data from the past ten years show that applicants to Wilhurst College have SAT...
Wilhurst College
You consult the records for one applicant and find an SAT score of:
points

Figure A.3 A Problem Context for Single Mean Hypothesis Tests

Problem Contexts for Two Means: File: TWOMEAN.HYP

<u>Beginning line</u>: **Number of problem contexts**: An integer value equal to the number of problem contexts that are described in the file. It is important to update this number every time problem contexts are added to or removed from the file.

The remaining lines describe the two-mean hypothesis testing problem contexts. Each problem context description consists of anywhere from 12-20 lines:

<u>First Line</u>: **Problem Context Information**: Ten components, separated by spaces or tabs:

1. **Title**: Alphanumeric text describing the title of the problem context. Limited to a maximum of 40 characters, appearing in double quotes.

2. **Mean for first population:** Numerical value.

3. **Standard deviation for first population:** Numerical value.

4. **Mean for second population:** Numerical value.

5. **Standard deviation for second population:** Numerical value.

6. **Restriction code**: An integer having the following value: 1 if the hypothesis test is to be restricted to integer values only, or 0 if there is no such restriction.

7. **Type of comparison**: A character consisting of the letter "P" or "I": use "I" if only an independent comparison is possible, use "P" if a paired comparison is appropriate.

8. **Number of observations**: An integer equal to the *maximum* number of observations allowed in the sampling experiment.

9. **Standard deviation of paired differences**. The numerical value of the standard deviation of the differences in a paired comparison (overrides the standard deviations entered in lines 3 and 5). For independent comparisons, this value is ignored.

10. **Multiplier**. The numerical value of a multiplier applied to the standard deviation of the differences in a paired comparison to obtain the standard deviation of populations (overrides the standard deviations entered in lines 3 and 5). For independent comparisons, this value is ignored.

<u>Second Line</u>: **Problem Context**: Text describing the problem context for the two mean hypothesis test. The text may be as long as 510 characters, and must occupy only the second line of this group.

<u>Third Line</u>: **Name of the claimant**: Text name.

<u>Fourth Line</u>: **Sampling Process**: Text describing the process of taking a sample.

<u>Fifth Line</u>: **Unit of measure**: Text naming the units in which the sample random variable is measured.

<u>Sixth Line</u>: **Number of items** in the list following. An integer value from 2 to 10.

<u>The Next Two to Ten Lines</u>: **List of items** (one per line). These lines represent a list from which the user must correctly select the names of the two populations, and for paired comparisons, the pairing variable. Some of the items in the list are red herrings, meant to cause the user to think about which populations are actually being represented, and what the actual pairing variable might be.

<u>Third to Last Line</u>: **Position of name of first population**: An integer equal to the number of the line in the above list that contains the name of the first population.

<u>Second to Last Line</u>: **Position of name of second population**. An integer equal to the number of the line in the above list that contains the name of the second population.

<u>Last Line</u>: **Position of name of pairing variable**. An integer equal to the number of the line in the above list that contains the name of the pairing variable. For contexts involving only independent comparisons, the value should be 0.

<u>Comment lines</u>: Any line beginning with the # symbol is a comment line and is disregarded by the program. The file must not contain any blank or empty lines.

Additional problem contexts are added in subsequent groups of 12 to 20 lines following the format above. Once created or edited, the file must be saved as an ASCII file in the *ConStatS* directory.

An example problem context for a two mean hypothesis test is shown in Figure A.4. It contains the problem context title, the first population mean of *75* and standard deviation of *16*, and then the second population mean of *70* and standard deviation of *18*. The next *0* implies that values are not limited to integer values. The *I* indicates that only independent comparisons are valid in this context, and that a total of *50* observations can be taken. The next two values are left zero, as they are not needed for independent comparisons. The second line contains a description of the problem context (much is omitted for reasons of space). The next three lines specify that the claim is being made by *Management*, describe the sampling process, and identify the unit measured as *parts produced*. The following list contains *4* elements. The numbers following the list give the location on the list of the first population and the second population, respectively. (So the third and fourth elements on the list are the red herrings.) The final value is *0*, since there is no pairing variable on the list, as this is an independent comparison.

"Worker Performance" 75 16 70 18 0 I 50 0 0
The management of the Sycamore Steel Co. wishes to determine if there is any...
Management
You look up the parts produced per day:
parts produced
4
Productivity of Day Workers
Productivity of Night Workers
Number of Workers sampled
Number of Parts produced
1
2
0

Figure A.4 Example Two Mean Hypothesis Problem Context.

Glossary

Abscissa: The X axis of a graph.

Alternative hypothesis: One of two mutually exclusive statistical hypotheses (the other is the null hypothesis) to be examined in a statistical hypothesis test. The alternative hypothesis carries the burden of proof in a hypothesis test, i.e., the null is assumed until it is shown to be unlikely.

Binomial experiment: An experiment involving n number of identical and independent trials. For each trial there are the same two possible outcomes, e.g., flips of a coin.

Bivariate: Relating two variables to one another.

Burden of proof: Strength of the evidence that must be gathered to warrant acceptance of a hypothesis.

CDF display: See cumulative distribution function.

Claim: An assertion about a condition or characteristic of a population.

Conditioning: Looking at the distribution of outcomes for one variable provided that another variable has a particular fixed value.

Confidence interval: Two statistics that serve as the end points of an interval. The procedure for generating the end points is successful in bracketing the population parameter a proportion of the times over a vast number of independent samples, i.e., the procedure results in an interval for each sample, and a proportion of these intervals bracket the population parameter.

Confidence level: The proportion associated with a confidence interval—i.e., the proportion of times that the interval will contain the parameter value under repeated sampling. The confidence level is $1-\alpha$ where α is the Type I error. See errors in hypothesis testing.

Constant: A fixed value that does not change.

Continuous probability distribution: A theoretical probability distribution for a continuous random variable.

Correlation: A measure of the relationship between two variables. See correlation coefficient.

Correlation coefficient: A measure of the degree of interdependence between two variables; can be expressed as the covariance of the two variables divided by the square root of the product of their variances. This measure varies between -1 (perfect negative correlation) and $+1$ (perfect positive correlation).

Cumulative distribution function: A function expressing the cumulative frequency (or probability) from the lowest to the highest values in a set of data (or for a probability distribution).

Data table: A tabular method of displaying the values of a sample of data.

Decision rule: A statement about the strength of the statistical evidence required to reject the null hypothesis in a hypothesis test.

Decisions in hypothesis testing: The action taken with respect to the null hypothesis in a statistical hypothesis test, i.e., reject it, or let it stand.

Defined situation: A detailed context for probability assignment.

Descriptive statistics: Measures such as the sample mean and variance that are used to summarize data; the branch of statistics concerned with summarizing data.

Deviation: The distance between a particular observation in a data set and the mean of that data set.

Discrete probability distribution: Probability associated with each value of a discrete random variable.

Distribution: When applied to a sample, a representation of the frequencies of the values of a variable when the values are arranged in increasing order; when applied to a population, a shorthand way of referring to a probability distribution.

Elementary outcomes: Possible outcomes that are not a composite of several other outcomes.

Error: The difference between a single value of a variable and its average or expected value.

Error of estimation: The distance an estimate falls from a true value.

Errors in hypothesis testing: The probability associated with false acceptance (Type II error or ß error) and false rejection (Type I error or α error) of a null hypothesis.

Estimate (verb): To calculate the value taken on by an estimator when applied to a sample; used to infer the value of a population parameter.

Estimate (noun): The value taken on by an estimator when applied to a sample; a guess about the value of a population parameter.

Estimator: A formula or method that can be applied to sample values to infer the value of a population parameter.

Estimation: The application of an estimator to sample values.

Exhaustive: All possible outcomes for a defined situation.

False acceptance: Failure to reject the null hypothesis when it is false; often called a Type II error or ß error.

186

False rejection: Rejection of the null hypothesis when it is true; often called a Type I error or α error.

Finite: Something having definable limits; not infinite.

Frequency: Number of observations of a particular type or class.

Histogram: A graphical representation of a frequency distribution; composed of a series of rectangles that have a width that is proportional to the width of the class interval and a height that represents class frequency. A type of univariate display.

Hypothesis: An assertion about a condition or characteristic of a population.

Hypothesis test: A formal statistical procedure for assessing the validity of a statistical hypothesis.

Independent: The occurrence of one outcome or event does not influence the probability of the occurrence of another outcome or event.

Inference: The process of drawing conclusions from samples.

Interquartile range: The distance between the first quartile (25th percentile) and the third quartile (75th percentile); contains the middle half of all observations.

Interval estimates: An interval used to estimate the value of a population parameter, e.g., a confidence interval.

Interval scale: A measurement system that has equally spaced limits of measurement, e.g., the centigrade scale for temperature.

Law of large numbers: The general principle that as you increase sample size the sample mean is more likely to be close in value to the population mean.

Least squares: A technique for fitting a line by minimizing the sum of the squared differences between the actual points and their predicted values; the same as ordinary least squares.

Linear relationship: A relationship between variables that can be expressed as an equation for a line.

Linear transformations: Transformations that take the form of a linear equation.

Log: The symbol for the common logarithm; it is the exponent to which a base of ten must be raised in order to produce a given number.

Logarithm (base 10) transformation and the natural logarithm transformation: Types of nonlinear transformations.

Mean: The average value, calculated as the sum of all measurements in a sample divided by the number of observations in that sample. A measure of central tendency in a set of data.

Median: The middle value in a ranked set of sample data such that half the observations fall above it and half below. A measure of central tendency in a set of data.

Mode: The most frequently occurring value in a set of observations. Another measure of central tendency in a set of data.

μ (mu): A commonly used symbol for the population mean.

Multiplicative consistency: If A is twice B and B is three times C, then multiplicative consistency requires that A is 6 times C.

Multiplicative inconsistency: A violation of multiplicative consistency in probability measurement based on ratios.

Mutually exclusive outcomes: The defining of outcomes so that an observation can be classified to only a single category.

Natural logarithm: Use of the natural number e as the base; it is the exponent to which a base of e must be raised in order to produce a given number.

Nonlinear relationship: A relationship between variables that is not capable of being expressed as a straight line.

Non-random variable: A variable that takes on changes in a predictable manner, i.e., the various values do not reflect a probability distribution.

Normally distributed: A random variable that takes on values as described by a normal distribution.

Normal probability distribution: The familiar bell-shaped curve, whose mathematical properties are often used in describing the distribution of many measured quantities with an interval or ratio scale.

Null hypothesis: One of two mutually exclusive statistical hypotheses (the other is the alternative hypothesis) to be examined in a statistical hypothesis test. The null hypothesis is presumed true and rejected only when the statistical evidence in the sample indicates that it is unlikely.

OLS: See ordinary least squares.

Ordinary least squares: A technique for fitting a line by minimizing the sum of the squared differences between the actual points and their predicted values.

Ordinal scale: A scale where the items are measured only by a rank (i.e., first, second, etc.). The same as a ranked scale.

Ordinate: The Y axis of a graph.

Outliers: A small set of observations that are far from the majority of observations.

Parameter: A constant (usually unknown) that is a characteristic of the population. Parameters appear in the formula for a probability distribution.

Paired observations: Outcomes of two random variables that are both associated with the same observational unit.

Point estimate: A single value that is used as a guess about the value of an unknown parameter.

Population: The entire group of items about which information is sought; the complete collection of all possible scores for a specified situation.

Population distribution: A probability distribution that describes the probability of occurrence of any set of outcomes, or events.

Population mean: A measure of the center of a population distribution.

Population parameter: The true value for the population characteristic that is estimated by a sample statistic.

Probability: The frequency of occurrence over infinitely repeated sampling or a measure of the degree of belief about the truth of a proposition—e.g., that a particular event will happen.

Power function transformation: A type of nonlinear transformation based on raising values to a power.

Random: A process that can be described probabilistically.

Random sample: A sample in which each individual score from the population has an equal probability and independent chance of being included, although some scores in the population are more frequent than others.

Random Variable: A type of variable whose values are characterized by a probability distribution.

Range: The difference between the largest and the smallest observations in a sample (or population).

Rank: The integer values assigned when a sample of n observations is arranged in order from smallest to largest values, with a rank of 1 assigned to the smallest value up to a rank of n assigned to the largest value.

Ranked scale: A scale where the items are measured only by rank. Same as an ordinal scale.

Ratio scale: An interval scale with a true zero, e.g., a measure of length in centimeters.

Regression: A statistical method for showing the linear relationship of one variable to another variable; the relationship is often estimated by a least squares technique.

Relative frequency distribution: A method of displaying data that shows the fraction of the total values lying within a particular interval.

Rescaling: Multiplying a variable by a constant in order to change the units in which it is measured.

Residual: The quantity remaining after the predicted value of a variable is subtracted from the actual value of the variable; often used interchangeably with the term error.

Sample: A randomly collected finite subset of observations from a population. Used to gain information about the entire population.

Sample mean: The sum of the sample values divided by the sample size.

Sample size: The total number of observations making up a sample of data.

Sample space: A set of mutually exclusive outcomes for a defined situation.

Sample statistic: A number describing a sample of data, such as the sample mean or variance.

Sampling: The process of selecting a sample from some population.

Sampling distribution: The distribution of a particular sample statistic, given all possible samples that can be generated by a sampling process.

Sampling error: Differences in the values in a sample of data that arise solely from the random manner in which the items in the sample are obtained.

Sampling experiment: The process of obtaining a sample of data.

Scatter plot: A diagram showing points that represent the values of two variables; the clustering of the points demonstrates the relationship between the two variables.

σ (sigma): A commonly used symbol for the population standard deviation.

Simulation: Use of a known process capable of being repeated as a representation of another process that cannot be repeated. Often used as a way of exploring the behavior of the unknown process under various conditions.

Skew: A measure of the asymmetry of a frequency distribution, with a perfectly symmetrical distribution having zero skew; negative or positive skew values indicate asymmetrical distributions with long tails to the left or right.

Skew index: The third central moment about the mean divided by the cube of the standard deviation.

Spread: The degree to which the values in a sample vary, often measured by the variance.

SSE: Sum of squared errors.

Standardization: Subtracting the mean of a random variable and dividing the result by its standard deviation to produce a new variable with a mean of zero and a standard deviation of one (see also Z score).

Standard deviation: A measure of variation or spread in a set of data; the square root of the variance.

Statistic: A function of sample values; often used as the estimator of some population parameter.

Statistical evidence: The value of a sample statistic.

Statistical hypothesis: A precise statement about the value of a population characteristic, such as a population mean or variance.

Sum of squared errors: The sum of the squares of the residuals of a least squares line.

Summary statistics: A set of values, such as the sample mean and standard deviation, that describe a particular set of observations.

Transformation: A function of a variable that can be either linear or nonlinear.

True-zero scale: A measurement scale where the zero corresponds to an absolute zero for the measured property. See ratio scale.

Univariate: Pertaining to a single random variable.

Variable: A characteristic of each item in a sample that is to be measured and recorded.

Variability: A lack of constancy in a series of observations.

Variance: A measure of variation or spread in a set of data. Represents the average squared deviation of all observations from the mean.

Z score: A linear transformation computed by subtracting the sample mean from a value in a sample and dividing this difference by the sample standard deviation.

LICENSE AGREEMENT

License Agreement

You should carefully read the following terms and conditions before breaking the seal on the disk envelope. Among other things, this Agreement licenses the enclosed software to you and contains warranty and liability disclaimers. By breaking the seal on the disk envelope, you are accepting and agreeing to the terms of this Agreement. If you do not agree to the terms of this Agreement, do not break the seal. You should promptly return the package unopened.

License

Prentice-Hall, Inc. (the "Licensor") provide this Software to you and license its use as follows:
   a. use the Software on a single computer of the type identified on the package;
   b. make one copy of the Software in machine readable form solely for back-up purposes.

Limited Warranty

The Licensor Warrants the physical diskette (1) on which the software is furnished to be free from defects in materials and workmanship under normal use for a period of sixty (60) days from the date of purchase as evidenced by a copy of your receipt.

Disclaimer

THE SOFTWARE IS PROVIDED 'AS IS' AND LICENSOR AND TUFT UNIVERSITY ("TUFTS") SPECIFICALLY DISCLAIMS ALL WARRANTIES OF ANY KIND, EITHER EXPRESS OR IMPLIED, INCLUDING, BUT NOT LIMITED TO, THE IMPLIED WARRANTIES OF MERCHANTABILITY AND FITNESS FOR A PARTICULAR PURPOSE. IN NO EVENT WILL LICENSOR OR TUFTS BE LIABLE TO YOU FOR ANY DAMAGES, INCLUDING ANY LOSS OF PROFIT OR OTHER INCIDENTAL, SPECIAL OR CONSEQUENTIAL DAMAGE'S EVEN IF LICENSOR HAS BEEN ADVISED OF THE POSSIBILITY OF SUCH DAMAGES.

SOME STATES DO NO ALLOW THE EXCLUSION OF IMPLIED WARRANTIES OR LIMITATIONS OR EXCLUSION OF LIABILITY FOR INCIDENTAL OR CONSEQUENTIAL DAMAGES, SO THE ABOVE EXCLUSIONS AND/OR LIMITATIONS MAY NOT APPLY TO YOU.

Limitations of Remedies

The Licensor's and Tuft's entire liability and your exclusive remedy shall be:
   1. the replacement of such diskette by Licensor if you return a defective diskette to Licensor during the limited warranty period, or
   2. if Licensor is unable to deliver a replacement diskette that is free of defects in materials or workmanship, you may terminate this Agreement by returning the Software.

General

You may not sublicense, assign, or transfer the license of the Software or make or distribute copies of the Software. Any attempt otherwise to sublicense, assign, or transfer any of the rights, duties, or obligations hereunder is void.

Should you have any questions concerning this Agreement, you may contact Prentice-Hall, Inc. by writing to
   Prentice Hall
   Editor-in-Chief
   One Lake Street
   Upper Saddle River, NJ 07458

YOU ACKNOWLEDGE THAT YOU HAVE READ THIS AGREEMENT, UNDERSTAND IT, AND AGREE TO BE BOUND BY ITS TERMS AND CONDITIONS. YOU FURTHER AGREE THAT IT IS THE COMPLETE AND EXCLUSIVE STATEMENT OF THE AGREEMENT BETWEEN US THAT SUPERSEDES ANY OTHER COMMUNICATIONS BETWEEN US RELATING TO THE SUBJECT MATTER OF THIS AGREEMENT.